CAMBRIDGE PAPERS IN SOCIAL ANTHROPOLOGY

General Editor: Jack Goody

No. 10   From craft to industry

The ethnography of proto-industrial cloth production

CAMBRIDGE PAPERS IN SOCIAL ANTHROPOLOGY

From craft to industry

The ethnography of proto-industrial cloth production

Edited by Esther N. Goody

Fellow of New Hall, Cambridge

CAMBRIDGE UNIVERSITY PRESS
CAMBRIDGE
LONDON   NEW YORK   NEW ROCHELLE
MELBOURNE   SYDNEY

Published by the Press Syndicate of the University of Cambridge
The Pitt Building, Trumpington Street, Cambridge CB2 1RP
32 East 57th Street, New York, NY 10022, USA
296 Beaconsfield Parade, Middle Park, Melbourne 3206, Australia

First published 1982

Printed in Great Britain at
the University Press, Cambridge

Library of Congress catalogue card number: 82–4205

British Library Cataloguing in Publication Data

From craft to industry – (Cambridge papers in
social anthropology; 10)
1. Textile fabrics – Manufacture
2. Underdeveloped areas – Manufactures
I. Goody, Esther N.
677'.02864'091724   TS1445

ISBN 0 521 24614 8

CONTENTS

FIGURES, MAPS AND ILLUSTRATIONS

Figures

Maps

Illustrations

Photographs 6.1 to 6.4 by Keith Tribe

TABLES

NOTES ON CONTRIBUTORS

Judith Ennew received her Ph.D. in anthropology from Cambridge in 1979, based on fieldwork in the Outer Hebrides. She is author of a book on contemporary Hebridean life, *The Western Isles Today* (1980), and several articles on political economy. She is currently researching on child labour in Peru.

Esther N. Goody lectures in social anthropology at Cambridge, having done fieldwork mainly in West Africa. A long-standing interest in kinship and informal education (*Contexts of Kinship* 1973; *Parenthood and Social Reproduction* 1982) led to the study of the teaching of weaving in Daboya and a concern with occupational differentiation and the division of labour.

Keith Hart, who holds a Ph.D. in social anthropology from Cambridge, is currently Visiting Professor of Anthropology at McGill University in Montreal. He has also taught at the University of East Anglia, at Manchester, and recently at several American universities. He is author of seminal papers on the informal economy, and *The Political Economy of West African Agriculture* (1982).

R. J. Pokrant is a lecturer in sociology at Salisbury College of Advanced Education, South Australia. A graduate of Leicester University (B.A. 1964) and Northwestern University (M.A. 1966), he is currently finishing a Ph.D. at Cambridge under the Social and Political Sciences Committee.

D. A. Swallow wrote her Ph.D. thesis on modern sectarian movements in eastern India at the University of Cambridge, and is currently Assistant Curator at the Museum of Archaeology and Anthropology there. She is the author of articles on contemporary Indian sects and cults, and is continuing her research into small-scale textile industries in India.

This volume grew out of an informal seminar on economic history and textile production, and we would like to thank Dr Mark Elvin, Dr G. N.

Notes on contributors

von Tunzelmann and Dr Michel Verdon for their contributions. The editor also wishes to thank Dr Chris Gregory and Dr J. Iliffe for comments on the introduction (for the final form of which they are, of course, not responsible). Background reading on the history of the English and Chinese textile industries was made possible by the editor's year at the Center for Advanced Study in the Behavioral Sciences, Stanford, California.

1 Introduction

Esther N. Goody

THE DIVISION OF LABOUR AND INVESTMENT IN PRODUCTION

Both Adam Smith and Karl Marx were fascinated by the way in which the process of production had been subdivided and specialized in eighteenth- and nineteenth-century industry. Smith describes the way in which the making of pins was broken down into 18 separate operations, which could be carried out by as many workers with an astonishing 240-fold increase in productivity, using the same technique and tools (Adam Smith 1776: vol. I, 6–7). Marx was intrigued by the different forms of cooperation which could occur in articulating the tasks separated by the division of labour. He saw this in a highly formal way, distinguishing between organic manufacture, in which the basic raw material passes through a sequence of stages in which it is converted into the finished product (pin-making would be one example), and heterogeneous manufacture. The making of a watch is used as an example here. It used to be the individual product of one craftsman. Then (in the nineteenth century) it became the social product of a large number of detail workers; there were mainspring makers, dial makers, hair-spring makers, jewelled-hold makers, ruby-lever makers, case makers, screw makers and gilders. And these had numerous subdivisions: among wheel makers the makers of brass wheels and the makers of steel wheels were distinct (Marx 1954:360). No advantage was seen in bringing these processes together under one roof: there were fewer overheads with outworkers, and more competition amongst them. The parts were collected for the final assembly by a worker whom Marx did not consider to be a craftsman, despite his skill, since he did not work directly for the customer but for the capitalist who organized the coordination of the various component parts.

We are used to a model of a factory assembly line where each worker carries out a single operation as the product passes from one to the next. So we tend to see the division of labour into detail tasks as linked to factory production and machine-powered tools. Yet the division of labour was already highly complex before these culminating achievements of the industrial revolution. The making of Swiss watches which Marx describes was based on cottage outwork, not done in a factory. And the 240-fold increase in production Smith remarked on did not depend on machinery, but on each worker becoming highly skilled in a separate stage of the production sequence. Indeed, these very elaborate subdivisions of the process of production which preceded the late-eighteenth-century and nineteenth-century explosion of the industrial revolution seem in some manner to have helped to bring it about. Clearly it is easier to design machines to do one step of a production process than to invent a Heath-Robinson super-machine to do them all at once. In this sense a detailed division of labour may well have been a necessary prerequisite to factory-based machine industry. But what was the force or process fuelling this progressively more detailed division of labour before the introduction of machines?

For Marx and Adam Smith the answer lay in the greater efficiency of production performed by detail workers. Greater efficiency meant greater profit for the manufacturer. While this is logically incontestable, the potential for such increased efficiency is inherent in any production process. But division of labour into detail tasks carried out by specialist workers is, in terms of economic history, very recent. Why? And how did it come about?

Like the chimera of the 'origin' of the industrial revolution, such a question has not a single answer but many facets. Three quite different forms of the division of labour in commodity production can be distinguished, though they are often superimposed: horizontal, vertical and functional. I want first to look at these three forms in some detail. Next, it is useful to consider schematically the history of the development of the textile industry in northwestern Europe in terms of the dynamics of these forms. What are their implications for the shift from craft to industry? The analysis suggests that a critical factor in the form of the division of labour is the nature of the integration between tasks. Integration in turn is closely linked with whether, in Hart's terms, capital is used to make a profit, or deployed as industrial capital, 'to purchase means of production – both produced (machines, raw materials) and non-produced (labour, land)' (this volume, p. 41). And, I would add, to whether capital is used to intervene in the *organization* of production. In terms of the organization of the textile industry in the period between the twelfth and the eighteenth centuries in northwestern Europe, this involves a distinction between mercantile capital and industrial capital, with a critical period during which they sometimes merge. It seems that substantial direct investment in the production process is associated with a division of labour into detail tasks designed to maximize efficiency. Finally, the four case studies in this volume are considered in relation to the form of division of labour they express, and to whether and in what way profits are converted to merchant capital or invested in production.

Forms of the division of labour

Obviously, there is no meaningful way in which we can recover the 'true' origin of the division of labour in commodity production, if only because this must have occurred repeatedly in different societies, under different conditions. There are, however, several forms that we can examine in accounts of commodity production in pre-industrial societies. The first is based on the increasing degree of skill of the individual worker as he becomes more experienced, and on the management of the production process in conjunction with training new workers. This is often seen as the division of labour by age, and from the individual worker's point of view is linked both to the learning of a skill and to maturation. In terms of articulation of the division of labour, the crucial roles are those of parent and teacher. In developed apprenticeship systems these roles are institutionalized on a non-kinship basis in the role of 'master'.[1] The division of labour by age can be seen as a *horizontal* division of labour, in that an individual worker proceeds through successive levels of age/skill specific tasks, and eventually reaches the position of master and teacher himself.

Recognition of the second form requires the distinction between the division of labour within the production process and the specialized production of different commodities. For specialized production of commodities can occur where there is no division of labour within the production process other than that based on developing skills. This second mechanism, which is evident in pre-industrial commodity production, is based on selective specialization in particular commodities. That this is a gradual process can be seen on two levels. In the early stages of commodity specialization, a worker continues to participate in subsistence activities in addition to specialist endeavour. Blacksmiths, the only specialist producers in much of pre-colonial West Africa, were also farmers. In Hart's terms the economy is very partially commoditized, and indeed hoes and knives often exchanged for livestock or grain rather than money.

The second level on which gradual specialization can be discerned is the degree of specialization within the economy as a whole. In the simplest societies there are no specialist producers of commodities. In simple agricultural systems one finds a few – potters, blacksmiths, weavers, carvers.

Esther N. Goody

But in the complex bazaar economies of the Middle East and south and southeast Asia the proliferation of more and more narrowly defined specialist producers is striking. In, for instance, tenth-century Russia, seventeenth-century Egypt and eighteenth-century Kashmir, there were many specialist occupations within which each craftsman made the whole product.[2] Contemporary bazaar economies like that studied by Geertz in Morocco still show this proliferation of occupational specialization (Geertz 1979).[3]

In contrast to horizontal division of labour based on age and developing skills, specialist commodity production can be thought of as *vertical* division of labour. Each specialist occupation encompasses the training process and progressive acquisition of skill, i.e. has its own horizontal division of labour. But there is no movement between specialist occupations. Skilled makers of hoes and axes do not 'evolve' into makers of brass swords, still less into glass-bead blowers (Nadel 1942: 257ff). Thus the economy comes to incorporate a number of specialist occupations, the products of which are exchanged through the market. Where specialist commodities have proliferated as in the examples from bazaar economies, producers tend also to be specialists only, and no longer to participate in subsistence activities. The producers become correspondingly dependent on the market for the satisfaction of their subsistence needs as well as for those specialist commodities which they themselves do not produce.

Under some conditions these specializations become the basis of regional differences in commodity production. In the medieval northern-European textile industry there was a highly elaborated specialization of different areas in different sorts of cloth, many of which came to be known by the part of the country, or even one town, in which they were first made: Kerseys were first made in the Suffolk town of that name; Dutch beys came originally from Holland but were made extensively in Essex during the sixteenth century; and Handshoote says were taken up in many weaving centres (Coleman 1969). Regional specialization may originate in a drawing into the market of locally idiomatic peasant production; in the history of the European textile industry this appears repeatedly as a response to competition on the wider market (Miller 1965; Coleman 1969). As such, this form of specialization represents a shift from production for local consumption to local specialization for an external market, i.e. to interdependence based on wider market forces.

Production of specialized commodities can lead to the separation and organization of those workers making a particular product or service, but this by no means always occurs. Where it does, organization has taken various forms: most distinctive are 'guilds' as in northwestern Europe, Turkey and Egypt (Thrupp 1963; Baer 1964), and the occupational sub-castes of India. In the latter, endogamy and ritual prohibitions have further reinforced the separation of occupationally defined groups.

The classic definitions of the Hindu caste system stress the interdependence of the various caste and sub-caste groups (e.g. Wiser 1936, Leach 1960). The *jajmani* system is based on permanent relationships of provision of services and commodities by specialist *jati*, usually of low status, in exchange for a set amount of food annually and certain customary protection. However Leach's argument that this allows the members of low-caste *jati* to impose constraints on their high-caste clients through the threat to withdraw services (Leach 1960) applies mainly to certain of the service castes (e.g. barbers and washermen) and the producers of basic commodities, such as potters and carpenters. Landless labourers have no specialist skills and are easily replaced should they become restive. Where the craft sub-castes produce highly specialized goods, it is also hard to see how this mechanism of control through reciprocity would operate; not many people can depend in a very meaningful way on the makers of scissors and nut crackers, wood carvers, scale makers or the makers of lacquered chests (*Census of India* 1961, *Gujarat*, vol. V, part VIIA). It is thus unlikely that they are in a position to threaten to withhold the products of their labour. These esoteric specialist commodities are the consequence of a market for luxury goods and specialist equipment. This is an interdependence of the market, and in the case of equipment is in fact based on a division of labour *within* a particular system of production.

Indeed, the specialized 'domestic industries' reported on in the 1961 Indian Census for Gujarat differ from Geertz's list of trades found in a Moroccan bazaar in one very interesting way. The Indian list contains a number of trades which do not serve the consumer directly, but produce commodities which are required by other trades in the production of their commodities. Thus *jari* makers produce the silver and gold thread used by the makers of certain saris; scale makers produce equipment for merchants of many sorts; wood-block carvers make the blocks used to print designs on cloth; there are also printers of cotton and silk cloth; and those who tie-dye designs in cloth (Gujarati *bandhani*; Hindi *bandhana*). This production of commodities which are themselves components for the production of other commodities constitutes a *functional* division of labour. These specialist sub-caste occupations are not ends in themselves in terms of commodity production, despite the fact that they have an independent system of recruitment and their own horizontal division of labour. Rather their products are essential to the makers of other commodities. Thus sari makers are dependent not only on spinners and weavers, but also on the producers of *jari* thread, the carvers of wood blocks, the printers of designs on cloth, and the *bandhini* tiers. Whereas in a vertical division of labour the craftsman makes the entire commodity, in functional division of labour, different components, or stages of production, are made by different craftsmen. It is this functional division of labour which Marx associates with the cooperation that characterizes manufacture, whether of Swiss watches with their many different components made by outworkers, or of coaches built by specialist upholsterers, painters, wheelwrights, cabinet makers, blacksmiths, carpenters and leather workers.

The various constituent industries which feed into the Indian textile industry are interesting from another point of view. For they are spatially dispersed. The census account of the carvers of wooden blocks for printing cloth, who were studied in three localities in Gujarat, notes that 'The engraved blocks are marketed in all the prominent hand-printing centres of India' (*Census of India* 1961, vol. V, part VIIA, 19:17). The account of the *jari* makers of Surat reports that 'Surat caters for the needs of manufacturers of Benares, Madras, Mysore, and other centres in India and abroad' (*Census of India* 1961, vol. V, part VIIA, 13:31). As the census reports make clear, the commodities of these functionally interdependent industries were articulated through the market rather than being incorporated within a single workshop or factory, or even being linked by a merchant capitalist, except on an occasional basis. It is clear from the material on the Indian textile industries that a functional division of labour developed independently of either centralized factory production or the industrial revolution (see especially Irwin 1966). However this is not unique to India. The organization of the Flemish wool industry in the twelfth to fourteenth centuries provides another very clear example.

One key role of functional specialization for technological innovation lies in its making obvious the bottle-necks in the production process. (See below, p. 23, for detailed examples.) Indeed, functional specialization leads to a new kind of interdependence in the production process; one stage cannot get on faster than the others. At the same time, by defining the sub-stages of the production process in smaller and smaller units, workers become specialists in one aspect of the production process, and able to see how it can be made more efficient.

I have roughed out what seems to me an important set of distinctions between forms of division of labour – horizontal, vertical, and functional – each of which have characteristic forms of interdependence. But what are the implications of these for the shift from craft production to forms which can be seen as leading more or less directly into industrial manufacture?

The organization of production in the pre-industrial northern-European textile industry

There are several themes which emerge as central in the pre-industrial period in Europe.[4] Among these are the growing complexity of the division of labour; technological innovation; the relations of production which articulate the division of labour; and the expansion and differentiation of the market for commodities. The beginning of the pre-industrial period is rather like an infinitely receding mirage. I will follow a long tradition in considering the period in terms of the development of the textile industry. This is less arbitrary than it might seem, as the first industrial complex that is clearly described is the Flemish woollen industry of the twelfth to fourteenth centuries, characterized by Eileen Power as 'a pocket of capitalism in a pre-capitalist world' (Power 1941). There is a striking continuity in the central role played by textiles throughout this period. Bautier says that the textile industry of the Flemish towns and northern France during the classical middle ages 'made an important contribution to the economic expansion and prosperity of western Europe' (1971: 209) and that, based on these towns together with many new centres, 'the textile industry had been the main type of business during the whole of the middle ages' (*ibid.*: 210). This industry served as the motive force in the formation of the merchant-adventurers' companies of northwestern Europe which sought new trade routes and new markets in the Baltic and Russia, and in the Mediterranean and the Far East. A rapid consequence of the Far Eastern trade was that cotton textiles from India became vital in the spice trade with Indonesia and the slave trade with West Africa, and gradually transformed the European textile industry itself (Irwin 1966). Ultimately it was the English cotton industry which led the emergence of industrial capitalism in the late eighteenth century.

In the *Cambridge Economic History of Europe* (Postan and Rich 1952), the section on the development of industry in the middle ages discusses only three industries: building, mining, and the Flemish cloth industry which flourished between the twelfth and the fourteenth centuries.[5] Although referred to as 'the' Flemish cloth industry, it was in fact based on a number of towns which were not only independent of one another, but were increasingly politically autonomous, being governed by councils made up of town elders and guild officials. Unfortunately the origin of the cloth

7

Esther N. Goody

industry in these towns is obscure, though it seems to have been linked to
the rise of a network of fairs in the late eleventh and early twelfth century.
By 1180 cloth was being sold under the name of its town of manufacture
in Mediterranean centres and the Levant. Export trade must have been
even older, as Italian merchants were already established in the Flemish
towns by this time.

Already in this medieval town industry the division of labour was surprisingly advanced. Flemish trade regulations enforced the separation of
each of the many processes through which wool had to go. Sorting it into
different grades was done at the warehouse by women. Beating the larger
pieces of dirt out was the work of men. Then it was put out to women
working alone or with children in town rooms or country villages for washing, combing, spinning and finally for oiling the yarn. Then to weavers – it
took two men to operate the looms for the heavy luxury cloth in which the
Flemish towns specialized. A master was limited to the management of
three looms, for which he was allowed only five assistants apart from the
services of women who went from workshop to workshop helping to set up
warps. From the loom the cloth went to a fulling trough to be scoured and
thickened with alkaline earth in hot water and urine, and then washed. The
Flemish drapers did not make use of the newly introduced fulling mills,
claiming that they damaged their fine-quality cloth. Instead it was trampled
by men's feet. A master fuller was restricted to four or five troughs. Dyers
were allowed up to eighteen vats, which if in continuous use would keep
twenty men busy. The final three finishing processes were stretching the
wet cloth on 'tenter hooks'; roughing the surface with teasels; and trim-
ming with huge, broad-bladed shears. These last three processes were usually
carried out in a single workshop.

> Industrial growth through the making of better cloth was in Flanders
> and neighbouring northeastern France . . . due entirely to merchant
> capital. Merchants took over all supply and marketing functions
> through the putting-out system, paying for work done, at piece rates.
> Production was dispersed in hundreds of workshops, the more skilled
> work being done under qualified masters, the less skilled in the
> workers' own tenement rooms, or in peasant homes in nearby vil-
> lages. The skilled masters equipped their shops at their own expense
> and paid their own staff out of the merchant-employers' payment for
> the week's output of the shop . . . It has been estimated that in
> Douai around the middle of the thirteenth century there were 150
> merchant drapers each keeping about one hundred people employed.
> (Thrupp 1972:248-9)

The distinction between capitalist and producer was maintained by the guild system, for it was the merchants who were guild members. They were manufacturers in the sense that they controlled raw materials and markets, and coordinated various stages of production (all activities requiring capital) but they were not themselves producers. Indeed guild members in the Flemish towns were forbidden to practise the craft they represented. If they were members of the dyers' guild, they could not actually dye cloth; of the silk weavers' guild, they could not weave silk, and so on. The corollary of this, of course, is the exclusion of the producers from the guilds. Thus they were doubly controlled: they depended for their raw materials and for selling the finished product on the guild members, and the guilds controlled the conditions of manufacture and indeed the very laws of the towns in which they lived and worked.

The success of the Flemish woollen trade led to increasing population density, and to a situation in which there was too little land around the cities for people to support themselves by farming. What seems to have happened was that those who had farmed became involved in the manufacture of cloth in one way or another, and combined this with growing what food their small parcels of land allowed. Thus production was not confined to the cities, but spread outside into the densely populated countryside. (The similarity with the 'close-settled zone' around Kano is striking.) It is not clear what relationship there was between the spread of cloth manufacture outside the cities and the tight control exerted within the cities by the guilds. However, this is a pattern which reappeared in England later.

The other response to the semi-urban population structure surrounding the cloth towns was the intensification of agriculture. Town cloth workers, having neither land nor time for agriculture, had to buy food. But little agricultural land was available around the towns. The response was the combination of dairy farming and market gardening, using the manure of the animals to allow permanent cropping of vegetables. Slicher van Bath (1960) has suggested that this was the origin of the Netherlands' concern with agricultural innovation which culminated in the so-called agricultural revolution.

The history of the northern-European cloth trade is entwined with political history. Flemish knights had been active in the Norman conquest and were given land, especially in eastern England. It is possible that this is linked to the close ties in the wool trade between eastern England and the Flemish towns. In any case, the Flemish industry grew more and more dependent on importing English wool. When political relations between England and the Flemish principalities became strained, successive English

9

kings retaliated by placing embargoes on the exporting of wool to the wool towns. From the fourteenth century, the Flemish share of the production of woollen cloth steadily declined, to be replaced by cloth of English manufacture.

As with the Flemish textile industry of the eleventh to fourteenth centuries, the early English industry was concentrated in towns, and closely controlled by merchant guilds, which in some cases virtually governed the towns as well. Yet in England already in the thirteenth century weavers were moving out of the towns and settling in the countryside. There are various views as to the reason for this movement out of the towns, perhaps all of them touching on aspects of the truth. In a fascinating paper entitled 'An Industrial Revolution of the Thirteenth Century', Carus-Wilson suggested that the introduction of fulling mills drew weavers away from the towns. These mills required fast-running streams to operate their water wheels, and were for the most part put up on 'the swift clear streams of the north and west, in remote valleys far beyond the bounds of the ancient chartered cities of the plains' (1941: 183–210). As a result she concluded, 'colonies of weavers began to settle around the fulling mills' and the industry as a whole moved from town to country.

But other factors were also clearly involved in this movement. Miller (1965) shows that the restrictions imposed on workers by the merchant guilds in the towns repeatedly led to the founding of craftsmen's guilds, mainly among weavers and fullers, in an attempt to secure better wages and conditions of work. This confrontation made it difficult for the merchant clothiers to cut production costs when in the thirteenth century increasing competition from Flemish cloth threw the industry into recession. Weaving and spinning accounted for something like 80 per cent of production costs, and lower wages could be paid to rural workers who lacked the guild organization of their town counterparts. Thus the town merchant clothiers themselves subverted the ordinances which restricted the manufacture of cloth to licensed boroughs, and bought from the countryside.

But the weavers appear to have moved into the rural areas as well. In part this was in order to avoid the taxes imposed by town governments, levies which sometimes fell on them but not on the better-off merchants (Miller 1965: 74). The lower wages of rural craftsmen were not only due to their lack of guild organization. They often appear to have had the use of some land, sufficient for a garden, a cow or two and chickens, with which they could augment their craft income. From the merchant clothiers' point of view they could be paid less than a subsistence wage.

The significance of the shift from production controlled by town guilds to weaving and spinning concentrated in the countryside lay in the pattern of combining 'cottage weaving' with farm labouring and small-holding, for an increasing proportion of the rural population had too little land to live by agriculture alone. Thrupp writes that by the early fourteenth century as much as 40 per cent of Europe's peasantry had less than the minimal amount of land necessary for subsistence (Thrupp 1972). While the decimations of recurrent plague redressed this situation for a time, by the sixteenth century marginal lands were again brought into cultivation in England (Postan 1972) and in southern France (Le Roy Ladurie 1974). The rural poor were a constant problem in England, at least from the fourteenth century when one of the provisions of the Statute of Labourers (1351) was a prohibition on almsgiving to 'sturdy beggars who do refuse to labour'. Further legislation was enacted at the end of the fifteenth century when by the 'Acte against Vacabounds and Beggars' (1495) all beggars and other idlers were to be put in the stocks for three days, whipped and sent back to their homes. During the sixteenth century both national and municipal laws forbade begging, required the able-bodied poor to work, and established taxes for the support of the indigent poor (Lis and Soly 1979: 48, 87–8). Later legislation specifically made provision for the training of paupers' children in rural industries so that they would be able to support themselves as adults. Significantly, King in his population survey of the seventeenth century lumps together 'cottagers and paupers' as 'the poor' (quoted in Lis and Soly 1979). Progressive enclosures of land, first for sheep and then for intensified agriculture, deprived the cottars, and later even small farmers of sufficient land for agricultural subsistence (see especially Dobb 1946: chap. 6). The landless often built crude dwellings and eked a living from gardening, agricultural day labour when available, and weaving, spinning, lace making, nail making and such other bye-employments as they could find.

Thus there developed a 'rural proletariat' who were dependent on cottage industry for augmenting the intermittent and low wages obtainable from working on other people's farms during the harvest season. Many probably had a little land, though many hadn't even that. But these people became dependent on their earnings from cloth production – at the same time making England the major producer and exporter of woollen cloth. Given this type of work force, it is perhaps not surprising that Italian and Flemish cloth was still considered by many to be the finest.

'Cottage industry' evokes an idyllic scene of the weaver seated at his loom, his children playing in the sunshine at his feet, with their mother singing as she feeds the chickens/cooks dinner/does her sewing . . . There are two main inaccuracies in this picture: first, all family members were likely to be involved in the production process (see below); and second, contemporary accounts imply an urgency and sense of struggle in an endless battle for survival. To add to the confusion, the term has been used for very different forms of production. For the purposes of comparative analysis two polar types can be distinguished. The cottage-craftsman mode, and the cottage-labourer mode.

Both cottage-craftsman and cottage-labourer production resemble what Sahlins termed the 'domestic mode of production' in that kinship relations are productive relations; kinship roles are also economic roles. But in cottage-craftsman production the process of manufacture and sale are controlled by the members of the domestic group itself. The independent cottage weavers of the Yorkshire district of Halifax, described by Defoe in 1727, illustrate this mode. These cottagers used wool from their own sheep, spun by their wives and daughters, which they wove on their own looms and sold individually to merchant clothiers at the weekly cloth markets in surrounding towns. Here the division of labour is contained within the household, and the producer not only owns his own tools, but both controls raw materials and has direct access to the market. This extreme autonomy was often modified by the need to buy more wool than the weaver's sheep could produce, or to pay for the spinning of part of the thread needed. And many households included besides the weavers and his wife and children one or two apprentices and perhaps one or two journeymen. These additional workers lived as members of the family, and, like the children, often later left to establish independent weaving households of their own. A surprising amount of cloth was produced by this household workshop system. The figures for the West Riding of Yorkshire, where cottage craftsman production flourished, were:

In	1740 – 41,441 broad pieces	and	58,620 narrow pieces
	1750 – 60,447 broad pieces		78,115 narrow pieces
	1760 – 49,362 broad pieces		69,573 narrow pieces
	1770 – 93,074 broad pieces		85,376 narrow pieces

(Mantoux 1961:61 n. 3)

At the other pole is the model provided by the weavers of the East Anglian textile industry beginning in the fourteenth century, and gradually throughout much of England thereafter. Here the merchant clothier bought the wool, placed it out for picking, carding and spinning, then sent it to weavers for making up into cloth, then to dyers, fullers and finally to finishers (tenters and shearers). As the owner of the raw material at each stage of production, the clothier also owned the finished product. The specialists who carried out the separate stages of production were in effect wage labourers, paid on a piece-work basis. In his account of the East Anglian woollen industry, Heard sees this form of organization as deriving from the earlier period when wool was mainly exported:

> The organisation of industry was established upon a pattern built up during the wool trade. The wool brokers and agents who had manipulated the wool sales understood all the technical and practical details of wool buying. Moreover with the decline of wool exports these were the men who had to adapt themselves to the new conditions. The individual craftsmen needed raw materials and a ready market for their manufactures. The wool broker quickly took advantage of this situation, becoming the supplier of raw materials, and disposing of the yarn, or cloth produced by the clothworker. Gradually these clothiers dominated the industry, and became the employers of a huge workforce. (Heard 1970: 62)

Due in part to a shortage of currency, clothiers often paid their workers in kind, with food or wool, rather than with money. This was known as the truck system and was considered wrong, becoming the subject of prohibitive legislation, widely ignored. Even where weavers bought their wool, they frequently lacked cash and took it on credit, against payment for the finished cloth. Then, when they sold the cloth, little was owed them after repaying the debt for the wool. In this way many became indebted to the wool merchants, who might come to own their looms as well. Weavers in this situation had to sell their cloth to their creditor, and thus had to take what he offered them. Wages fell accordingly, for the clothiers were constantly alert to ways to cut their costs. The process is vividly described in a song from the time of William III.

The Clothier's Delight, or, the rich Men's Joy[6]

Of all sorts of callings that in England be
There is none that liveth so gallant as we;
Our trading maintains us as brave as a knight,
We live at our pleasure, and take our delight;
We heapeth up riches and treasure great store
Which we get by griping and grinding the poor.
    And this is a way for to fill up our purse
    Although we do get it with many a curse.

Throughout the whole kingdom, in country and town,
There is no danger of our trade going down,
So long as the Comber can work with his comb,
And also the Weaver weave with his lomb;
The Tucker and Spinner that spins all the year,
We will make them to earn their wages full dear.
    And this is a way, etc. . . .

And first for the Combers, we will bring them down,
From eight groats a score unto half a crown;
If at all they murmur and say 'tis too small,
We bid them choose whether they will work at all:
We'll make them believe that trading is bad;
We care not a pin, though they are ne'er so sad.
    And this is a way, etc. . . .

We'll make the poor Weavers work at a low rate,
We'll find fault where there's no fault, and so we will bate;
If trading grows dead, we will presently show it,
But if it grows good, they shall never know it;
We'll tell them that cloth beyond sea will not go,
We care not whether we keep clothing or no.
    And this is a way, etc. . . .

The next for the Spinners we shall ensue,
We'll make them spin three pound instead of two;
When they bring home their work unto us, they complain,
And say that their wages will not them maintain;
But if that an ounce of weight they do lack,
Then for to bate threepence we will not be slack.
    And this is the way, etc. . . .

But if it holds weight, then their wages they crave,
We have got no money, and what's that you'd have?
We have bread and bacon and butter that's good,
With oatmeal and salt that is wholesome for food;
We have soap and candles whereby to give light,[7]
That you may work by them so long as you have sight.
    And this is a way, etc. . . .

When we go to market our workmen are glad;
But when we come home, then we do look sad:

We sit in the corner as if our hearts did ake;
We tell them 'tis not a penny we can take.
We plead poverty before we have need;
And thus we do coax them most bravely indeed.
      And this is a way, etc. . . .

The sort of dependence which the cottage-labourer system produced was most evident during the periodic slumps of the textile industry when the weavers were desperate for work. E. P. Thompson writes: 'As their conditions worsened, so they had to spend more and more time in unpaid employments – fetching and carrying work, and a dozen other processes' (1965: 287). And he quotes an observer in the late nineteenth century who wrote of weavers:

> If they succeeded [in finding work] it was mostly on condition that thay helped to break the wool for it; that is, opened the bales, then the fleeces, taking off the coarse parts called the *britch*, put it in sheets, then go to the mill and help to scour it, then 'lit' or dye it . . . All this was for *nothing*, except in some cases a small allowance for a little ale or cheese and bread . . . When the slubber had doffed the first set of slubbing, it often became a serious question as to whose turn it was to have it, and casting lots would frequently be the mode of deciding it . . . (J. Lawson 1887, quoted in E. P. Thompson 1965: 287)

These two models are basically different in two ways. The cottage craftsman carried out all, or most of, the stages of production himself, with the help of other members of his household. Those he could not do he paid for on the open market. The functional division of labour implicit in textile production was often encompassed within one, domestic unit. The cottage labourer, on the other hand, was a specialist, performing only one stage of the production process. Whether he combed or carded, spun, or wove, he depended on the work of others for his raw materials. The cottage craftsman was independent, in that he raised or bought his raw materials, owned his spinning wheels and looms, and sold his product on the open market. The cottage labourer was not only dependent on the merchant clothier for raw materials, sometimes for his loom and for the disposal of his wool, thread or cloth, but often was in debt to a particular merchant and so tied to him and forced to accept the wages he offered.

The question is, to what extent are dependence and the functional division of labour related, and, if so, why? Mantoux suggests that, once the craftsman produces for more than a local market, he must depend on an intermediary for the sale of his work. To this must be added that, once the craftsman needs raw materials which he cannot himself produce or buy locally, he also depends on an intermediary for these (see especially Bowden 1971: chap. 2). We have seen, for instance, that the merchant clothiers' control of the manufacture of old draperies in East Anglia grew out of their control of the wool needed by the weavers (Heard 1970; also Thrupp 1972). It is interesting that apparently only relatively late in the development of the English textile industry, in the seventeenth and eighteenth centuries, does the merchant clothier sometimes own the loom as well as control the raw material and the sale of cloth. That is, there is some evidence that control over the tools of production is less problematic in the history of this industry than is the control over raw materials and access to the market.

There is another sense in which the elaboration of the division of labour was linked to the dominance of the merchant clothiers. The later stages of the production process – dyeing and finishing – required more capital, equipment and skill than the others. Thus it was virtually impossible for the independent artisan cottager to do any but the simplest dyeing himself and most of his cloth was sold as 'whites', i.e. undyed. If there was a local public fulling mill he could get his own cloth done there at a fee. But where these facilities were monopolized by the merchant clothiers, the weaver had no choice but to sell his unfinished cloth, at a relatively low price, to him. Capital was required for dyes and dye vats; and fulling mills were even more expensive to build.

An often-noted puzzle of pre-industrial textile production is the curious absence of factories. Not only was there rural 'cottage' mass production, but there was hardly any urban factory production to go with it. Workshops existed, but these generally remained small. Stranger still, they did not utilize the division of labour already existing between workshops and in rural industry. There were weaving workshops, dyeing workshops and finishing workshops, but few attempts to bring these processes together.

The only examples we do know of were either created by the state, as in France under Louis XIV (Mantoux 1961: 29ff), or lasted only a brief time and failed to attract successors. A subsequent, sixteenth-century, account of one of the few attempts to establish a textile factory occurs in Deloney's novel *Jack of Newberie.*

> Within one roome being large and long,
> There stood two hundred Loomes full strong:
> Two hundred men the truth is so,

Wrought in these Loomes all in a row.
By every one a pretty boy,
Sate making quils with mickle joy;
And in another place hard by,
An hundred women merily,
Were carding hard with joyfull cheere,
Who singing sate with voices cleere.
And in a chamber close beside,
Two hundred maidens did abide,
In petticoates of Stammell red,
And milke-white kerchers on their head:
Their smocke-sleeves like to winter snow,
That on the Westerne mountains flow,
And each sleeve with a silken band,
Was featly tied at the hand.
These pretty maids did never lin,
But in that place all day did spin:
And spinning so with voices meet,
Like Nightingals they sung full sweet.
Then to another roome came they,
Where children were in poore aray:
And every one sate picking wool,
The finest from the course to cull:
The number was seven score and ten,
The children of poore silly men:
And these their labours to requite,
Had every one a penny at night,
Beside their meat and drinke all day,
Which was to them a wondrous stay.
Within another place likewise,
Full fifty proper men he spies,
And these were Shearemen every one,
Whose skill and cunning there was showne:
And hard by them there did remaine,
Full fourscore Rowers taking paine.
A Dye-house likewise had he then,
Wherein he kept full forty men:
And likewise in his fulling Mill,
Full twenty persons kept he still.
Each weeke ten good fat oxen he

Spent in his house for certaintie:
Beside good butter, cheese, and fish,
And many another wholesome dish.
He kept a Butcher all the yeere,
A Brewer eke for Ale and Beere:
A Baker for to bake his Bread,
Which stood his hushold in good stead.
Five Cookes within his kitchin great,
Were all the year to dresse his meat.
Sixe scullian boys unto their hands,
To make cleane dishes, pots and pans,
Beside poore children that did stay,
To turne the broaches every day.
The old man that did see this sight,
Was much amaz'd as well he might:
This was a gallant Cloathier sure,
Whose fame for ever shall endure.

(Deloney 1929: 24–5)

Even granting a large measure of idealization, such an enterprise must have had a substantial output, and can hardly have failed to benefit from the relatively greater work discipline and supervision. Yet, it remained a marvel, not a model, to later generations. Why? Thrupp suggests that, given the existing technology, manufacture may not have been very profitable. Comparison of trade and manufacturing enterprises in medieval Italy shows the level of return to be substantially higher from trade (Thrupp 1972: 261). This calculation refers to manufacturing based on the putting-out system. But in Jack of Newberie's factory he had additional costs to pay which in cottage industry were borne by the worker. He clothed his workers and fed them. In this he treated them as he would have servants or apprentices. But the cumulative expense must have cut very considerably into whatever profits he made. If he also felt obliged to carry his employees in slack periods this would have been a further expense not shouldered with respect to workers on the putting-out system. This in turn may well have made him cautious about hiring additional workers when demand was high. In short, the undertaking of the same obligations to factory workers as were recognized towards apprentices and servants must have led to an expensive and rigid system of production. Although at least some clothiers recognized the potential advantages of rationalizing textile production by centralizing the several stages, when this rationalization was combined with customary obligations to employees it does not appear to have been profitable enough to attract imitators.

It is of the cottage-labourer form of domestic production which Medick writes in seeing the emergence, expansion and decline of rural industries as 'industrialization before the factory system', or 'proto-industrialization' (1976: 296). Important between the sixteenth and nineteenth centuries on the continent and earlier in England, proto-industrialization appears everywhere in Europe to have had a common structural foundation in the close link between household production based on a family economy and the capitalist organization of trade, putting out and marketing of products.[8] Home-industrial weavers, knitters, nail makers or scythe makers were always directly or indirectly dependent on merchant capital.

> The functional interrelationship between family economy and merchant capital, and the peculiarly stable and at the same time flexible character of this configuration, constituted a comprehensive set of social relations of production, giving to the historical process of proto-industrialization the traits of a socio-economic system. (*ibid*.: 296)

Medick contends that given the pre-conditions of the emergence of a large underemployed class of small peasants and rural landless people,[9] and at the same time the expansion of world markets dominated by merchant capitalists (see Dobb 1946; Hobsbawm 1968; Wallerstein 1974), the rural poor had no alternative but to make part-time or full-time shift from land-intensive agrarian production to labour-intensive craft production. Organized by the merchant capitalists, this resulted in a system of rural mass production.

Proto-industry was domestic industry. And as such it was closely tied to the inner dynamic of the family under conditions of market and monetary relationships and capitalist organization of trade, putting out and marketing. Like the peasant economy, this rural-industry economy was based on a small household of producers, which was also the unit of organization of reproduction and consumption. These multiple, superimposed functions gave the proto-industrial economy its special characteristics, in particular the similarity of the rural industrial household to the peasant household in its relationship between labour and subsistence. In Chayanov's terms, both peasant and proto-industrial family try to maximize the gross product, not the net profit. If, for example, the returns of the family economic unit fell (as they might do with the repeated slumps in the world market which characterized this period), the family sought to increase its output of work, even beyond that which could be exacted from wage labourers. It was precisely because all members of the family were engaged in production, and might be able to eke out some sustenance from a small garden and possibly a cow, that they could 'afford' to work for less than the amount required to reproduce their labour – the constraint which set limits on the amount of work that a capitalist could squeeze from factory wage labour. For the cottage-labourer family economy, on the other hand, the work effort, regardless of the amount of labour expended, appears as an invariable overhead cost, since the family members must be supported somehow, and must eat whether they are working 3 hours or 8 hours or 18 hours a day so long as more work represents even a small increment in income.

If, on the other hand, with improved economic conditions – or perhaps an increase in the family work force – the income necessary for subsistence can be secured with only a few hours work per day, there is no incentive to work longer hours. Additional 'time resources' are converted to consumption or leisure.

Thus the family economy is responding both to external pressures and to internal balance of production and consumption within the family itself. The logic of family economic production is effective only because of the inclination of the poor, proto-industrial workers, to resort to 'self-exploitation' in their productive efforts if this is necessary to ensure customary family subsistence and economic self-sufficiency. In macro-economic terms, Medick holds, this mechanism of self-exploitation by the family enables the merchant or putting-out capitalist to realize an extra 'differential profit'. In Engels' words: 'Competition enables the capitalists to subtract from the price of labour what the family produces in its own gardens and small plots' (quoted in Medick 1976 – preface to 2nd edition, 'Zur Wohnungsfrage' (1887), in Marx–Engels *Werke*, vol XXI, Berlin 1962: 331). Medick contends that the differential profits that can thus be had exceed those available in the guild system or from comparable wage–labour relations in manufacture. He hypothesizes that: 'The primary social relation of production in the transition from traditional peasant society to industrial capitalism was established not in manufactures, but in the characteristic interaction of small and sub-peasant family economy and merchant capital.' Thus Medick sees the producing family of the rural-industrial lower classes as the essential agent in the growth of emergent capitalism. 'The family functioned objectively as an internal engine of growth in the process of proto-industrial expansion precisely because it *subjectively* remained tied to the norms and rules of behaviour of the traditional familial subsistence economy' (*ibid.*: 300). In other words, it was the willingness of the proto-industrial family economic/productive unit to impress men, women and children into long hours of poorly paid labour which allowed the merchant capitalists to realize the 'extra differential profit' which in turn produced the industrial explosion which became industrial capitalism.

Furthermore, says Medick, the proto-industrial system contained within its structural foundation the essential seeds of its own destruction and replacement by industrial capitalism. This contradiction was anchored in the regulating system of the family mode of production as, in effect, opposed to productivity and surplus, i.e. the reverse side of the labour/ consumption balance of the family mode of production. Here labour was diverted into feasting, playing and drinking in exactly those situations of potential growth in which the capitalist putter-out could have obtained maximal profits. The answer of the merchant capitalists was, finally, to bring the labour force into the factory where it could be controlled.

The division of labour and technological innovation

In northwestern Europe, after a very early period of monopoly of textile production within the towns, there was an irregular but irreversible shift to rural production, to the cottage-craftsman mode and increasingly to the cottage-labourer mode. The central role in the industrial revolution of technological innovation in the textile industry raises the question of whether these shifts too were linked to technological innovations. It is a surprising fact that it is at the very beginning, with the Flemish woollen industry, and then again at the very end, with the north of England's cotton industry, that major technological innovations occur. The long period in between sees the major changes in relations of production discussed above, but little significant improvement in technology.

The introduction of the horizontal treadle loom to northern Europe (originally from Syria via Persia?) probably occurred in the tenth or eleventh century (Broudy 1979: 102ff). The horizontal treadle loom makes possible the use of a simple foot-pedal mechanism for opening and reversing the shed through which the warp must pass, and it thus has the potential for greatly speeding up the weaving process. Is it only a coincidence that the first textile industry in Europe renowned for its exported cloth appeared in Flanders at the time the horizontal treadle loom was introduced?

The spinning of wool thread must have provided a constant occupation for women of this region. The introduction of the treadle loom, together with the demand for more and more cloth, meant an increased demand for thread. By the thirteenth century an early form of spinning wheel had appeared (Baines 1977: 53) which was much more efficient than the simple spindle which previously was the only source of thread. However, the distaff and spindle continued to be used alongside the spinning wheel into the nineteenth century. The spinning wheel reduced the number of spinners who were required to provide the thread for one loom. Estimates of this number vary widely but, even using the spinning wheel, it was somewhere in the order of a ratio of five to one loom. The origin of the spinning wheel is variously claimed by India, Persia and China; in any event it came to Europe from the East.

At about the same time, the water wheel was adapted to operate fulling hammers producing the fulling mill. Such mills are first mentioned in northwest Europe in the eleventh century. By the thirteenth century fulling mills were distributed throughout much of England, particularly in the mountainous valleys of the northwest and the Cotswolds. Fulling was considered necessary to the manufacture of woollen cloth, and had previously been done by stamping on the cloth in a stone trough. This required heavy and energetic workers, who very early formed a separate occupation within the textile industry. Initially many fulling mills were built on estates and subject to the same regulations as flour mills, that is, those resident on the estate were required to use the lord's mills, and had to pay him for the privilege. During the late thirteenth and fourteenth centuries there are records of prolonged dispute between the Bishop of St Albans and the townspeople over the Bishop's insistence that the fulling be done at his mill. The townspeople apparently preferred to full their cloth at home in the old way rather than pay for the use of a fulling mill. Here again there is continuity of old technology alongside the new. It seems probable that the fulling mills were more efficient where there was much cloth to process, while individual households could just as easily full the few cloths they wove at home. It is clear that fulling mills represented a level of capital investment quite different from loom or spinning wheel. They were not necessary for the home production of cloth for the family's use, but accompanied the growth of a market-oriented textile industry in England.

There seem to have been no major technological changes in the production of textiles for several hundred years, though the loom and the spinning wheel were subject to improvement and variation.[10] In 1733 came 'the first of the inventions by which the textile industries were transformed, and that which must be considered as the origin of all the others' (Mantoux 1961: 206). This was a simple modification to the loom which allowed the shuttle to be sent across the full length of the fabric and back again with one hand – the 'flying shuttle' as it came to be called. The consequences of this new device were immense. Initially it meant that wider cloth could be woven by a single operative (the old 'broadcloths', since they were wider than the reach of one man's arms, had actually required two weavers sitting side by side). But far more important, the speed of weaving was greatly increased. This led very quickly to a shortage of thread, since even the old looms needed several spinning wheels to keep them working and suffered from chronic undersupply. This shortage led to a series of attempts to invent a machine for spinning wool and cotton thread. The first such machine was patented in 1738 but did not prove successful (Mantoux suggests because the full effects of the new flying shuttle had not yet made themselves felt). Complaints of shortage of thread increased, and in 1761 the Society for the Encouragement of Arts and Manufactures advertised prizes for the invention of a spinning machine. The consequences are extremely interesting. Two quite different machines were patented, virtually simultaneously: Arkwright's water frame in 1769 and Hargreaves' spinning jenny in 1770. The spinning jenny marked an intermediate stage between hand spinning and powered spinning machines, for it was operated by hand but allowed the simultaneous spinning of many threads. Subsequently jennys were powered by water, but they were most widely used in the hand-operated form by cottagers seeking to extend their output. In 1788 there were thought to be at least 10,000 jennys in England. In a few years they virtually ousted the spinning wheel. The jenny was simple to build and inexpensive; it took up little room and did not require a special workshop. If anything, the spinning jenny extended the period of cottage industry by keeping spinning in the hands of individual, dispersed workers.

The water frame, on the other hand, required power – initially from water mills. This made it useless for cottage production, but led to the building of spinning mills, and the final centralization of textile production in factories. Further, the thread spun by the water frame was stronger than that produced on a wheel or jenny, and thus made it possible for the first time in England to use cotton thread for warp as well as weft.[11] Finally Crompton's mule, combining the best features of both the jenny and the water frame, was able to produce thread both strong and very fine. This was the prototype of modern machine spinning.

Now the imbalance was on the weaving side. More thread was machine spun than could be used by the available looms, even when these were equipped with flying shuttles. At first the response was to export thread, and large amounts went abroad. But there were outcries against this from cloth manufacturers who feared that the ample supply of strong thread would lead to dangerous competition. Now there was pressure to develop a powered loom which could weave even more quickly than the flying-shuttle loom. In the meantime the surplus of thread and still-expanding market for cloth led to the recruitment of even more cottage weavers. There was thus actually an increase in the handloom sector of the textile industry at the end of the eighteenth century, just before the introduction of power looms during the first half of the nineteenth century (Cartwright's power loom was first patented in 1785; E. P. Thompson 1965).

Apart from the mechanization of the printing of cloth and chemical dyes, these were the major technical inventions that produced the industrial revolution in textile production – the first industry to be so transformed. Significantly, the key advances in the eighteenth century arose from the successive increase in output in weaving and then spinning, the same two processes transformed at the beginning of the period of mercantile capitalism by the introduction of the horizontal treadle loom and the spinning wheel. The basic division of labour in textile production was set at that time and was not effectively altered until the transformation from hand to powered machines. The power of the interdependence, which is a consequence of the functional division of labour, is underscored by the pressure for improvement generated when steps are out of phase. Significantly both the flying-shuttle loom and the spinning jenny were designed for and used in cottage production. It was the consequences of this series of inventions, the imbalance in output first of weaving and then of spinning, followed by attempts to improve the lagging stage, which led to the utilization of new power sources and ultimately to the centralization of production in factories.

Forms of division of labour, mechanisms of integration, and the reproduction of relations of production

As long as the unit of production remained the household – whether in simple hierarchical division of labour, vertical division of labour, or as one phase of a functional division of labour – productive relations continued to be based on kinship roles. At the domestic level the mechanism of labour replacement was the bearing and rearing of children. If the family had enough to eat, some of the children survived to augment the domestic labour force. However, they sought in turn to establish their own domestic units. In doing so they withdrew resources from the parental production unit – both their own labour, and whatever endowment of land, cash, or tools the parental unit could allow them. Thus the new units were of the same tiny size and minimal capitalization as the parental unit. As Shanin has noted for the more prosperous Russian peasantry, a particularly successful domestic production unit would tend to rear more children and to be able to allow more of them to marry. But eventually their larger resources would be parcelled out, and the size and prosperity of the new units regress to the norm (Shanin 1971).

Another limitation may have operated to keep the size of these domestic production units small. Lowe (1972) suggests that when a cottage craftsman was particularly successful, he tended to cease producing cloth himself, and used his capital to move into the merchant-manufacturer mode, buying up raw material and giving it out to cottage labourers. Such a process would be consistent with the relatively large number of those engaged at this level of textile production.

The pattern of horizontal division of labour occurs so widely because it is based on the utilization of children in the production process, and on their gradual acquisition of skills to the point where they are able to perform the same production tasks as the parents. The parental domestic unit of production is replaced in time by those founded by the children. The developmental cycle of the production unit is based on the developmental cycle of the domestic group itself. So long as the production unit is the household, the two cycles are inseparable.

However, more complex economies develop additional, more complex, higher-order forms of articulation of the division of labour. Thus where there are specialized commodities, there must be some mechanism for their distribution. One such mechanism is through patron–client relations. Here inequality is typical of the exchange. The courts of kings and princes often acted as foci for skilled specialists who produced luxury goods on commission. Sometimes, as in North India, princes assembled craftsmen in order to create more and better prestige goods. Another form of patron-client relationship is the *jajmani* system in India. Here the landowner who paid for services and commodities with grain entered into many different transactions, securing many types of services and goods (Neale 1957; E. N. Goody fieldnotes). He also had a medium of exchange with which he was able to move outside the patron–client domain: by selling grain for money with which to procure services and goods on an external economy. The market itself constitutes the other major means of articulation of the division of labour in systems of vertical specialization. This is evident in the use of the metaphor of the bazaar to describe economies in which vertical specialization is very highly developed, but in which functional division of labour is rudimentary or non-existent.

Esther N. Goody

With the predominance of functional division of labour, the nature of interdependence between commodity producers shifts from optional to obligatory. It may be a matter of preference, or of affluence, whether a man buys scissors, nutcrackers, or a lacquered chest. The decision of a weaver who is a cottage craftsman to buy extra wool if his own sheep do not produce enough is of an entirely different order. If he does not, or cannot, buy the wool, then he cannot continue to make a living as a weaver. Similarly, a printer of cotton cloth in India had to have carved printing blocks; a maker of tie-dyed saris had to have both cotton cloth, and dyestuffs; a maker of gold-embroidered saris had to have *jari* thread. This need of access to raw materials (even when they are themselves objects of prior stages of production) creates a recurrent source of indebtedness, which is evident in accounts of the medieval Chinese cotton textile industry (Chao 1977) no less than in the careers of Kano tailors (Pokrant, this volume) and in northwestern Europe. It is here that the role of merchant capital becomes crucial. Indeed, the history of pre-industrial Europe from the middle ages could be read as an account of myriad experiments and explorations with various modes of manipulating merchant capital in order to control commodities. At first reliance was on the market; workshops and cottage craftsmen produced goods which merchant clothiers bought. Then, with further differentiation of function, dyers and finishers (Thrupp 1972) *successful* cottage craftsmen (Lowe 1972), wool merchants and ex-wool merchants (Bowden 1971; Heard 1970) moved into the merchant-clothier role, and by manipulation of debt-dependency relationships, merchant capital moved gradually into the organization of rural or proto-industrial production. This phase extended for some time before the next transition to centralized production in a 'factory', probably as the joint consequence of the need to have greater control over the rate and quality of production, and the requirements of machinery run by water power. This central role of merchant capital was recapitulated in the later development of capitalism in Russia (Lenin 1964).

Table 1.1 *Forms of division of labour and types of integration*

	Type of integration
Horizontal division of labour	(1) dependence relationship based on youth, informal training or apprenticeship, reciprocally with:
	(2) authority relationship based on age and skill, plus the teacher's ownership of raw materials, tools and finished product.

Table 1.1 (*cont.*)

Although it is inherently unequal, over time the horizontal division of labour is integrated by the maturation of the apprentice who progresses to the status of master. Pupil/teacher roles may be filled by kin (child/parent; foster child/foster parents) or by non-relatives (apprentice/master). There is a cyclical reproduction of the production unit.

Vertical division of labour	Within a production unit there is typically, but not necessarily, a horizontal division of labour.
	Between production units making the same specialized commodity there may be integration on the basis of guild rules and offices, or there may be a sub-caste council. But there is not necessarily any form of integration between such production units.
	Between producers of different specialist commodities, and between producers and consumers, there are two main forms of integration:
	(1) patron/client relationship – e.g. courts, *jajmani* system;
	(2) the market.

The major feature of vertical division of labour is specialization of the final product as a commodity.

Functional division of labour	Within a production unit there may be a horizontal division of labour, or, if based on one of the more complex forms of integration, the production unit itself may be characterized internally by either vertical or functional division of labour.
	Between production units integration of commodities may be based on:
	(1) the market;
	(2) commercial capital/merchant capital;
	(3) producer capital/industrial capital.

Functional division of labour involves interdependence in the making of a final product. The various stages of work in the making of cloth are one example. In the medieval textile industry there were often independent workshops engaged in each of the several stages of the functional division of labour: combing, spinning, weaving, dyeing and finishing. Functional division of labour need not be localized in a factory, as the continuing use today of sub-contracting and putting out demonstrates. The nature of the integration of functional division of labour is clearly critical, as the finished product depends on the linking of the stages.

Esther N. Goody

In terms of the relationship between forms of the division of labour and modes of articulation, there would seem to be two interesting questions. First, what are the factors which lead to the internal organization of those engaged in a vertical division of labour (as in 'guilds'), and under what circumstances does this become involuted in closed kinship units (as in occupational sub-castes)? And then, what is it that leads to the shift from dependence on the market for integration of functional division of labour to the intervention of merchant capital? And, especially, what factors are involved in the shift of merchant capital from operation through the market, as in a bazaar economy, to active engagement in organizing the factors and relations of production, as in industrial capitalism? The striking proliferation of specialist production in bazaar economies without this involvement of capital in the *organization* of production is of particular interest, as many of the third-world countries seeking to 'industrialize' have highly developed bazaar economies yet seem to find this final transition difficult.

The role of rural industry in the transition from craft to industry

It is in this context that I want to consider the implications of the long and intensive period of rural industry which preceded factory industry in Western Europe. Medick's analysis of this domestic 'proto-industry' concludes that it was a necessary prelude to full-scale industrial capitalism because, owing to the self-exploitation of the workers, the rural capitalist was able to realize extra profits which formed the basis of investment in the expensive plant and machinery of factory industry.

However, it could be argued that once the transition had been made from investment in trade to investment in production itself, under conditions of an expanding market (see Hobsbawm 1968: chap. 2) the movement into factories was 'overdetermined'. There probably are many mechanisms involved. The expanding market set up pressures for increased production which led to technical improvements that operated in an uncoordinated way, such that each new improvement removed one bottle-neck but created a new imbalance (see above). This led to incorporating new forms of power, first water power and then steam, and, with a central source of power, centralized production was an obvious sequel.

It is in the nature of the processes of textile production that it is impossible to calculate, and to account for, all raw material. Cleaning of wool and carding it precede spinning, and in the process some fibre is lost; when a cloth is cut off the loom, warp threads at the start and end are lost, and

28

others through breakage. Weaving tensions vary, and even for a given number of warp threads per inch the exact amount of thread used in a cloth of a given length will differ. If cloth workers were convinced of the clothiers' dishonesty (as in *The Clothier's Delight*, p. 13ff.), for their part the clothiers believed that spinners and weavers cheated them, keeping back wool or thread which they either sold separately or used themselves. Under such conditions of mutual hostility and suspicion, and the manufacturers' inability to supervise work done by cottage labourers, factory centralization promised greater efficiency in use of both materials and labour.

Medick seems to be arguing that rural industry provided an opportunity for accumulation of capital – primitive accumulation? – that was necessary before factories could be built and equipped and run efficiently. There are several problems about this view, although the case for exploitation and the reaping of surplus profit is a convincing one. First, it has never been argued that successful merchants did not make huge profits, quite the contrary (see Dobb 1946: chaps. 4 and 5). The problem has been why were these profits transferred from trade into land or titles or other forms of investment, but not into improving production? The most convincing reply seems to be that investment in production didn't 'pay off' before the use of powered machinery (Thrupp 1972). Thus, if Medick is right about the crucial role of rural industry, there must be something more involved than the realization of differential profits; merchants and financiers also had profits, but did not invest them in industry.

Indeed, the very scale of profits realized, linked to the low overhead costs of cottage labour, might well have delayed investment in expensive factories and equipment, as Dobb has argued for the emergence of factory production in England. And here it may be relevant that Medick is focusing on the development of industry on the continent rather than in England. For in England the role of a voracious overseas market was enhanced by ties with colonies which were carefully prevented from producing in competition with the mother country. There were mercantile profits as a source of investment capital on a major scale, not only those of rural industry. Hence the significance of the surplus profits from rural industry may well have been different on the continent than in England; in any case continental factory industry had the English model to follow and thus its development poses a different sort of problem from the 'invention' of factory industry in England. It may be that continental imitations of factory industry were financed by differential profits from rural industry, but only when competition with the products of factory industry forced this move.

What then was the role of rural industry in the transition to industrial

Esther N. Goody

capitalism in England? One thing which it clearly did do was to establish a pattern of investment in the organization of production on a wider-than-workshop basis, across several stages of production. For functional integration through the market, rural industry substituted functional integration within a single enterprise, by a merchant-manufacturer. Repeatedly, in the Flemish towns, the Italian cities and the English towns, guild control prevented the expansion of enterprises beyond a fixed point. Guild regulations were also extremely conservative in prescribing type and quality of cloth, thus preventing flexible adaptation to changing market conditions. Rural industry was impossible to control by regulations, in either size of production units or in uniformity of product. However, the very dispersal of the different stages of production required the development of skills of management and organization very different from those required to run a workshop based on a horizontal division of labour. Perhaps equally important, rural production became so extensive that it fed, and indeed required, markets on a vast scale. It is doubtful whether factory industry would have been profitable without such markets.

There is some information, but not much, concerning rural industry in the case studies of developing societies of this collection. In northern Ghana raw materials for weaving and dyeing were products of domestic labour in the basic sense that cotton was grown on household farms, and spun by women in their spare time. Indigo leaves were collected from wild bushes, and processed at home by women. All this work was on an individual basis, and the products reached the weavers and dyers through the market. In the mid-1970's there was no tradition of earlier slave labour for spinning, weaving or dyeing. However, there was one patronymic group in Daboya, the Sakpare, whose men it was said did not traditionally weave because weaving had been slave work. I never heard this prohibition mentioned by Sakpare elsewhere in Gonja, and it was impossible to get any further information on use of slave labour. In Kano, in northern Nigeria, the pattern in the nineteenth century was very different. The large amounts of cloth exported[12] were mainly woven by men, at home, during the long dry season when there was no farming. There was some growing of cotton on slave plantations, and almost certainly some slave weaving. But most of the cloth appears to have been woven on an individual basis and sold in local markets or to itinerant traders. Both dyers and merchants bought up cloth for dyeing and finishing as required for the export trade. There is, however, no indication of cottage-labourer production in the sense of the merchant or dyer giving out raw materials and paying for their manufacture. Thus there was rural industry in the sense of production for the market through sale to middlemen by men and women partly dependent on agriculture. What does not seem to have happened – or at least what we have no evidence of – is the organization of production by a merchant-manufacturer on a cottage-labourer basis.

These West African examples are interesting since there was no direct contact with the technology and organization of industrial capitalism until the early twentieth century in these areas. Patterns of production until then are West African patterns. In India, as Swallow shows, the picture is much more complex. During the twentieth century there was rural manu-facture of textiles of several different kinds, including a putting-out system of the cottage labourer type. However, India was a major exporter of tex-tiles before the advent of the trade with Europe in the sixteenth century. How this early production was organized is not yet clear. By the seven-teenth century there was the equivalent of a cottage-labourer system in South India, with European brokers or their agents supplying thread on credit, and the usual indebtedness of weavers (Irwin 1966: 32). What remains to be worked out is whether there was a cottage-labourer form of rural industry prior to the extensive involvement of European traders in the Indian textile market.

An equally fascinating and less obscure case is that of Chinese textile manufacture. The widespread use of cotton for clothing by ordinary people was established late in China, and was a direct consequence of the policies of successive governments in the thirteenth and fourteenth centuries. In 1365 a government edict required those holding between five and ten *mon* of land to plant at least half a *mon* of cotton; those with over ten *mon* had to plant at least one *mon* of cotton. This ruling did not take account of variations in soil and climate which made it impossible for some farmers to grow cotton, and was soon modified so that every farmer had to pay a cer-tain percentage of his tax in cotton or cotton cloth. Farmers who couldn't grow cotton had to buy it to meet their tax obligations. Further, the official exchange rate between grain and cloth greatly favoured cloth. This situation created a thriving market in cotton and cotton cloth, and ad-ditional incentive to grow cotton wherever this was possible. Spinning and weaving as bye-employment were frequently used to raise money for taxes or to meet debts. Thus a dispersed but extensive rural industry in cotton textiles was established during the fourteenth century.[13] However, Chao considers that it was not until the middle of the seventeenth century (after further government measures) that cotton replaced linen for common use. The tradition of a division of labour by sex was very strong in China; men did the farming and women did the spinning and weaving. Chao writes that 'there is ample documented evidence that females were the main source, if not the exclusive source, of labour in the domestic system producing cotton textiles during the entire Ming and Ch'ing periods' (i.e. between 1368 and 1850; Chao 1977: 38).

This immense, nationwide cottage industry was not based on a putting-out system. Rather it operated through the market. A woman with no money at all could get credit on cotton bought one day which she returned to sell as thread the following day; in the same way thread could be taken and paid for out of the price of the finished cloth. The cotton-textile industry remained a rural cottage industry until the end of the nineteenth century.[14] The absence of cotton-textile factories is particularly interesting, since both private and government factories are amply documented since very early times. A private silk factory is first mentioned in Chekiang between 1356 and 1367, which had ten workers on five looms, who were paid a daily wage. Private silk factories developed rapidly during the Ming period, and in 1601 in Soochow alone there were 'thousands' of silk weavers on the labour market. When the law limiting the size of silk factories to 100 looms was repealed at the end of the seventeenth century, factory size jumped to 500 and 600 handlooms. This makes the absence of cotton-weaving factories all the more surprising, though there are really two questions here: (1) Why did the widespread rural manufacture of cotton textiles never become organized in a putting-out system by the equivalent of the European merchant-manufacturer? and (2) Why was silk production brought into the factory, but not cotton?

The production of silk in factories was probably related to several ways in which it differs from cotton. First, the raw material, silk thread, though raised by rural households, was very much more valuable than cotton, and must have been too expensive for rural weavers to buy and risky for merchants to give on credit. Perhaps more critical, elaborately patterned silks were woven on complex looms requiring a second person to sit above the loom and manipulate the heddles by pulling strings according to the pattern. Such looms had to be built by skilled craftsmen, and must have represented a considerable investment. Factory production of silk textiles allowed for control of the valuable raw material and looms, and avoided the problem of providing large expensive looms to outweavers. The high degree of skill required in working with the silk looms may have been a further incentive to centralize production in a factory, as the manufacturer could closely supervise the work and avoid costly mistakes. In contrast, cotton was widely available and cheap; cotton looms were simple, one-person treadle looms, requiring little skill to make or operate.

As this contrast suggests, silk was produced for the wealthy and for export, for a luxury market. Cotton, on the other hand, was mainly for the everyday wear of the common people. There was a huge market, but the cloth had to be cheap and, given the level of technology and transport, this left a very narrow margin of profit. Both Chao and Dietrich (1972) argue that cotton remained a rural domestic industry because the labour came from women who had no other source of employment; anything they were able to earn made at least a marginal improvement to the household's standard of living. The men of the household brought in something from agriculture or labouring, so the women's work did not have to meet all the family's subsistence costs.[15] With very low labour costs cotton cloth could be made to sell at a price low enough to meet the market, with some margin of profit for the merchant.

If Dietrich and Elvin are correct that cotton-textile production was integrated only through the market in China, without the development of a putting-out system, this may also be related to the very low level of profit involved. There does not seem to have been for China at this period any equivalent of England's expanding overseas market where large profits could be made by selling at a price much higher than the cost of production. Instead, China had arrived at what Elvin calls a 'high-level equilibrium trap' in which pre-scientific industrial technology is utilized to maximum efficiency in a very large market, and in which demand and supply are balanced at a very low level of technology in a way that makes small increments in efficiency trivial in relation to the vast scattered enterprise involved (Elvin 1973: 298ff). Scarcity of land and rural poverty in China were such that 'self-exploiting' rural women would work long hours for very little, even without the intervention of a merchant capitalist, of whom no mention is made in the following song.

Complaint of the Weaving Wife

Hungry, she still weaves.
Numbed with cold, she still weaves.
Shuttle after shuttle after shuttle.
The days are short,
The weather chill,
Each length hard to finish.
The rich take their rent;
The clerk the land tax,
Knocking repeatedly with urgent insistence.
Her husband wants to urge her on,

> But has no heart to do so.
> He says nothing,
> But stands beside the loom.
> (Li Wen-Yao, 1750, V, 69b–70b. Quoted in Elvin 1973: 274–5)

Low-priced cloth for a mass market may have offered such a low profit margin to the merchant that there was no incentive to invest further in the organization and management of a putting-out system. Chao's account suggests that even with the systematic exploitation of debt and control over raw materials and market, such a system could not have significantly further reduced the amount paid to women for spinning and weaving. Significantly, what seems to have happened in the Chinese cotton-textile industry is 'self-exploitation' without the systematic organization of rural industry by the merchant-manufacturer who is both the villain of Medick's analysis – and, according to that analysis, the origin of the final transition to factory industry. What is clear is that Chinese manufacturers were quick to organize the factory production of luxury textiles on a very large scale, even before the introduction of powered machinery. But in the absence of an expanding market the capitalist organization of rural cotton-textile production did not occur.[16]

These preliminary comparative comments would suggest that the extended period of rural industrial production which preceded the industrial revolution in England, and also subsequently on the continent, may have served to begin the shift of investment capital from trade to direct involvement in production on a scale aimed at supplying a very large market. It seems that this may happen only where, as in England, the functional integration of the component stages of production occurs through the direct intervention of someone who is both merchant *and* manufacturer, in the sense that he uses his capital to control raw materials, tools and labour, and not simply, as does the merchant, to buy and sell these on the open market. It is particularly interesting in this context that the organization of Chinese markets has been shown by Skinner to be elaborately hierarchical, with the result that products move efficiently from small local markets to larger district markets and hence to the major regional markets and finally between regions (Skinner 1964). Perhaps, as Elvin persuasively argues (*op. cit.*), the very efficiency of the market system shielded Chinese merchants from pressure to organize supplies of raw materials and then production, as happened in Europe.

Patterns of investment in production in developing societies

The case studies in this volume represent differing degrees and modes of investment of capital in the industrial process. The Daboya weavers might seem to be a clear example of producers reinvesting in production, and of course this occurs. However, even among the weavers there is a significant difference between individual men, weaving alone without any apprentices, and a man like Abudulae who manages the production of ten looms and the selling of their cloth. Yet Abudulae's 'firm' is possible because his father is dead and he himself has several adolescent and young adult sons. As his sons marry and weave independently, Abudulae's authority will become indirect, like that of Mallam Abudu. This cyclical nature – developmental cycle – of the production group establishes a limit to its size and complexity. With the marriage of the sons, and then the death of their father, a large unit fragments into small ones at earlier stages of the cycle.

There is another sort of limit on the reinvestment of profits in production which is linked to this cyclical development. This is the transfer of capital into trade of various sorts, and into religious status. Established master weavers often become directly involved in trade in some aspect of weaving, such as the buying of hand-spun thread, securing of manufactured thread and dyes, and the selling of cloth and smocks. Here investment in trade and in the weaving industry coincide. But profits are also put into livestock for breeding and sale, and into wholesale trading in such commodities as kerosene, soap, sugar and cigarettes. It is probably only with profits from additional trade that substantial wealth (in local terms) is earned. It is the dream of every Muslim, as well as a duty, to make a pilgrimage to the holy city of Mecca. This is very expensive, though nowadays with chartered planes the trip takes only a matter of days or a few weeks, rather than years. With help from all his sons, and their several trading and weaving activities, Mallam Abudu went to Mecca in 1975. As Alhaji Abudu, he is now recognized as a religious leader as well as the most competent elder of the Bakarambasipe weaving section.

Some of these same features are evident in the pattern of reinvestment of the Kano tailors studied by Pokrant. Most men either work alone or with a single apprentice. However, there are some large workshops in which tailors work for wages. In Hart's terms this is 'a crucial step in the abstraction of social labour since human beings now buy and sell their own productive capacities' (p. 41). Despite this, there remains a strong element of cyclical development in the organization of these workshops. An apprentice aspires to set up as an independent tailor once he is trained, and many indeed hope to find another occupation altogether. As in Daboya, many tailors' apprentices are kin, but there is not the same formality about training each other's sons. Nor are the obligations to continue working for a teacher so clear, though there are vestiges of this in Pokrant's case material. Significantly, even the payment of wages does not ensure the workshop owner either of the full-time work of his employees, or of a dependable number of employees. But in Kano a workshop owner can hire another man to replace an apprentice or employee who leaves, which the Daboya weavers cannot do.

In Kano profits of an individual tailor are sometimes put into a more complex form of production, the workshop based on a combination of wage labour and apprentice labour. But as in pre-industrial Europe there is also the pattern of accumulating profits in order to move out of production into trade. The use of profits as trading capital is still seen as promising better returns than its investment as industrial capital. Pokrant describes contract and credit relations between workshop owners and market traders, but not complex firms in which a large-scale trader also operates workshops which supply him with clothes to sell.

With the Swallow study of the Indian garment firm the pattern changes radically. The firm was founded not with producer capital, but with merchant capital invested in production. Labour is performed for wages and not as a phase of the horizontal division of labour. There is thus no problem of cyclical fission of the production unit to contend with. Nor would this be a possibility in the garment export industry, since design, equipment and marketing must all be centralized owing to constraints of capital, skill and organization. Initially, profit was reinvested in production in the form of a new factory building and new equipment. But the transition to investment in production is not yet complete. When market fluctuations, government intervention and labour troubles threaten profits, investment strategy reverts to that of the merchant-manufacturer. Work is 'put out' to small firms to which the company has no long-term obligation. Investment is in raw materials and contracts, no longer in plant and equipment.

What is particularly fascinating about the Swallow study is that she documents this same pattern of tentative and reversible investment in production for the handloom-weaving industry in Southern India. One important difference between the West African and Indian patterns of division of labour is of course the occupational castes of India. There has long been a strong tradition of trading in the West African savannah. The Islamic faith played an important role in its spread and operation, with conversion to

Islam almost certainly linked to entry into trade in many areas. There were often dominant Muslim trading kindreds in major trading towns (see for instance Braimah and Goody 1967; and Launey 1982). This very strong tradition of trading in certain patronymic groups never, however, reached the degree of closure of the Indian trading castes (Vania/Bania and the functionally equivalent local groups of Jain and Parsee sects in north-west India). It is hard to know, in the Indian case, how much significance to attach to the tradition of the trading castes of investment in merchandise rather than in production. However, in a short pilot study of a Gujarat town I encountered two men of the trading caste who had invested in pro-duction of soap and pottery. Initially neither knew anything about the production process, but by hiring members of the respective artisan sub-castes they were able to design simple factories. In both cases business skills (in accounting and marketing) were combined with modernization of production methods to produce small but viable businesses. Thus, at a more modest level than that represented by the export industry studied by Swallow, specialization in trading does not necessarily prevent investment in production. It may be that the smaller scale of these two enterprises would make them less vulnerable to the external threats which led to rever-sion of investment in trading for the exporting industries.

With the Harris Tweed industry described by Ennew this transition to investment in production is complete, in that the factory owners are so committed to investment in production itself that they seek full control, including both ownership of all the tools and raw materials, and direct, full-time supervision. Crises in the industry, which have indeed occurred, did not lead to a policy of minimizing vulnerability by minimizing invest-ment in production and obligations to the workers through extending the scope of work done outside the factory. Rather the response was the reverse policy of full control through bringing the weaving into the factory, with further investment in new looms.

Of course, these four studies do not represent absolute points on some fixed continuum of change in the pattern of investment of capital. But they do provide a series of windows through which this change can be observed.

2 On commoditization

Keith Hart

I. Human society has evolved in our epoch to an unprecedented level of economic integration. The central feature of this development is a division of labour which embraces ever-widening circles of humanity in a single nexus of commodity production and exchange. Almost all modern social theory is an attempt to grasp the implications of this fact. At the heart of the issue lies the definition of a process identified variously as the growth of capitalism, market economy, industrialism, etc. The elementary concept in this process is the *commodity*. The limited objective of what follows is to clarify the meaning of this term and to define the evolutionary tendency which, for want of a better expression, I will call *commoditization*.

It is usually not difficult to find a word for something distinctive. But, once we have found it, certain logical consequences normally ensue. The most important of these is that phenomena excluded by the term form a single category opposed to it in a dualistic negation. Moreover, language has the effect of reducing the infinite variations of matter in time and space to ideal abstractions (i.e. words) whose principal virtue as vehicles of communication is that the meanings they convey are presumably static. It is thus not an idiosyncratic quirk of modern social science that it be obsessed with polarized dualities. It is very hard for us to think in any other way. If we label something 'x', our discourse depends on supposing that its meaning will stay the same long enough for a linguistic community to come to share it. This 'x' then defines, at least residually, what it is not ('not x') and sometimes generates a paired opposition ('minus x'). When 'x' is a historically emergent feature assumed to be dominant in our day, it is not unusual for history itself to be represented as the restructuring of 'not x' by 'x' or even as the dialectical struggle between '−x' and 'x'. It is one thing to recognize this mundane aspect of our thought. It is something else again, however, to escape from its intellectual limitations.

The pervasiveness of commerce in modern life begs us to conceive of its negation..The idea of the absence of buying and selling evokes what has been called variously 'natural economy', 'self-sufficient subsistence' and 'primitive communism'. This state is in turn destroyed or replaced by the market and ultimately by industrial capitalism in its several forms. One reads frequently of a transition from subsistence to commercial economy or of a modernization process which depends on the growing significance of commodities where they were previously absent.[1] If the commodity is thus an expression of divided labour made social by means of some transaction, then its antithesis is self-sufficiency, i.e. labour performed by oneself for oneself. No one can gainsay that modern society rests on an advanced division of labour made possible by the production and circulation of commodities on a large scale, nor that this process was less developed in all previous periods of human history. But, once we seek to identify this evolution with words, the many gradations of history give way to huge leaps across ideal barriers established by our definitional vocabulary.

Thus, let us define a commodity. For example, 'a commodity is something useful that may be bought and sold'. Whatever 'buying' is, we now know that, where it is absent, there are no commodities. We must next find other words for non-commodity transactions, and the distinction between one type and the other assumes great categorical significance. History itself may be reconstructed as a problem of transition or as a nonlinear oscillation between two great categories of social thought. Moreover, the way is open for scholars to dispute what the commodity *really* is: 'all commodities have both use value and exchange value', 'the essence of the commodity is reciprocity'. Before long we have forgotten why we wanted to define the commodity in the first place and learning degenerates into an argument about reified words. Nor is this phenomenon restricted to economic history: the pattern is repeated whenever social enquiry is made to hinge on defining some great trans-historical object such as the state, the city or science.

There is, of course, one way out of the dilemma, which is to deny that it exists. The logic of the above is inexorably dialectical: the commodity grows out of and continues to transform that which it is not. But modern economics conceives only of a world of commodities structured by its own marginalist logic. In this way what Adam Smith saw as a historical process, whereby every man becomes in part a merchant, has been transformed by his latter-day successors into a universal calculus knowing no empirical negation of itself. This is the root of the failure of economic science – that it cannot grasp the human past, present or future.

I argue that the definition of commodity economy should be set firmly within an understanding of human social evolution as a totality, that is, as a process of commoditization which is always partial and therefore dialectical. Moreover, I insist that the definition of what the commodity is and is not should be organized as a hierarchical set of descriptions which reflects both a kind of logical abstraction and the course of human history itself. The central idea is that commoditization is synonymous with one major aspect of our species' evolution; as such it has many concrete manifestations in our past and present and may take several courses in the future. From this point of view, while we are condemned to accord our own times great prominence in any attempted definition of commodity economy, it would be mistaken, for example, to allow the historical dominance of the market in the growth of civil society to influence our investigation in too one-sided a fashion.[2] For direct commerce is only one of the ways people have found to make their labour social through the circulation of its products.

If 'labour' is the activity of an organism engaged in producing the means of its continued existence, that labour may be said to be divided when more than one organism depends routinely on some mutually constituted specialization in order to produce the needs of each. As the scope of such a division of labour increases, so too does social interdependence. The greater the volume of social labour, the more prominent are the mechanisms adopted to organize the process. The commodity is human labour embodied in a good or service offered to society rather than consumed directly by its producer. As such, commoditization may be defined as the progressive abstraction of social labour, i.e. as the separation of generalizable qualities and inherent properties from the concrete persons whose activities make up the social whole. This process is intrinsic to the evolution of species in general, but particularly to the history of our own species.

II. The following is a set of definitions of the commodity, each of which stands in a specific relationship to the rest within a hierarchy of logical abstraction that is also a putative historical sequence. Each member of the set presupposes those preceding it, but does not necessarily entail those following it. For all its Hegelian overtones, this is not teleological history. The sequence is best described as identifiable stages in the progressive abstraction of social labour. No one definition may be taken to stand for the set as a whole, nor is the set finite, but rather a preliminary attempt to transcend some of the limitations of existing approaches to the problem.

A. The commodity is:

(1) *A thing produced for use.* The first stage in the abstraction of labour is its embodiment in an object standing outside the producer.

(2) *Alienated*. It is made social by being produced for the use of another, someone foreign to the unit of production and reproduction.

(3) *The product of divided labour*. Productive specialization requires and enhances social interdependence: an interlocking system for the provision of individual and social needs necessitates organization of mutual rights and obligations. The founding principle of divided labour in the human species is sexual.

(4) *Circulated by means of exchange*. Two-sided reciprocal transfers are a common, but not the only, way of circulating the products of divided labour.[3]

(5) *Exchanged through the market mechanism*. A giant step in the abstraction of social labour occurs when people make an immediate determination of quantitative equivalence or exchange value, often in a routinized setting.

(6) *Crystallized as pure exchange value, i.e. money*. Money is a commodity whose only use is as a means of exchange.

(7) *Used as capital to make profit*. When money is used to make more money, it constitutes a new active principle in social life.

(8) *Deployed as industrial capital*, to purchase means of production – both produced (machines, raw materials) and non-produced (labour, land). The wage form is a crucial step in the abstraction of social labour since human beings now buy and sell their own productive capacities.

(9) *Predominantly human labour itself*, when services come to outweigh goods in the sphere of commoditized production.

(10) *An abstract cipher*. Social labour is measured directly, without material transfer, as computerized transactions which represent human subjects as numbers in information-processing machines.

Each of the ten steps listed above represents a further degree of abstraction of human labour from the original condition of organic life, namely from an immediate material symbiosis between the individual and nature. The progress of the social division of labour requires the detachment of human activity from its material context, so that heterogeneous goods and services may find some measure of equivalence in society. In this process, value is quantified and generalized, the formal apparatus of social life is made more elaborate and dominant.[4] Finally, stripped of its embodiment in things, human labour is revealed as a fully social, abstracted quantity. This evolution is a process of commoditization, in which a series of commodity forms succeed in enhancing the social potentialities of humanity, while undermining the concrete authenticity of a simpler past. Not one form alone ('the commodity is x'), but the series as a whole ('commoditization is steps 1–10 . . . n') best defines the economic tendency of human history.

The first step in the definition of the commodity (A1) generates a residual category (B1), what the commodity is not. A1 spawns A2, the next step in defining the commodity, thereby creating within A1 a residual category (B2) which falls outside the further restriction imposed by A2. Within A2 the definition is refined further to include A3 and exclude B3. This progressive sequence of definitions and negations may be represented as a hierarchy of abstraction, in both the conceptual and descriptive senses of the word (see Figure 2.1).

The point is that commoditization is a dialectical process: the series A 1–10 is not sufficient by itself. Every step generates a new category of excluded phenomena which are just as crucial to an understanding of the social evolution I am describing. The set of negations is as follows.

B. The commodity is not:

(1) Something which is not the product of human labour; something produced which is not useful; an aspect of human interaction (e.g. a service) which is not objectified as a produced thing.

(2) Produced for one's own use or for the use of a unit with which one is identified. The concept of alienation, depending as it does on an insider/outsider distinction, is clearly relative to the boundary defining the other.

(3) A thing given in the absence of a division of labour, for the sake of sociability and even reproduction; for example, certain marriage transactions in primitive homogeneous societies.

(4) One-sided transfers in which direct reciprocity is denied and asymmetry is emphasized: tribute, extortion, public finance, sacrifice,

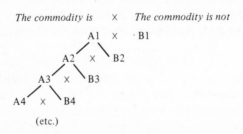

Fig. 2.1 Commoditization as a hierarchy of abstraction

redistribution, charity. This is the economic dimension of all hierarchical structures of domination, both temporary and lasting.

(5) Transfers in which there is no determination of value by reciprocal
exchange of equivalents, e.g. some systems of delayed gift return.

(6) Commodities that have some use in addition to serving as a form of
currency and all items which are sold merely for use.

(7) Money spent passively on consumption, rather than being invested to
accumulate more money.

(8) Earlier forms of capital – merchant's capital (buying and selling
products) and usurer's capital (making money with money alone);
neither form is directly involved in production.

(9) The first phase of industrial capitalism, when primary and secondary
production predominate and much labour is still not sold for wages.

(10) When commodity relations still involve material things more than
computerized abstractions.

One curious feature of this set of definitions is that the commodity has
shifted from being a material product of human labour (A1) to a rational
abstraction of the labour process (A10). Commoditization is thus the evolution of the social division of labour from an embryonic stage, where
human activity is alienated in the form of material products, to the advanced condition of modern service economies in which people are paid
and evaluated through complex information systems. This dematerializ-
ation of some aspects of commodity economy has been a major impedi-
ment to analyses which seek to place primitive and modern economies
within a single framework of structural comparison. It is because the dialectical processes discussed here are real, and not just the products of a
philosophical imagination, that they cannot be abolished by positivistic
incantations.

III. It is clear from the above that the evolution of commodity economy
has been in large part synonymous with the expansion of the market. But
the market reflects and enhances the progress of the division of labour,
whereby producers become increasingly differentiated. Intensification of
specialized production for an expanded market often requires larger inputs
of money capital. The entry of capital into production (which is at first
mostly agricultural) speeds up technological innovation, with impressive
consequences for the growth of human productivity. Looked at as a
material process, this is industrialization. But, when the bulk of workers
buy what they need out of wages received from the owners of capital, we
may speak of industrial capitalism. This has been the main force for change

in the modern world. Industrial capitalism (a term which embraces the mechanization of agriculture) is thus the most advanced phase of a process of economic development which begins with small-scale production and exchange of commodities.

Within the overall sequence of commoditization, therefore, it makes sense to emphasize the distinction between capitalist commodity production and those other forms of commodity production (pre-capitalist or non-capitalist) where people do *not* normally sell their own labour as a commodity. These latter forms may – and often do – coexist with organized capital in the shape of merchants, bankers and industrialists from both home and abroad. The offer of goods for sale by direct producers is most often found where economic organization is small-scale and the division of labour weakly developed. The sale of wage labour to capitalist production units opens up the way to a massive unleashing of industrial and commercial forces.

All that I have said on this topic so far is a selective paraphrase of Marx, omitting most of what he had to say on the subject of surplus value and class struggle.[5] But Marx stuck closely to the liberal market model of economic evolution and thereby limited his vision to those steps in the definition of commoditization where the market was dominant (A5–8), losing sight of the origins of the commodity (A1–4) and of its possible further evolution (A9, 10). It is, of course, perfectly acceptable to restrict the concept of the commodity to acts of purchase and sale, but such a categorization leads us to draw too strong a line between commerce and other economic forms, including those dominated by the state. Above all, a definition along these lines obscures the manifest similarities between all the societies which have developed an advanced division of labour, including the planned economies of the communist bloc. When the commodity is seen to be a device linked to the abstraction of social labour, the market may be understood as only one possible mechanism out of several.

Marx defined a commodity as an object produced for others having both use value and exchange value.[6] Exchange *value* can only be determined where products enter routinely into immediate exchange with each other. So, for Marx, the commodity is synonymous with markets, and his definition embraces all of steps 1–5 above, leaving the emergence of money capital and the commoditization of labour as the distinctive features of the modern age. The universalization of capitalist commodity production makes it possible for the first time, according to Marx, to see the simple, general categories underlying human economy. So the most primitive forms are entailed in the most developed expression of commodity economy; and his main analytical effort is directed, teleologically, at the most recent part of a historical process of evolution. In taking this position, Marx is not alone: most of us, self-consciously or otherwise, derive our concepts from the emphases most apparent in our day.

An alternative approach, typified by the work of Mauss (following Durkheim and inspiring Lévi-Strauss),[7] is to define the commodity very generally as something synonymous with human society itself, as reciprocity – a two-sided material flow through which elementary social relations are constituted. Utility is denied (i.e. division of labour as a precondition), the transfer may be asymmetrical and the market mechanism is subsumed under a universal category corresponding to step 2 above – primitive alienation of things or persons as the means of expanding society's horizons. The burden of analysis thus falls, according to a genetic logic, on the most primitive manifestation of the general propensity, on the origins of human society in the gift, exogamy, or whatever. Despite their confused treatment of the process of human social evolution (which they both accept and deny at once), Mauss *et al.* are particularly good at illuminating that part of the process which Marx more or less left out, namely the emergence of advanced commodity economy out of a social order that was at first constituted according to other principles (i.e. the self-reproduction of small, 'natural' groups). In this way the otherness of primitive humanity is not sacrificed to a teleological vision of our common destiny; but the distinctive forces driving modern history are lost through their non-dialectical emphasis on the universal in human social life.

Despite their complementary focus on production and exchange, on the telos and genesis of economic life, Marx and Mauss identify much the same elements in the growth of commodity economy. At this point a detailed comparison of *Pre-capitalist Economic Formations*[8] and *Essay on the Gift* can only be represented by a brief summary. For Marx human history is a dialectic of man–nature interaction, marked by growing social activity in which two processes are dominant – (1) individualization of the animal herd (evolution of the 'self' and of the 'free-thinker'); (2) separation of mankind from the earth as natural laboratory.

> The original conditions of production cannot initially be themselves produced. What requires explanation is not the unity of living and active human beings with the natural, inorganic conditions of their metabolism with nature and therefore their appropriation of nature; nor is this the result of a historic process. What we must explain is the *separation* of these inorganic conditions of human existence

from this active existence, a separation which is only fully completed in the relationship between wage labour and capital (Marx 1973: 489).

Capitalism is the highest form of human social development (and the most developed manifestation of commodity economy) because (1) the individual is objectified in private property and therefore in thought and social life: (2) both labour and means of production (capital) are 'free' and therefore capable of self-expansion; (3) as a mass of produced objects standing outside mankind, capitalism reveals our humanity to us and destroys religion. In contrast, the primitive commune through which mankind originally settled down on the earth is dominated by nature and by social forms binding men to the earth – (1) the chief, objective condition of labour is nature, not the products of labour and (2) membership in the community generates an attitude to the land which is antecedent to the working of it. The final dissolution of old communal forms of production only occurs when capital (1) dissolves the relationship between the mass of labour and the earth; (2) destroys labourers' ownership of the instruments of labour; (3) eliminates labourers' access to social means of consumption prior to production; (4) dissolves relations where the labourers themselves (e.g. slaves or serfs) are a direct part of the objective conditions of production as such. In the end, capital replaces men with machines and new forms of society may be constructed on the basis of a wholly new balance between the forces of society and those of nature.

Mauss' implicit evolutionary model runs remarkably parallel to Marx's argument in *Grundrisse*. Humanity develops exchange as a means of mitigating danger, both of nature and warfare. It does so at first by establishing social relationships with mystical beings. The primitive community performs labour on nature in order to consume and reproduce itself: it sacrifices to the gods to maintain supply and ensure peace. This is the model for external relationships with other groups. The reciprocity of sacrifice (*do ut des*) emerges as a basic principle of social justice. Social life depends on men engaging in intercourse with each other through the circulation of *spiritual matter*, the gift. The gift collapses the distinction between self and other; but the separation of the moments of exchange in time creates the possibility, at least temporarily, of dominance on the part of the gift giver. The modern contract, guaranteed by state law, contrasts starkly with the gift in that the immediate equivalence of the things exchanged and their separation from persons speak of a social equality which is not threatened by the hostility of bargaining. For Mauss there is clearly an evolution from

sacrifice to total prestations between primitive groups to individual gift
exchange between representatives of groups to impersonal commerce. This
corresponds to a shift from the religion of the primitive commune via
increasing internal differentiation and hierarchy to state contract law.
Hence the revolutionary significance of the Roman distinction between
ius in rem and *ius in personam*, fracturing the original unity of man and
nature in social life.

There are thus several evolutionary sequences present in the history of
exchange: (1) the separation of things from persons; (2) the increasing
individuation of the contract; (3) the growing significance of equality in
exchange (the principle of equivalent returns); and (4) the progressive
abstraction/objectification of concepts applied to the analysis of exchange.
In this way Mauss echoed Marx's assumption that the secularization of
society involves a separation of human activity from the material world;
that advanced commodity economy is a source of social equality; and that
individuation is linked both to all of the above and to the growth of
abstract logic. Both Marx and Mauss saw the contradictions in these devel-
opments, but they drew different political conclusions from their obser-
vations.

This brief excursion into intellectual history may serve to place my
earlier remarks on commoditization within a context that is larger than
one man's private musings. There are differences enough between Marxism
and the *Année Sociologique*: I have chosen here to highlight a common
element in the thought of Marx and Mauss, individuals whose thought was
more complex than that of many of their followers. I suggested that the
commodity is at first a produced object standing outside the producer and,
later, a price put on labour which may never be materialized as an object.
This contradiction defines, as genesis and telos respectively, a single evolutionary process in which the commodity becomes ever more abstract.
The work of Marx and Mauss shows how such an understanding reflects the
historical separation of active human society from the material nexus of
production and reproduction that is basic to organic existence.

IV. The test of this semantic discussion of commoditization is whether or
not it clarifies our analysis of industrial capitalism's contradictory march
through our age. No such analysis will be attempted here, but some general
remarks about modern economic history may give the abstract language of
earlier passages a more concrete application.

The main historic task of industrial capitalism has been to transform the
self-sufficient labour of domestic groups into a social circuit of commodity

production and exchange. The destruction of tribal and feudal organization around the world is well known: commodity economy must expand into that which it is not and replace existing forms with more suitable institutions. But more general than this is the process whereby people everywhere are driven to substitute commodities (paid for out of remunerations for their own specialized services) for what they had previously done for themselves. This dialectic of commoditization was not finished with the explosion of factory work in the West during the nineteenth century. The period since the second world war has seen a fantastic invasion of domestic life by commodity economy, especially in the industrialized countries – children are looked after outside the home from the cradle to their mid-twenties and home cooking has begun to be replaced with fast-food restaurants and other commodity substitutes. Yet, on a global scale, the socialization of domestic economy is barely begun and still has far to go, even in the countries with the most advanced division of labour. The mechanism promoting this growth is the rising productivity of labour which constantly raises the value of personal time and cheapens the cost of replacing unspecialized domestic labour with commodities. It cannot be overemphasized that commodity exchange is intrinsically linked to, even driven by, tendencies in the organization of production.

I have said that commoditization is a dialectical process, by which I mean that forces of opposition and negation are generated by its evolution. For example, naturalistic ideologies of self-sufficiency and conservative reaction in many forms are a clear manifestation of hostility to some aspects of commoditization in industrial capitalist societies. At the same time, many people now spend a high proportion of their days in activities for which they are not paid. If commoditization seems to diminish the quality of life, this growing zone of private work affords many opportunities for the elaboration of forms of production which are relatively free of the larger society's alienating presence. As the scope of public intervention in private lives increases, so too does the sphere of personal choice. Some may not count the two tendencies equal, but it should be recognized that the latter is not necessarily enhanced by retreat from the advanced commodity-producing division of labour.

But the biggest question raised in this enquiry refers to commoditization and socialism. Is the communist state built around the negation of commodity economy, or is it just a variant of the complex society that grows up around any advanced division of labour? The answer depends largely on whether one defines the commodity narrowly, as Marx and orthodox enonomics did, or more widely, as I have done in this paper. Even on the narrow definition, it would be hard to deny that Russians mostly live by earning wages, or that forced transfers to federal and state governments are significant in the American economy. It may be that the range of possibilities in any advanced economy is relatively limited. Although I have focused here on the problem of conceptualizing commoditization, it is an urgently necessary task to investigate empirically what concrete difference it makes when commodities are produced and circulated under the auspices of the market or by means of state organization. It would be ironic if we were all to be blown up in the name of 'fundamental' oppositions which are illusory in practice.

3 Daboya weavers: relations of production, dependence and reciprocity

Esther N. Goody

The weaving yard is a rectangular open area sloping down to the river bank, with the three Bakarambasipe compounds framing one long side, and waste ground on the other. The two weaving sheds are set back-to-back in the centre, the warps of the looms in the first shed stretching 10, 20, 30 yards up the rise, those of the second extending down the slope. The clacking of shuttles, each with its own tempo, sets a complex, restless rhythm to which the elders – sewing, silent and almost immobile on the mosque porch – seem oblivious. 'It must be some kind of a factory' is one's first thought.

In terms of the scale of production, and the fact that cloth is mainly sold to traders rather than directly to consumers, one may speak of the Daboya textile industry rather than artisan or petty-commodity production. But what sort of an industry is it? What is the nature of the division of labour? How is this articulated? Is specialization organized by a merchant-middleman as in the classic putting-out systems? By an entrepreneur who distributes raw materials, pays the equivalent of wages for the finished component, and then passes this on to the next specialist, thus owning the product at all its stages of production and finally selling it to retailer or consumer? Or is specialization mediated by the market – with the components of each stage of production bought and sold by a series of producers? These are the two obvious Western proto-industrial models for organizing the cooperation between specialists made necessary by the division of labour. And where does the fact that the men of Bakarambasipe are all members of three related kindreds fit in? Is the work force perhaps just one huge kin group, under the authority of the senior member – a true collective?

I went to Daboya to learn about the teaching of weaving, as an example of institutionalized 'informal' education. The scale on which weaving was carried out was a surprise,[1] and the factory-like nature of production set

50

new problems concerning the division of labour and its organization. There was also the question of how the organization of production was related to the teaching process on the one hand, and to the authority of close kinsmen and of the head of the kin group (*kanang*) on the other. And I came to realize that the technical aspects of weaving themselves played a critical role in relations of production.

The state of Gonja lay in orchard bush country, directly above Ashanti in what is now northern Ghana. It has been described as an 'over-kingdom' (J. R. Goody 1967), since the paramount had few powers and was chosen in turn from among the semi-autonomous divisions. Daboya is famous throughout Gonja as the centre of dyeing and for its fine cloth. There are usually a few weavers in the other divisional capitals, and sometimes one or two in other villages. But thread has long been sent to Daboya for dyeing with the rich indigo shades that form the old patterns, and smocks of Daboya cloth are the traditional garb of the chiefs who assemble for the annual Damba ceremony.

The town of Daboya is located on the banks of the White Volta, at a point where the receding annual floods uncover sands saturated by brine springs. For centuries the local people have extracted salt, and people used to come from all over northern Ghana bringing slaves, livestock and produce to trade for salt. This local and middle-range trade made Daboya a market centre and it also came to serve as one of the key entrepôts in the long-distance trade in which kola from the Ashanti forests was exchanged for slaves from Mossiland and northern Nigeria.

The rich but obscure history of the town is built around a succession of attempts to control the salt wells and the market. Originally under the authority of the JembulugoWura (chief of the 'salt' wells) and the Jembulugo or BuruguWuritche (queen of the 'salt' wells), it was within the Dagomba sphere of influence when conquered by the founder of the Gonja state, NdeWura Jakpa, in the seventeenth century. Jakpa made his daughter the BuruguWuritche, and left her in control of the town, known at that time as Burugu (lit. 'wells', in the language of the Dagomba). However, the Dagomba continued to raid the town, and a younger son of NdeWura Jakpa, then ruling the western-Gonja town of Wasipe, was sent to her aid. The WasipeWura routed the Dagomba, but stayed as chief of the area, henceforth known as Wasipe. That the wealth of the town continued to be a valuable prize is clear from the turbulent history of the Wasipe chiefship, which has survived conquest by the Ashanti, renewed battles with the Dagomba, an attack by the Mamprusi kingdom to the north, and at least one civil war (fieldnotes J. R. Goody and E. N. Goody).

51

Esther N. Goody

Although there has 'always' been weaving in Daboya, it is apparently only in the last twenty or thirty years that this has been more important commercially than indigo dyeing. Dyeing was the pride of the town, and the major source of craft income. If the political history of Daboya is complex, it is equally difficult to identify with certainty the original introduction of dyeing. Accounts do agree that knowledge of deep-pit indigo dyeing was brought by traders from Bornu and Hausaland in northern Nigeria. There are several sets of dye pits still visible or remembered in Daboya, and several of these were asserted by different people to be 'the first dye pits in Daboya'. It is clear that the centre of dyeing activity has shifted over the years from one section of the town to another, and these conflicting versions probably all reflect an element of truth if 'first' is taken to be 'preeminent at a given time'.

The earliest identified site lies near N'kantchenso, the compound of the Bornu Limam's people, on the edge of the old market. Dye pits were introduced here in the middle of the eighteenth century by a trader and scholar from Bornu. Many years later this kin group split, one part under Yayadodu moving to an area known also as N'kantchenso, on the banks of the river. Here they built new dye pits and continued to dye and weave. Probably in the middle of the nineteenth century another trader, Idi dam Bornu, arrived in Daboya. He was sent by the WasipeWura to live in the GarimaWura's section, where he married and built dye pits along the river at Sewii. Also in the mid-nineteenth century, two Hausa traders, Abudu Bokwara and Abudu Sokoto, settled in the GarimaWura's section and cut dye pits at Sewii; and Niame Karamo Idisa made three dye pits in Dakumpe where he lived. At about this time or a little later, Alassan from Kano cut the first of the Yulume dye pits. He didn't stay and marry, but gave his dye pits to Karamo Braimah Bakarambasipe and Karamo Jaato. Later, probably after Karamo Braimah Bakarambasipe returned from Wa at the end of the nineteenth century, he gave hospitality to a Hausa trader, Baba Serife, who is remembered as being descended from white Muslims (Arabs). He married a daughter of Braimah Bakarambasipe and taught his people how to cut dye pits and brew dye. He is remembered as one of the most prosperous and successful of the dyers in Daboya in the early years of this century.

These several separate dyeing enterprises indicate a high level of demand for dyed cloth and thread between the mid-eighteenth century and the mid-twentieth century. They also reflect the close links between northern Nigeria and the Daboya market, where large amounts of kola were brought from Ashanti and traded for salt, slaves, cloth and livestock. The proliferation of separate dyeing units, each with its own attested origin, is consistent with the high degree of secrecy which is today associated with dyeing skills. They are a jealously guarded resource, to which a man has full rights only through inheritance in the male line. This is perhaps not surprising in view of the money a successful dyer can expect to make. A dispute between two sections of weavers in 1974 was partly argued in terms of inheritance rights to the deserted dye pits by the river.

The Bakarambasipe elders, men of 65 to 75 in 1974, often remarked that when they were young only the old men wove. It was gentle work, done while sitting in the shade, suitable for those no longer strong. The young men were sent to collect thread for dyeing from the far-flung villages of Gonja. On their return they would help the mature men with the dyeing, and then carry the dyed thread back to the villages where it was woven, bringing still more newly spun thread on their return to Daboya. A man with grown sons would remain in Daboya, brewing dye and dyeing thread, and seeing to the management of farms and livestock. (Daboya men did not farm in those days; food was grown by slaves or bought from village people.)

This pattern appears to have continued until the mid-1930's, when two traders from Tamale began to bring unbleached calico cloth to Daboya on bicycles. This was tie-dyed in the same dye pits used for thread, and sold as women's cloths, *alikodu* (from 'calico'). At this time, gaily patterned cloth of European manufacture was the preferred wear for West African women, but the women of northern Ghana had little cash with which to buy such luxuries. The locally tie-dyed calico was sold much more cheaply than imported patterned cloth, and there was a ready market for as much as could be made. Some of the dyers dyed cloth for the traders, who took it back to Tamale for sale there. Others bought the unbleached calico, dyed it, and sold it themselves.

The men who sold the tie-dyed cloth in the villages bought hand-spun thread when they could, to take back to Daboya for dyeing and weaving. One woman's cloth at that time cost £1, and a large stick of thread 10 shillings. Thus two large sticks of thread could be traded for one woman's cloth. This new source of thread may have been instrumental in the growing importance of weaving, which has now largely replaced both dyeing and tie-dyeing as the main industrial occupation. One man in Bakarambasipe was still tie-dyeing cloth in 1974 and selling it in the very poor remote Tampluma villages. But by then Daboya women dressed in printed cotton cloth either imported from Europe or made in the factories of southern Ghana. There was little demand for tie-dyed cloth. As a result, the men had again altered their production strategy and were dyeing thread, both hand-spun and manufactured, and, with this, weaving cloth in the traditional patterns. In 1974 there were four sections of Daboya in which the main male economic activity was weaving: Bakarambasipe, Kalampo, Yulume and Kakulibiito. These men, and a few individuals in other sections, totalled 74 weavers out of the total population of Daboya that in the 1970 census was 1,579.

THE STRUCTURE OF DABOYA AND THE SENIOR WEAVING SECTION

Daboya, as the capital of Wasipe division, contains representatives of all three social estates: Muslims, commoners and the ruling group, the Ngbanya. The residential sections of the capital reflect several organizational principles. The WasipeWura's section, Kowesi, contains, in addition to the divisional chief's own compound, those of several of his attendants: the *wundzum* (barber), the *akurma* (drummer) and the Mbongwura (war leader). Between Kowesi and the rest of the town lies the site of the old market, now marked only by tall silk cotton trees. South, near the river, lies Kasetendon, where the priests of the shrines of old Burugu, the Kupo and the KasawaleWura, live. Near them is the NtereWura, head of the ferrymen. Compounds of dynastic segments of the ruling group are scattered through the town, while the various Muslim patronymic groups in their separate sections cluster in the centre. On the northeastern side lies the Zongo, the 'strangers'' quarter, on the path to the dry-season ford.

In the pre-colonial period, and indeed until commercially processed salt became readily available, most households participated in the dry-season work of extracting salt from the river sands. Huge amounts of firewood were required for the fires used to evaporate the brine until salt crystals appeared. Slaves and commoner men from the villages came into Daboya at this time to maintain the stocks of firewood, and to carry brine from the salt wells into the town where it was processed. The women of the family which provides the priest of one of the oldest shrines, the Kupo, are formal leaders of the first salt extraction each year, and present a bag of this first salt to the WasipeWura.

In the pre-colonial period, when the Daboya market thrived, many of the residential sections were identified with occupational specializations. Several of those along the river, including both commoner Ntereso and royal GbiteWurape, specialized in fishing. The Wangera Muslim sections made bags for the Mossi, who carried Ashanti kola nuts north into the savannah by donkey. They also made cloth caps. It is striking that it is these compounds today which operate the 'bag trade'. Young men head-load hand-operated sewing machines to grain-producing villages, and set up there as tailors, mainly repairing clothes. From this base they arrange to buy grain, particularly in the period before the harvest when people will accept low prices because they need the money. At harvest time the grain is collected in cloth bags and carried to Daboya, where it is stored until the next pre-harvest season when it is sold at premium prices due to the scarcity of grain.

This ethnic and occupational differentiation of the capital stands in sharp contrast to the composition of the villages, and indeed is more complex than that of many other divisional capitals, especially those whose links with long-distance trade were weaker.

Each section is headed by one or more elders – many but not all of whom hold some sort of office at court. On Mondays and Fridays the Ngbanya chiefs who are in Daboya assemble at the compound of the YazoriWura, who is heir-apparent to the WasipeWura. From there they proceed to the compound of the GarimaWura, who leads them to formally greet the WasipeWura. Commoner and Muslim elders make their way individually to greet the WasipeWura and join the assemblage at court. The Monday and Friday gatherings at court thus effectively represent the heterogeneous population of the town. Here are presented and reconciled potentially competing interests of trader and producer, Muslim and pagan, citizen and stranger. It is before them that disputes between members of different sections, and sometimes disputes from the outlying villages, are heard. And it is to this group that the WasipeWura announces decisions and plans affecting the town.

Dyeing and weaving were thus not the only forms of market-oriented production in pre-colonial Daboya. They are, however, the ones which have proved most adaptable to the immense economic changes which have followed the end of the long-distance caravan trade from northern Nigeria and Mossiland, and the coming of colonial over-rule and the opening of transportation and trading links with the Atlantic coast and with Europe.

Local tradition and the evidence of disused dye pits testify that there were in the nineteenth century several centres of dyeing and weaving in Daboya. The pits belonging to the Bornu Limam's section are now hidden by grass. Indeed, in 1974 only the pits of Bakarambasipe, Yulume and Kalampo were in use; Kakulibiito is a weaving centre but has no dye pits. Bakarambasipe is the largest of the weaving sections and its elders are

Esther N. Goody

recognized by the WasipeWura as senior among the Daboya weavers.[2] There are also scattered compounds where one or two men weave.

Bakarambasipe today: structure and authority

There are three compounds in Bakarambasipe (Figure 3.1), all identified in relation to the founder Braimah Bakarambasa. The compounds are known as the Big House (Langbunto), the Small House (Langbiito) and Baba Serife's Place (Baba Serifepe). The names of the first two reflect both the closeness of their links to the founder, Braimah Bakarambasa, and their relative size a generation or two ago, when the Big House contained many more people than today. Now the Small House is the largest of the three Bakarambasipe compounds, and it is the elders of the Small House, Mallam Asiiku and Mallam (now Alhaji) Abudu, who are recognized as senior.

The three constituent compounds of Bakarambasipe contain kindreds (*kanang*) descended from men of three different patronymic groups. The descendants of Braimah Bakarambasa in the male line are greeted *kwaare* (m) and *gbaani* (f). The agnatic descendants of the husband of the founder's sister, Wuria, are greeted *konate* (m) and *sonsoni* (f). Baba Serife's descendants through males are greeted *turi* (m and f). Although men of other patronymic groups also live here, the core patronymic groups reflect the compounds' different agnatic origins, and this is reaffirmed with each exchange of greeting. While to outsiders all are Bakarambasipe people, internally they are very conscious of their separateness.

Both the Small House and the Big House are internally subdivided into courtyards, each under the authority of a man whose father has died. This internal structure is reflected in the pattern of commensality between and within courtyards. Until 1973 the senior elder of Bakarambasipe was Limam T$\phi\phi$ma, the eldest resident grandson of Bakarambasa (ϕ = open 'o'). While he was alive, the elders of the Big House and of the Small house normally ate the evening meal together on the mosque porch.[3] It was following Limam T$\phi\phi$ma's death that Mallam Braimah returned to live in Daboya, and assumed the headship of the Big House, as the eldest of the surviving Bakarambasa grandsons. He is a generation above that of Mallam Asiiku and Mallam Abudu, but is younger than they are. This disjunction between age and generation seniority is exacerbated by the WasipeWura's recognition of the two elders of the Small House as the representatives of Bakarambasipe, and thus as senior to Mallam Braimah. Whatever the cause, the elders of the two houses now eat their evening meal as two separate groups, those of the Big House in Mallam Braimah's courtyard, those of the

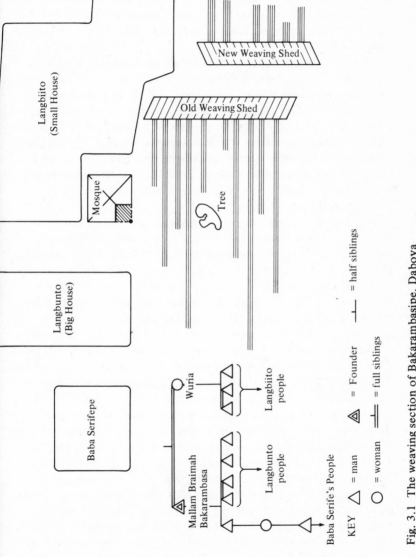

Fig. 3.1 The weaving section of Bakarambasipe, Daboya

Small House in the courtyard of Mallam Abudu. In the Small House the members of the generation of mature men, the *mberantia*, also eat together, in the courtyard of Abudulae who is the eldest among them. The young men and youths eat together in their own courtyards, with the young boys roaming about from one group to another in search of any leftovers. Women eat with their own daughters and young children, co-wives together if they are on good terms.

Within each courtyard the married women take turns cooking the evening meal for everyone. Older women who have 'retired from marriage', new brides and recent mothers are omitted from the rota. Each woman who cooks sends one large pan to the elders, another to the *mberantia*, and makes a pan for the youths and young men of the courtyard, and one for each woman and her children. The man whose wife is cooking must give her money for ingredients; few weavers farm, most buy their own food. Women themselves are responsible for condiments for flavouring the soup. In this way each married man takes his turn feeding the whole courtyard. In Gonja idiom, they all 'eat from one pot'.

The nature of the authority of the *kanang* head is at once evident and elusive. In the early morning the elders of the Small House, apart from Mallam Maman (see genealogy, Figure 3.2), come and greet Mallam Abudu.[4] They may simply enquire after his health and slip away, or they may stay to discuss compound affairs. The morning greeting is strictly analogous to the obligation of the elders and sub-chiefs of the town to greet the Wasipe-Wura on Mondays and Fridays. It is a sign of respect, an admission of subordinate status and an opportunity to settle business that jointly concerns them.[5]

Every married man has authority within his own domestic group, and this means in the first instance over wife/wives and children. When a man's son marries, his own authority is further enhanced, despite the fact that his son will have domestic authority over his own wife and children. The son in this way carves out a small sphere of autonomy, but he himself remains the child of his father, and cannot act outside the domestic setting without consulting him. In economic matters, for instance, the son must provide food for his own wife to cook when it is her turn to feed the courtyard and contribute to the commensal groups of elders and *mberantia*. This is a matter of pride as well as duty. But the son's resources are not his alone, for any savings will be at the disposal of his father should he need them. And of course his father still controls the capital which will eventually pass to his brothers and then to their sons. The signifance of this balance between domestic autonomy and external dependence becomes clear in the discussion of a weaver's progressive independence.

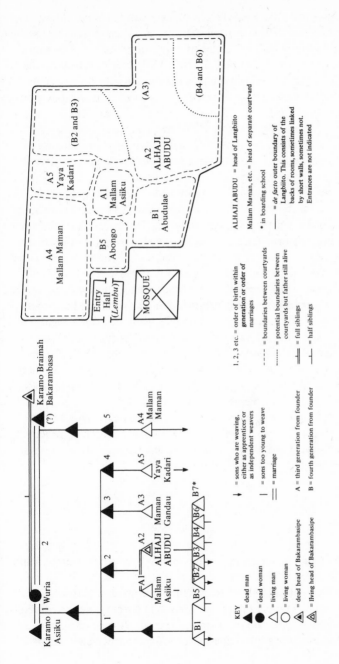

Fig. 3.2 Courtyards within Langbiito, Bakarambasipe Section, Daboya, with genealogy showing relationship of courtyard heads to Braimah Bakarambasa, founder of section

59

When a married adult man's father dies he finally becomes fully economically independent. This is not necessarily an advantage if a man is
young with few resources and no inheritance, for his male relatives will
expect him to manage for himself. They will help him in a crisis, and cooperate financially if this promises to be advantageous. But they have no
responsibility for looking after his welfare as a father does. All the courtyards indicated within the Small House are headed by married men whose
fathers are no longer living (Figure 3.2). Occasionally, as with Maman
Gandau, an adult man whose father has died is unmarried and has no dependants. He then contributes to the expenses of feeding the courtyard in
which he lives, but does not head his own domestic group.

Courtyards are progressively differentiated by the placing of new rooms
to partition off sections of a previously open area. This process can be seen
by comparing the courtyards of Abudulae and Mallam Maman, with that of
Mallam Abudu (Figure 3.2). The first two courtyards are both large, containing the rooms of many youths and young men in the son's generation,
but few of these have married, and those only recently. The rooms still
open outward on a large central yard. Mallam Abudu, however, has several
married sons, the older ones having more than one wife, and the eldest
himself the father of a married son. This courtyard has several slightly
detached enclaves (dotted lines) which are not as yet fully enclosed. If they
do not all open on a single central yard, they still share an irregular open
court. This shared space represents their common subordination to their
father, Mallam Abudu. So long as he lives it is unlikely that any of the married sons will enclose a separate courtyard of his own.

Before looking at the pattern of cooperation and dependence in production within the *kanang*, it is necessary to outline the technical processes
involved in weaving and dyeing. For these exert their own constraints on
the division of labour and relations of production.

FROM COTTON TO CLOTH: TECHNICAL PROCESSES

There are three main, linked, technologies in the contemporary Daboya
cloth industry: dyeing, weaving, and the sewing of cloths, smocks and
gowns. In addition, there are the problems of supply of raw materials and
of sale of the finished products.

The three main technologies are linked at key points and thus so are the
problems of input (supply of raw materials) and output (sale/distribution).

In the weaving yard the various stages of production go on simultaneously, with no apparent sequence. This Marx saw as characteristic of

manufacture, for when many cloths are being produced at the same time, some will be at each stage of production. Here, however, the technical processes are discussed as though we were following a basket of raw cotton through its transformation into a finished garment.

Raw materials

Hand-spun thread is known as *gbanya jesse*, literally Gonja thread. Gonja women, particularly of the ruling and Muslim estate, used to spin thread from local cotton for their own cloth and for sale. Today few women still spin, and the weavers must travel to distant markets to buy even enough for a part of their output. The rest of the thread they use is manufactured in southern Ghana and bought through kinsmen in Kumasi (in the forest zone) and in Tamale, the administrative centre of northern Ghana. I.C.I. commercial indigo dye crystals and manufactured coloured thread for embroidery are also bought in this way.

No materials are openly on sale in Daboya, and one man whom I knew dealt in thread denied doing so. The buying and selling of thread and commercial dye crystals is based on a fine balance of cut-throat bargaining and personal obligation, which is contrary to a market contract ethic. One man's price is not the same as another's; a trader from one section may not want to sell to competitors from another if supplies are scarce. It is hard to see how seventy looms can be kept in operation with no open selling of thread or commercial dye; but each weaving section has one or more men who specialize in the supplying of these materials.

Laying out the warp and weft

After the thread has been found, it must be laid out in the correct length and number of threads for each colour of the warp; the weft is also laid out at this time. Hand-spun thread can be laid out directly from the sticks on which it is purchased, but machine-made thread must be wound off the cones, two to four threads together, on to a spool which can be used for laying warp and weft. This task is assigned to bobbin boys (apprentices) and even the younger boys may take a turn at winding the spools.

The warp and weft are laid out between iron pegs driven into the ground to form a rectangle with two long sides (of between 30 and 50 yards) and a short side of 2 to 4 yards. The distance between pegs depends on whether the warp is for two, three, or four (women's) cloths. The weaver, or bobbin boy, then carries the spool of thread back and forth until the right number of.threads has been laid for each colour of the warp and for the weft. Each set is tied off into a separate bundle, ready for dyeing.

Dyeing

The right to 'open a dye pit' (*bu garamang*), that is to brew dye oneself, is jealously guarded. If a man's father was a dyer, then he has the right to dye. Otherwise, no matter how closely associated he is with Bakarambasipe, a man may only supplicate for the privilege of using one of the old dye pits. There were ten men regularly brewing dye in Daboya in 1974. Balls of *gara*, fermented and dried indigo leaves, are bought from women who collect the leaves in the early rainy season. *Kadii*, ashes of a forest tree burned with thorn bushes, and *zata*, burned cakes made of the sludge from exhausted dye pits, are also needed. These a dyer makes himself. The elder of one of the kindreds with dyeing rights should pray as the first four indigo balls are crumbled into the dye pit. Then the rest of the ingredients are added, with water, and the whole mixed with a long stick. *Baba*, commercial indigo crystals, is also added at this time. Once the brew has been mixed, it must be left to ripen for several days, and be stirred every second day. An experienced dyer judges it to be ready by the colour of the froth after stirring, the smell, and the colour of the surface liquid under the foam.

When a pit is ready, the man who opened it usually uses it himself for the first few days. He will have collected enough thread or tie-dye cloths to make the brewing worthwhile. When he has completed the thread and cloth he had prepared, the dyer lets others use his pit. This may be done for payment, or on a reciprocal basis, or sometimes two men cooperate in procuring the materials. Most dyers are also weavers and such a man will open a pit at intervals when he needs more thread for his weaving, and will dye a substantial quantity at one time, to be kept in reserve for future use. However, some women still send thread to Daboya for dyeing, and there are many weavers who are not dyers, but must arrange for someone else to dye their thread. Thus, opening a dye pit is done both to provide thread for a man's own looms and to make money by dyeing for others.

Skeining

When the dyed thread has dried it is ready to skein. This requires two men who stretch the threads taut and parallel, then repeatedly double it on itself, all the while maintaining the tension. Finally, the warp threads are bound into neat oval bundles which ride on the weighted warp sled and are progressively unwound as the warp is woven.

Tying in the warp

When the warp threads of each colour have been skeined, the ends must be tied through the reed in the correct pattern for the design desired. Few men know how to do this, although it is neither very difficult nor time consuming. It does, however, require knowledge of the number of threads of each colour in their proper sequence. One of the master weavers is asked to take the three warp bundles, of white, pale blue (*fer ntchu*, lit. washed in water) and dark blue (*jesse niu*, lit. mother thread) and tie in the pattern.

Weaving

The weaver then fixes the ends of the warp to the waist beam of his loom, and sets about the tedious job of untangling the threads. For each must lie taut in the correct order, and the dye makes them stick together and catch at first. The warp is placed on a weighted sled, which used to be an antelope or cow skull, with the bands of thread looped around the horns to

3.1 The Bakarambasipe upper weaving shed. Warps in foreground

Esther N. Goody

3.2 Lazii at his loom, Bakarambasipe

maintain the correct tension. Nowadays either a flat piece of wood or an
old bicycle chain guard is used, weighted with a stone. The warp sled is
placed at a distance from the loom – perhaps 20 yards to start with – and
drawn slowly nearer as the weaving proceeds. Every evening, and when it
rains, the warp is taken up, carefully looped over the waist beam of the
loom, and the whole taken inside. Next morning the stretching and
untangling process must be repeated before it is possible to begin weaving.
Throughout the weaving, bobbins must be filled with weft thread. This is
another time-consuming but necessary task that weavers delegate when
possible.

The selling of cloth

There are five main forms in which cloth is sold:
(1)   As the strip is woven, it is wound around the waist beam of the loom

making a large disc or round of cloth (the *kalobaw*). When the warp is finished this round is eased off, and tied. It can easily be stored or transported, or unwound as needed for sewing into cloths. Elders who deal in finished cloth buy entire rounds.

(2)   If there is a buyer ready when the warp is finished, strips are laid out in lengths of a woman's cloth or a man's cloth (measured by hand spans). In this way enough is cut for one or two cloths, and sold in the strip. The rest of the *kalobaw* is kept for future use or sale.

(3)   One of the staple products of the weaving sheds is white funeral cloth. It is relatively cheap to make as no dye is required, and less trouble is sometimes taken with its weaving. Youths who are just learning will be set to work on funeral cloths, for here their ragged selvedges and open weave will not be noticed. Each of several close relatives is expected to contribute a funeral cloth following a death, so there is a constant demand for such cloths.

(4)   Commissioned cloths. Occasionally even now, a woman brings thread she has spun to a weaver and asks him to make her a given number of cloths of a certain pattern. This is still done for a relative in the traditional way, without payment. Otherwise she is charged ¢10 (= £3 in 1974) for two cloths for the dyeing and weaving, and the weaver takes 'surplus' material and thread. Commissioned cloths are made up. There is a man in Kupope who specializes in sewing strips together into cloth, and beating flat the seams.

(5)   Some of the material woven in Bakarambasipe is made up by the elders into smocks. Indeed, this appears to be their one occupation, as they sit sewing on the mosque porch, chatting, receiving visitors, and keeping an eye on the weavers. It is much more profitable to sell a smock than to sell the same amount of material in strips or made up into a cloth. Where a woman's cloth cost ¢16 in 1974, a smock using about twice the amount of material cost ¢50–¢70. There are several types of smock, and various styles of embroidery, some done by hand, but the most elaborate done by machine. Hats are also made up and sold at a considerable profit.

A few of the weaving elders act as middlemen, buying rounds of cloth and smocks from individual weavers for resale to visiting buyers, or to be peddled around the villages. Such men must have considerable capital, and appear to do a brisk trade with itinerant traders who deal with them in preference to seeking out individual weavers for the particular patterns that they want. I visited the NsaoWura many times, and on every occasion we were interrupted by a would-be buyer or seller. The Daboya weavers have

Esther N. Goody

links with certain tailors in Tamale who machine-embroider smocks for them, but, significantly, they do not sell in Tamale market. They claim to be able to sell all they make by the traditional methods, through itinerant buyers, commissions, and peddling to the Gonja towns. They do not admit the inconsistency between this position and their worry about alienating the itinerant buyers if they raise their prices.

Smocks are sold to individuals who come to Bakarambasipe; sometimes two or three a week make the forty-mile trip from Tamale to find a Daboya smock. They are also sold to itinerant buyers who regularly make the journey, usually from the northern towns of Gambaga, Navarongo and Bolgatanga, to buy rounds of cloth, strips, finished women's cloths, caps and smocks. Such a buyer may spend several days in Bakarambasipe, sewing his purchased strips into smocks while he waits for more material to come off the looms. Some buyers regularly buy from the same weaver; some deal directly with the elders; others make the rounds of several weavers in the same weaving section. But regular buyers stick to one weaving section, and establish strong patterns of expectations about the amount and type of material they will want and the price they will have to pay. Because these buyers come all the way to Daboya, and thus save the weavers the trouble of sending their cloth out for sale, they are able to get very favourable terms of purchase. This was highlighted by the rising costs during my time in Daboya, for the weavers found it very difficult to pass on these costs to the buyers of their cloth. Indeed, there was a major dispute between two sections of weavers over whether or not the standard price of a length of cloth should be raised or not. A relatively recently formed section maintained that they were not making any profit (which I judge probably to be correct) and ought to put up the price. The Bakarambasipe men, who consider themselves to be the senior Daboya weavers, insisted that the price should be kept at the previous level for fear of driving away the buyers whom they depended on. At the time I left, the Bakarambasipe men were preventing the others from using the dye pits because they had unilaterally raised their prices. This embargo virtually brought their weaving to a halt.

SKILL, SPECIALIZATION AND THE DIVISION OF LABOUR

It is possible to classify the tasks involved in the production of cloth as unskilled, semi-skilled and highly skilled. Corresponding to this is what might be called a horizontal division of labour on the basis of age.

66

Unskilled tasks

Young boys from the age of 5 or 6 are encouraged and persuaded to participate in unskilled tasks, but are not forced to do so. Such tasks include
washing new thread (it is put in the river and jumped on), laying out warp
and weft skeins (this involves carrying a spindle up and down between the
pegs on which the warp is strung; it takes hours to complete a set of warp
and weft skeins); and bobbin winding on the *korokoro*. Boys also help to
empty out the contents of exhausted dye pits.

Semi-skilled tasks

There are several tasks which require some skill, but which adolescent boys
seem to master easily. Weaving itself is the major job of this kind. Once the
synchronization of feet (on heddle harness) and hands (throwing and
returning the shuttle, and beating with the reed) has been accomplished,
even boys of 8 or 9 can weave, but the older youths are adept at maintaining a firm but easy tension, untangling warp threads and tying broken
threads, which constitute the main weaving problems.

3.3 Boys of 6 or 7 are given simple tasks like the washing of thread in preparation for dyeing

Esther N. Goody

Using the weighted spindle to wind shuttle bobbins by hand from the weft skein is a skill which takes patience and rhythm to learn, but is not really difficult. Except for the youths just beginning to learn, every weaver is expected to wind his own bobbins; but bobbin boys may be asked to wind for their master.

Highly skilled tasks

(1) The setting out of the warping pegs is a skilled task because one must understand the relationship between the pattern it is intended to weave and the number of threads of each colour that will be needed in the warp. Also it is necessary to estimate how to allocate the available thread between warp colours and the woof, and how to translate this to the distance between warping pegs.

(2) Correct skeining of the threads after dyeing is vital if the warp is not to become tangled as it is repeatedly set up and taken down. A properly skeined set of warp threads can be tied into the reed and stretched taut from the weighted warp sled with a minimum of untangling of the individual threads.

(3) Dyeing. The brewing of the dye is highly skilled. A man must not only know the necessary ingredients, but be able to estimate relative quantities. He must know how to tell when dye has matured sufficiently to use, and when it is no longer strong enough to take successfully.

Dyeing thread requires a knowledge of the interaction between dye and air. The thread is first submerged and then wrung and stretched by hand. This exposure to the air is necessary if dye is to take effect and be fast to washing later. This is repeated several times and the dyer must be able to judge what the colour of wet thread will be when it is dry.

(4) Tying in the warp. Surprisingly few of the weavers know how to tie in the different traditional patterns. Not until a man becomes a loom manager is he responsible for planning the pattern of the cloth he weaves, and even then it is perfectly possible to ask another to tie in a warp of the desired pattern. Such services are given freely, but it is a matter of independence. An important senior weaver who could not tie in his warps would be an anomaly.

(5) Measuring cloth for sale. It requires both skill and confidence to measure off cloth for sale to a visiting buyer who sits eagle-eyed waiting for a mistake and anxious to argue the price.

(6) Buying hand-spun thread. Both skill in judging quality and estimating quantity are needed, as no two spindles look alike. The buyer must also know how far to try and push down the price, and when to give in, because he buys from the same women regularly.

(7) Sewing smocks. Seams are made by hand, the smocks lined with cloth from old flour bags (specially bought for the purpose) and some are hand-embroidered in simple stitches. Matching the pattern and making up styles with gussets to give fullness require skill in cutting and sewing.

(8) Buying manufactured raw materials. This requires capital, judgement of quantities and reasonable prices, and the necessary contacts in Tamale or Kumasi. No materials are openly sold in Daboya, because selling is embedded in other relationships.

(9) Selling of strips, cloths and smocks. This requires experience in dealing with itinerant buyers, or in peddling. It also requires capital for buying from weavers if a man wishes to play a retailing role, and the ability to hold out if price is not right – i.e. it is important not to *need* to sell.

There is a correlation between degree of skill and age. Boys up to the age of 10 or 12 provide unskilled labour. Adolescent boys and young men are semi-skilled. Virtually all married men in Bakarambasipe are able to carry out most of the skilled weaving tasks and many become expert in one or two specializations – buying, dyeing, tailoring, or selling. These specialist skills represent a shift from the horizontal division of labour by age to a functional division of labour based on differentiation. The interdependence which results from the horizontal division of labour is cyclical. A weaver begins as a boy working for his teacher, and eventually becomes a teacher for whom boys work. But the interdependence based on the functional division of labour between specialists depends on kinship authority and reciprocity. With a special skill to exchange for that of others, a mature man is in a position where he can manage several looms if he wishes. The organization of these processes concurrently so as to keep several looms in operation requires real managerial skill. An accumulation of knowledge and reciprocal service relationships is necessary before a man can make the transition from weaver to loom manager, to master weaver.

The seven ages of the weaver

There are, then, different levels of skill involved in the various aspects of cloth production. A boy beginning to learn is given the tasks requiring least

69

skill, and these tasks are drawn from several stages of the weaving process. In Marx's terms he begins as an unskilled labourer and progresses to detail work. Only after many years will he become a craftsman in command of the full range of skills that are required to produce a finished cloth from a basket of thread. Learning is roughly synchronized with physical and social maturation according to the following stages:

(1) Infants and young children play by the loom. Little boys are incorporated into the weaving fellowship by being asked to run simple errands, and through the toy looms their older brothers make for them.

(2) Boys between 5 and 10. There is a conscious policy of not forcing boys to participate regularly in the productive work of the weaving sheds. They may be asked to run an errand, or to carry a spindle of warp thread up and down between the warping pegs. But it is recognized that at this age they lack the patience and concentration to stick to a task for very long, although they do have the ability to follow simple instructions. The weavers say that it is important not to force boys beyond their abilities or they will rebel and not settle down to work later on. However, boys of this age delight in constructing toy looms from sticks and the bits of thread the men save for them, and weaving lamp wicks. Occasionally boys will make a more substantial loom and spend hours trying to warp it and weave 'real cloth'.

(3) Apprentices, or bobbin boys. When a boy is judged ready to settle down and work on a regular basis, he is assigned to, or chooses, a weaver to work with and learn from. The weavers do not teach their own sons but in effect trade sons, though, as with apparently formal systems of marriage exchange, this works out in the long run rather than simultaneously. The teacher is referred to either by a kinship term or as *nyinipe*, the term used for a male foster parent; he is addressed by a kinship term. A man's older sons will go either to his father or brothers – sometimes to a more distant kinsman. Younger sons sometimes learn from their older brothers, though they too may go to a father's 'brother'. Mallam Abudu's second son, Mallam Yahaya, decided himself to learn from Limam Tϕϕma, the senior elder of the Big House, who was a distant 'grandfather'. The apprenticeship of all the sons of Mallam (now Alhaji) Abudu is given in Figure 3.3. Apprentices, or bobbin boys, divide their time between weaving and doing chores like laying warp and winding bobbins. Other weavers occasionally ask their help, and this fits into the diffuse kinship authority of the older men over the younger in the section. Relations between weavers and their apprentices are easy-going, but the boys work relatively steadily. There is a

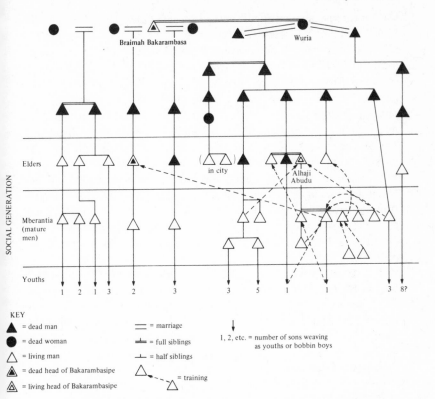

Fig. 3.3 Partial genealogy of decendants of Braimah Bakarambasa and his
sister, showing the training of the sons of Alhaji Abudu. Living
males are allocated to the 'social' generations of Elder, *Mberantia*
and Youths as for dining groups

gradual progression from intermittent to regular work, which leads into the
next stage in which a young man works mainly on his own, but still weaves
'for' his teacher.

The transition from bobbin boy to dependent weaver is a gradual one.
Even an apprentice of a few months can weave shroud cloths, but much of
his time will be spent on laying warps and winding bobbins. Gradually he
spends more of his time weaving, and carries out more of the stages in the
production of the cloth he weaves, until his master can hand him a basket
of sticks of thread and expect him to be fully responsible for producing the
finished cloth. When he has reached this stage and has woven for his

71

teacher for several months, he may spend some of his time weaving for his father. It is simply a question of whose thread he weaves.

(4)   Young men: dependent weavers. When a young man has mastered most of the tasks involved in weaving – not only weaving itself, but laying out warp threads and setting up and taking down the loom – he will 'cut' his own loom if he has not been given one by his teacher. A loom has two sets of parts, one fixed, in the weaving shed, and the other – including the reed, heddle and pulley, and the warp – which is taken down each evening. All parts can be made from material available locally. Indeed, there is a prohibition against taking the frame of a loom away to another town, which probably reflects the fact that it is usually incorporated into a row of loom frames under a single roof. This is no hardship, however, as sticks from any tree can be used to construct another frame. Nowadays several elements of the movable part of the loom are for preference made from manufactured materials: heddles from nylon cord, shuttle pins from bicycle spokes, etc.

It is neither expensive nor difficult for a young weaver to acquire his own waist beam, pulley, heddles and reed, but to do so does not give him independence from his teacher. There are two material embodiments of this continuing dependence: the loom frame, and ownership of thread. A weaving shed containing from 2 to 15 loom frames is constructed by a master weaver, or by two or three together, for those weaving under them. Each frame in the weaving shed is 'owned' by one of the master weavers, though it may be loaned by him to an independent weaver if he does not need it. Positions in the weaving shed can also be inherited by sons or favourite pupils. A youth who is trained in a given weaving section will be allotted a loom frame which he continues to use as long as he is weaving there. If a member of the *kanang* returns from an absence to find that 'his' loom frame has been occupied, he can either seek permission to use another which is empty, or, with the agreement of the elders, build a new one. Of course, if he moves out of the section's weaving yard altogether, he does not need permission to build his own frame. Such a move is usually a sign that the builder of the new weaving shed wishes to be seen as independent of the other senior weavers in his *kanang*.

The major constraint on independence for a young weaver, once he has acquired the necessary skills, is lack of capital with which to buy thread and pay for its dyeing. For the critical rule is 'he who owns the thread owns the finished cloth' – i.e. has the right to the money from its sale. As long as he cannot buy his own thread, a man must continue to weave the thread of others. There is no formal end to apprenticeship, although a youth is expected to continue to weave for his master for several years after he has learned the basic skills of weaving. His labour is not explicitly stated to be in compensation for teaching, because the relationship has been a diffuse one from the start. But it is understood that the master has a right to expect that the youth will continue to weave for him, usually until he marries, or at least through adolescence and into young adulthood.[6] The young weaver is not paid for the work he does for his master, but he is given pocket money, and bought a pair of trousers or a shirt from time to time. The senior weavers are very aware of the need to avoid arousing the resentment of their dependent weavers. It is too easy nowadays to leave Daboya and go 'south' in search of adventure. I was told that fathers often encouraged a son to marry at an earlier age now than in the past, in the hopes that the responsibility for wife and children would keep him in Daboya. This is something of a sacrifice, since previously a young man did not marry until he had been able to save enough to begin to buy his own thread and thus be able to support a wife from his independent earnings. Encouraging earlier marriage means both finding the capital for a son to become an independent weaver, and, thereby, either the master or the father losing his labour.

Formerly, a young man had two ways of saving the money necessary to buy his own thread. He could, as all weavers did, save thread left from preparing a loom. His master having given him thread 'for three cloths' expected three cloths in return, but both of them expected that there would be some thread left over. Anything more than what was necessary for the three cloths ordered belonged to the apprentice. The other way was to weave for someone other than his *nyinipe* (but only with his permission). For this work a man was paid a commission on the final sale. It took several years of partly working for his master or his father, and partly doing paid work for others, before a man had enough capital to regularly buy his own thread. Whenever he had enough thread to set up his loom on his own, the finished cloth belonged to him, and he kept all the profit from its sale. When a man can expect to weave for himself sufficiently to support a wife, it is recognized that it is time for him to marry.

(5)   Married men: independent weavers. All weavers who are married weave mainly for themselves. Few of the unmarried ones do so. An independent weaver is responsible for finding the thread, getting it dyed, laying out the warp, and selling the finished cloth. (None of the men at this stage was able to tie in a new warp pattern.) An independent weaver may be given youths to train by his kin. This is a tremendous advantage because he then has control over their labour – they weave his thread. He may reassign

such a youth to another young man who is weaving for him. This may mark the transition to another stage, that of master weaver.

(6)   Some independent weavers are content to carry on as weavers only, or with one occasional apprentice. Lazii, Mallam Abudu's eldest son, does this, and also farms. Others seem to follow one of several strategies in becoming master weavers – that is, managers of their own 'businesses'. This may be done by:

(i) *Managing many looms*. By taking several apprentices, or breeding many sons, a man can have a number of youths and young men weaving for him. Abudulae, the senior member of the *mberantia* generation (see Figure 3.2), has already two married sons and his four wives have borne several younger sons who weave for him. In 1974 they had several of the looms in the Bakarambasipe sheds as well as four looms on an old dye-pit site by the river. When I returned for an afternoon in 1976, Abudulae had moved all his looms to the river site and thus apparently declared independence from the immediate authority of the elders.[7] Abudulae is responsible for finding thread and dyeing it and setting up warps for ten looms. This is a full-time job, but one which must pay handsomely. Allowing for the variation in skill among his many apprentices, he must sell the equivalent of ten cloths a week for an income of ₵160 – against which, of course, he must set the cost of thread, dye, and food and clothing for about 30 people. (At official exchange rates in 1974, ₵160 = £48.) He also raises guinea fowl. Abudulae dyes his own thread.

(ii) *Dyeing*. Few men are in the position of genealogical seniority which allows them to marry many wives early and establish the basis of such a personally created business organization. But any Bakarambasipe man whose father was a dyer may learn to dye, and this is remunerative, but very hard work. To be a dyer gives a weaver an advantage because the charges for dyeing are high, so the profit on weaving is increased substantially if a man can dye for his own looms. In addition, of course, as a dyer he will make money by dyeing thread for others; he may enter the tie-dye trade if he wishes; and he can participate in the reciprocities between dyers which ensure a steady supply of dyed thread, even when one has no pit of one's own in use, or when commercial indigo is in short supply. Mallam Abudu's second son Mallam Yahaya both dyes and weaves, making more from dyeing than from his weaving, despite his acknowledged expertise in the latter.

(iii) *Trading*. Amadu (Langbunto) has concentrated on the trading side of

3.4 Mallam Yahaya (seated, right) selling his finished cloth to an itinerant buyer

the weaving industry. He maintains a home in Tamale as well as in Daboya. He keeps two looms in operation in Daboya (his weavers are an adult son and an apprenticed sister's son), and is responsible for the four Daboya looms in Tamale – though these do not seem to be in regular use. He buys thread and dye on commission and for resale in Daboya, sews smocks and caps from woven strips, and peddles finished cloths and smocks around the Gonja villages. He was one of two Bakarambasipe men who planted rice on a large scale in 1974, using commercial fertilizers and hiring a tractor for the ploughing. To engage in this sort of farming one must have substantial capital. It is probable that Amadu will eventually slip into the place of the present main supplier of manufactured raw materials from the south, Alhaji Ibrahim, when he grows old. Amadu is building up his capital, keeping in close touch with the market (by peddling cloths around the villages) and, perhaps most important, maintaining his contacts in Bakarambasipe among the weavers who are his customers.

Managing many looms, dyeing and trading are the three main patterns of specialization which characterize the master weavers. However, there are others followed by one or a few men:

75

Esther N. Goody

(iv) *The tie-dye cloth trade.* This involves buying unbleached muslin in Tamale in twelve-yard pieces; cutting it into quarters and sewing the patterns in raffia thread; dyeing the cloths; and then carrying bulk lots, by bicycle, to middle-women who retail the cloths in each of several villages. In terms of cash outlay, there is about 100 per cent profit in this trade. However, it requires a back-up work force for the time-consuming tasks of sewing in the pattern, and then unpicking the raffia afterwards. Yaya Kadari in Langbiito, who specializes in this trade, keeps his four wives and several pre-adolescent children fully occupied. In Yulume the elders sew tie-dye cloths rather than gowns.

(v) Usually one man from each weaving section specializes in the *buying of hand-spun thread* from distant markets and villages. He will take commissions for others, and also resells in Daboya.

(vi) Each of the elders has some cattle, *bought either as a form of investment for profits, or for trade.* In Bakarambasipe one of Mallam Abudu's younger sons has the responsibility of looking after these animals, in addition to the two looms he manages. He does no hearding himself, but engages Fulani herdsmen, decides on where the cattle shall be penned (the enclosures must be moved regularly to avoid hoof rot), finds and administers medicines when beasts are sick, and deals with selling and buying.

(vii) One of the sub-section heads in Langbunto, Nda Allassan, is the senior among those who *own sewing machines.* He does enough machine sewing, mainly making caps, to add substantially to his income from farming and from keeping three looms in operation. He was hoping in 1974 to get enough capital to purchase a machine that would do the embroidery around the neck and hem of Western-style tie-dye shirts which he now sews.

(viii) A few men *trade as a middleman*, buying kerosene, matches, tinned food in bulk from Tamale and reselling to Daboya women who retail either from their homes or the neighbourhood markets.

(ix) One of the Langbiito men has a *shop where he repairs bicycles.* His shop is in a neighbouring section, where he was reared by his mother's brother who taught him to be a 'fitter'. He also dyes and has two youths weaving for him. Since many of the small tools and parts of weaving apparatus use bits from bicycles (especially spokes, inner tubes and chain guards), it is very useful to have one of the members of Bakarambasipe in a position to obtain these easily.

(x) Daboya, on the edge of the White Volta River, supports a thriving *fishing* industry which, during the rainy season, brings two lorries

daily from Tamale with women to buy fish. One of the Bakarambasipe men was reared in Kasetendon by his mother's brother who
was a fisherman, and in whose boat he crewed for several years. He
now lives in his father's house, but in addition to his weaving goes
fishing regularly, both for food for his family (otherwise he would
have to find the money to buy fish or meat two or three times a
week) and to sell.

The partial transition from maturity to elderhood is marked by the
death of a man's father. He then controls whatever inherited wealth he has
direct claims on (wealth his father earned himself during his lifetime). At
the same time he ceases to be subordinate in matters concerning day-to-day
affairs. Even grown men greet their father early in the morning and receive
instructions about family affairs for the day. When a man's own father is
dead he still remains formally subordinate to the other men in the section
of his father's generation, the elders.

(7)   The final age of the weaver is elderhood. This is essentially a genealogical position and in each compound includes all the men of the senior
generation in relation to the founder, Braimah Bakarambasa. These elders
(*enumu*) eat together, and separately from the mature men of the generation below them (*mberantia*). Genealogical seniority in turn represents
authority over those beneath them in the system; and it represents control
of the assets of the kin group. Inherited wealth is vested in the senior generation, and at the same time their adult sons continue to present part of
their earnings to their fathers. Some elders continue as master weavers,
managing several looms directly. Others concentrate on sewing expensive
smocks and on buying up cloth for resale to visiting traders and in the villages. At present the mark of the elder is that he sits sewing in the shade
while others weave or dye. The other major occupation of senior elders is
the representation of their kin group in community affairs. It is obligatory
for Muslim elders to attend funerals, to send representatives to birth and
wedding ceremonies, and to greet the WasipeWura on Mondays and Fridays.
Thus elderhood represents the taking on of a quasi-political role in the
wider community. This in turn adds to an elder's status, and reinforces his
authority within the kin group and with traders.

THE DEVELOPMENTAL CYCLE OF THE WEAVING
ENTERPRISE

Kinship and economic roles are closely interdependent for the Daboya
weavers. A male continues to be subordinate to his father so long as the

Esther N. Goody

father lives, unless he leaves the community. This means that the father has
a major say in all decisions made by his sons, and has a claim on their
labour and resources. A father draws on these claims as he wishes, but if he
is too demanding the son may leave. Older men with adult sons thus command substantial labour and may also command substantial wealth. Within
this nexus, a youth moves from complete dependence as a bobbin boy, to
relative independence as a weaver responsible for his own wife and children,
to a position of management as a master weaver organizing the labour of
his sons and apprentices. A man like Mallam Abudu, who lives to be the
father of several master weavers, has claims on his sons' specialist expertise
and the labour of their production units, in addition to those of his own.
His paternal authority gives him the position of director of a complex business. Mallam Abudu has claims on the farm produce of his eldest son, the
dyeing skills of Mallam Yahaya, the trading judgement and contacts of
Idisa, and Musa's buying of hand-spun thread. While the sons are economically separate in relation to each other, and either trade services or pay for
them, their father receives these services as his right. A weaving enterprise
thus reaches its maximum extent as a result of the delay in fission of the
domestic group which occurs on the death of the father. Such a delay in
the separation of adult sons is not automatic, however. A father who is not
himself a competent businessman may find that his sons leave Daboya
rather than remain under his authority. Similarly, whether or not adult
sons recognize the kinship authority of a dead father's full or half brother
probably depends on the latter's effectiveness as a director.

Success as a master weaver means that a man can marry several wives,
and thus raise several sons on whose labour and skills he in turn has claims.
If his father dies while he is still relatively young, he also comes into his
direct inheritance (that part of his father's resources which the father himself has earned) at a time when he can invest it in either wives, or raw
materials or trading. Abudulae's father was himself a highly successful dyer
who helped him marry several wives at an early age, and on his death left
wealth which allowed Abudulae to support and extend his large household
and enterprise. His adult sons are not yet established as master weavers,
though they teach their younger brothers and supervise their weaving. Thus
Abudulae himself still has to dye thread for the ten looms he manages,
though his sons and the apprentices lay out the warps and set up the looms.
In 1974 Abudulae's married sons were weaving in the main Bakarambasipe
sheds, but for the younger boys he had established four looms behind
Bakarambasipe, on the high bank of the Volta next to the abandoned dyeing pits. When I returned briefly in 1976 I found that all Abudulae's sons

78

and apprentices were weaving on the river-bank site, and he had opened the dye pits there also, making a fully independent weaving yard. Abudulae's transition to elderhood, marked by his inclusion among those who represent Bakarambasipe at weddings, naming ceremonies and funerals and at the chief's court, will probably not occur so long as Mallam Abudu, his father's brother, is still active in this role. However, in the meantime his economic independence is clear for all to see in the busy dyeing and weaving yard by the river.

RELATIONS OF PRODUCTION AND CONSTRAINTS ON INNOVATION AMONG THE WEAVERS

The recent history of the Daboya weaving industry is a record of successful adaptation of product and technology to externally introduced changes. The introduction of Hausa pit dyeing in the mid-eighteenth century represents the first 'visible' adaptation of technology in response to external influence. The resulting dyeing industry must have been very successful, judging both by the many disused dye pits in Daboya and the fame of the town throughout Gonja as the centre for dyeing thread. The next major known innovation was the use of the dye pits to tie-dye calico for sale to women who could not affort imported printed cloth. This occurred in the mid-1930's, and represented a radical shift from the previous collection of thread for dyeing and return to the villages. The same network of contacts in the villages provided the marketing outlets, but new contacts had to be established with the Tamale merchants, and new techniques of sewing cloth with raffia thread either invented or learned. One particularly interesting feature of the tie-dye trade which is still remembered is its responsiveness to fashion. One pattern is still known as 'all Daboya' because, for a time, all the women wore it in preference to others.

The decline of the tie-dye trade was apparently gradual – some still continues. But women prefer the brightly printed cottons which used to be known as Manchester cloth, and which became increasingly available throughout the 1950's and 1960's, and now are made in Ghana itself. At the same time machine-spun thread became available, through market contacts in Kumasi. As the spinning of local cotton has declined markedly, a more dependable source of thread was necessary before weaving could become a market-oriented activity rather than artisan production for particular customers. By the 1970's weaving had ceased to be the occupation of old men, and become the major commercial activity of Bakarambasipe.

The shift of emphasis from dyeing to weaving did not involve any new

79

Esther N. Goody

technology. But there have been many changes in weaving and dyeing as a result of manufactured imports. These fall roughly under the headings of raw materials, tools and technology, and style.

Raw materials

Dyers now use a combination of local indigo leaf and imported commercial indigo crystals. They say the combination is more colour-fast than either alone, and that it allows them to get the very dark blue/black colour that makes their cloth preferred to all others. Manufactured cotton thread is used in probably three-quarters of the weaving done in Daboya (1974). In addition, *lele*, imported coloured thread, has always been used for decoration. This used to come from North Africa via northern Nigeria, but is now much more readily available from coastal imports.

Tools and technology

Nylon cord is used for the heddles instead of hand-spun cotton thread; wooden reels on which imported sewing cotton is sold are used for loom pulleys. Many parts of bicycles are used by the weavers: the most important are chain guards as warp sleds, spokes as pins for shuttle bobbins, and the rubber inner tubes for binding weft threads for *ikat* dyeing. Candles are now used to grease hand-spun warp threads to stop them catching on the heddles, instead of the shea butter which was formerly employed. Two devices are regularly used to speed up the warping process: one, the *korokoro*, was introduced to Daboya by a Bakarambasipe man who was working as a lorry driver. He saw it in use by Ashanti weavers of *kenti* cloth, and constructed one for his brothers in Daboya. The *korokoro* allows threads from two or more cones of machine-spun thread to be wound together onto a spindle ready for laying out warp or weft; it is also used to wind weft bobbins. A small boy can turn the handle and guide the thread, and so this device is doubly useful in that it has added to the unskilled tasks that can be allocated to them. The other device is a frame holding four or eight large spindles of commercial thread (prepared on the *korokoro*). Warp can be laid 4 (or 8) times faster by walking up and down between the warp pegs holding several spindles at once. The bobbin boys can use this warping frame, which requires some skill to keep the tension even on all the spindles and to avoid tangles. Both the *korokoro* and the multiple-spindle warping frame are responses to the introduction of machine-spun thread, which has quite different characteristics (strength, thickness, uniformity) than hand-spun thread, and presented new problems in use.

Apart from these adaptations to machine-spun thread, the main innovation has been the shift from using two different shuttles, one for white and one for blue thread, to *ikat* dyeing of the weft threads. This appears to have been 'invented' by the Daboya weaver-dyers themselves, by extending the principle of tie-dyeing used for cloth to the binding of the skein of weft threads with strips of rubber (inner tubing). There is no need to judge measurement exactly, since the repeat of the pattern will always be regular for a given skein of thread. There is, in any case, no 'correct' distance between bars of white in the weft-patterned designs. The use of *ikat*-dyed weft is universal among the weavers now. They say it makes weaving much quicker not to have to shift shuttles to introduce the bars in the pattern, and that now they don't forget to put in the bars!

Style

There are ten patterns used by the Daboya weavers, all variations on a blue-and-white striped warp with white or blue weft, the blue sometimes having white bars. At least one of these patterns has seen a change of name in the past twenty years, with a nick-name being gradually substituted for the 'real' name, which few people now know. The old cloths I have been able to see use these same patterns. However, old cloths were mainly woven to order, and were often gaily decorated with geometric patterns of imported coloured thread that were laid in at irregular intervals by hand. One man spoke of having seen a loom with an extra set of heddles for patterning, but none of the men weaving now in Bakarambasipe had used it. Such patterns take extra time and the weavers believe there is insufficient demand for them now to make it worthwhile. It is quite possible that the prolific supply of gaily printed machine-made cloth has filled this demand. Mallam Yahaya himself experimented from time to time with new colours in both warp and weft. However, he said that they didn't sell well, and each time he had returned to the traditional patterns.

The recent history of the Daboya textile industry is thus one of continuous adaptation to changes in market conditions and new raw materials and technology. Yet some new techniques have been rejected. From the outsider's point of view, the most obvious bottle-necks in cloth production are the time taken to lay out warp and weft threads, and the time involved in setting up the movable part of the loom and untangling the warp every morning, and taking it down every evening (as well as when it rains).

Shortly before I came to Daboya, Mallam Yahaya, acknowledged as the most skilled of the Bakarambasipe weavers, had made a trip south, to the industrial complex at the Akosombo dam, in order to look over the textile factory there. A night-watchman friend showed him the machines and explained how they worked. He returned anxious to find ways of improving the Bakarambasipe industry, and I was asked for advice on how they might build a big roof over the weaving yard to enclose the looms and their warps, thus making it unnecessary to take them down each day. However, various schemes were successively discarded as impracticable. Eventually I arranged to take him to the weaving unit at the University of Science and Technology at Kumasi, where he saw hand-operated revolving warping frames and European hand looms which incorporate a warp beam into the loom frame. The looms he rejected outright, as being too wide for the Daboya cloth strips.[8] He spent a long time examining the warping frame, which clearly intrigued him. However, when I offered to buy him one, he declined, saying first that he could not agree without consulting his father, Mallam Abudu, and then that he had more need of money for metal sheeting for a new roof. The first objection was pious, but not really a problem, as his father would have welcomed any improvement in weaving technology backed by Mallam Yahaya. The second reflected his assessment of priorities for available resources. He got the metal sheeting.

But why was the warping frame not taken up as other devices had been? It would seem to be exactly the sort of middle-range technical aid that would improve production without requiring new skills or resources, like electricity, beyond the weavers' means. And why was the loom rejected out of hand? A shift from narrow to broad cloth seems no more radical than a shift from dyeing thread to tie-dyeing cloth.

The rejection of the loom was immediate and complete. It was very expensive by Daboya standards, and must have seemed too complex to be made locally. While a master weaver might have been able to afford one loom, he would not have been able to buy additional ones for each of the youths and young men weaving for him. Abudulae certainly could not have paid for ten. A shift to the European broad loom would thus have meant no longer making use of the weaving labour of dependent weavers and bobbin boys, because there would not be enough looms for them. This loom would have promoted weaving, at least at first, from the semi-skilled to the skilled category. But if the master weaver was himself using the new loom, he would no longer be free to manage the processing of thread, warping and dyeing for the remaining traditional looms. This was not a decision based on relative technical merit, but on relations of production.

The more reluctant rejection of the warping frame is somewhat different. Warping enters the skill sequence at an earlier point, and particularly concerns the utilization of bobbin boys. The calculations of how many spindles of thread to wind onto the frame at one time, and the number of complete sets, winding from top to bottom, would have to be made by the master weaver. Older bobbin boys could probably manage the winding process itself, but the master weaver would have to stay close at hand to finish off each set and start the next. No longer could boys of the awkward age between 5 and 10 be brought into help intermittently with the totally unskilled job of walking with a single spindle between the far-spaced warping pegs. And the younger bobbin boys would be without their main work. To have adopted the warping frame would have meant shifting the balance of unskilled and semi-skilled tasks in favour of the latter, with a sharp drop in work suitable for older boys. Although efficiency in terms of the time required to prepare a warp would certainly increase, efficiency as measured by the utilization of labour at different levels of skill would decline.

One solution could be to let the boys play until a later age than at present, and wait to train them until they could manage the more complex procedure. However, the present balance of unskilled, semi-skilled and skilled tasks provides a progression which allows boys from an early age to make a real contribution to the weaving process. Their participation is carefully managed so as to engage their interest while leaving them considerable freedom until they are old enough to have the patience to develop skills that they can take pride in. A major task in kin-based enterprise is motivating the next generation to participate effectively. This is not only a matter of control, because too severe control simply drives a young man to move away, and this must always have been an option in a trade-oriented community. Another readily available alternative for a disaffected youth is to join the household of a maternal kinsman. Many of the Daboya weavers' practices, like a man's avoidance of teaching his own son, and the permissive attitude to boys' work, can be seen as a deliberate balancing of the need to utilize labour and train youths in weaving skills, against the dangers of arousing a boy's antagonism to male kin, and to weaving itself. Again, a decision to adopt the weaving frame could not be made only in terms of technical efficiency, but had to take account of the implications of doing away with the major unskilled task of the weaving process.[9]

The introduction of 'labour-saving' technology also has direct implications for the maintence of effective economic control over bobbin boys and dependent weavers, youths and young men. It is almost certainly the cyclical aspect of the horizontal division of labour which makes it tolerable.

That is, a youth weaving without payment for his teacher can look forward to the time when he will himself be a loom manager, and others will be weaving for him. His acquisition of his own loom is for him an important stage in reaching this goal, as is the gradual acquisition of his own thread, and eventually the ability to support a wife from his own earnings. If the use of costly tools became necessary to Daboya weavers, then either weavers would have to wait much longer before they had the capital to become independent, or they would remain as dependants of the master weavers permanently. The latter situation, however advantageous to the master weavers, would certainly lead to the younger men leaving Daboya. The former would have the same result. And there is another facet to the picture. For at present it is positively advantageous to the elders to have mature, independent sons, since they retain effective claims on their assets and labour. But if these sons had much greater need for capital themselves, in order to buy the new equipment, would they be able or willing to share resources with their fathers?

And this of course is why Bakarambasipe is not really like a factory. For, although many weavers work in the same weaving yard, they represent a number of independent economic units each internally hierarchically organized. The division of labour within each unit is articulated on the basis of an age/skill seniority reinforced by kinship authority, or by obligations to a teacher which are modelled on kinship authority. The division of labour between units is articulated by a mixture of commercial transactions and reciprocity. But the single capitalist controlling the entire enterprise, which Marx saw as the essential feature of manufacture, is missing. The elders who represent Bakarambasipe at the WasipeWura's court do so in a political role, not as entrepreneurs. And, indeed, they represent in this way the residents of courtyards which are entirely economically independent.

4 The tailors of Kano City

R. J. Pokrant

From the number of assertions made about the elimination of traditional
crafts, it might be supposed that the subject had been thoroughly investi-
gated. This is not the case.   (Hopkins 1973: 250)

The aim of this paper is to examine one particular Hausa craft, tailoring,
which, far from being eliminated, continues to play an important role,
albeit in a changed form, in the economic life of the Hausa. I shall confine
my attention largely to the situation prevailing among the tailors of Kano
City, the ancient core settlement of what today has become the Kano
Metropolitan Area (K.M.A.), the largest urban area of northern Nigeria and
the third largest city in Nigeria.

The paper will concentrate upon the present-day (*c*. 1975–6) organization of tailors in the old city of Kano, drawing most of my illustrative
material from three Kano City wards which either have been, or continue
to be, noted for their tailoring activities.[1] Major emphasis will be placed on
the highly differentiated character of the tailoring process, variations in the
organization of production, training and recruitment of tailors, markets
served, and the division of labour.

HAUSALAND AND THE HAUSA PEOPLE

From the tenth to the nineteenth century Hausaland saw the development
of a number of autonomous city-states, each of which imposed a measure
of political and economic control over a largely rural farming population
whose surplus product was extracted by a ruling class of kings or chiefs
(*sarakuna*), titled officials (*masu sarauta*) of both free and servile origin,
and a wide range of titled and non-titled subordinates (Fuglestad 1978;
Hogben and Kirk-Greene 1966; Hunwick 1971; Sutton 1979; A. Smith
1970, 1971; M. G. Smith 1978).

Trading and religious communities developed in the capital cities
(*birane*) which, besides performing important administrative functions in
the various royal courts, extended commercial and religious links between

85

various parts of Hausaland and between the Hausa and other peoples of the central Sudan. These communities were often the main carriers of Islam, which increasingly became a means by which the indigenous animistically based systems of political authority were challenged (Al-Hajj 1968; Lovejoy 1978a).

New types of craft goods, weapons of war, crops and food-stuffs were introduced during this period and by the nineteenth century there existed a regional economy based upon long-distance trading networks controlled by groups of long-distance traders (*fatake*) and merchants (*attajirai*), who were the connecting links between the mass of rural producers of food-stuffs, livestock and craft goods in different parts of Hausaland and markets beyond the region's border. Like the bulk of the peasant farming population, the trading communities were subject to various kinds of taxes and tribute in return for which they were provided with a measure of security in their trading operations.

The unstable alliance which the indigenous rulers of Hausaland maintained with these trading and religious communities came to an end in the late eighteenth century when reformer Usman dan Fodio, supported by sections of immigrant Fulani and indigenous Hausa, declared a holy war (*jihad*) against what were considered the corrupt and non-Islamic ways of the Hausa or Hab'e rulers, and established over large parts of Hausaland, including Kano, an Islamic theocracy with its spiritual headquarters at Sokoto (Adeleye 1971; Arnett 1922; Hiskett 1973; Last 1967; Martin 1977; Waldman 1965).

Over the nineteenth century the *jihad* leaders, their followers and successors pursued a policy of territorial expansion and consolidation, by means of which they increased the size of the area subject to Sokoto authority, increased its population, incorporated new raw-material-producing areas, encouraged the emigration of peasants, merchants, traders, aristocrats and craftsmen to new regions of settlement and trade, and farmers into the Hausa heartlands. It was during this period that Hausaland in general, and Kano in particular, reached the peak of their pre-colonial economic and political development (Abubakar 1970; Adamu 1978; Aliyu 1974; Balogun 1970; Usman 1974).

KANO CITY AND KANO EMIRATE

The economic and political centres of this expanding pre-industrial empire were the emirates of Katsina, Kano, Zazzau and Zamfara, and the districts of Sokoto and Gwandu. (Adamu 1978; Fika 1978; Lovejoy 1978b, 1979).

Of these, Kano came increasingly to dominate the rest in terms of the productivity of its agriculture, the variety of commercial services it could provide, the range of its manufacturing activities, the size of its population, and the importance of its markets and trade-terminus points for the buying and selling of locally produced and imported commodities and their distribution to all parts of the empire and beyond. One measure of Kano's growing prosperity and commercial importance at that time is that by the 1880's it provided the largest proportion of all the tribute paid by the various vassal states to Sokoto authority. (Fika 1978: 56).

Most craft producers were peasant farmers of free and servile status who worked small family farms. The main period of craft work was during the long dry season from October to May when agricultural activity was at its lowest. Within these peasant households, dependent males were provided with private plots (*gayaunu*) separate from the family farms (*gandu*) and were encouraged to take up craft work, trading and other activities, the products and profits being their own (Hill 1972; M. Smith 1954). During the dry season many farmers also migrated to other parts of Hausaland in search of opportunities to trade and practise their crafts. In these ways, pressures upon central *gandu* grain stores and other demands upon household heads were reduced.

The largest number of craft workers in the emirate engaged in the production of textiles and clothing for local, regional and export markets and included spinners (who were mainly women), weavers, indigo dyers, cloth beaters, and tailors and embroiderers. Other craft specialists included leather workers, tanners, blacksmiths working with iron, whitesmiths working with other metals, potters, builders and wood workers (Ferguson 1973; Fika 1978; Jaggar 1973; Shea 1975).

Besides the many thousands of farming households whose individual members were responsible for much of the emirate's craft production, there were larger rural estates, attached to royal, royal-slave, and aristocratic positions, and worked by a permanent labour force of farm slaves, with extra labour provided from the free peasantry at peak periods of the agricultural cycle. Many wealthy merchants, particularly those engaged in the kola and cloth trades (Lovejoy 1973a, 1973b), some craftsmen, and religious clerics (Tahir 1975) owned smaller private estates on which agricultural produce and craft goods, especially cloth, were produced both for local consumption and export. The main work force on private estates consisted of slaves, but also included members of the estate-owner's family, other kinsmen and their families, clients, and people of the same geographical-cum-historical origin (*asali*).

Like the majority of family farms, estates were located outside Kano City, but all ruling-class estate owners and many private-estate owners also maintained homes in the city.

Some of the larger private estates were not simply centres of agricultural and craft production but also acted as terminus points for the long-distance-trading system, with merchants receiving long-distance traders, putting them up in their own homes, arranging for the purchase and sale of imported goods, and selling to these traders craft products produced on the estates or by other craftsmen, who were both financed in their production by merchants and used the latter for their own independently produced output.

The major craft exports of the emirate were textiles and clothing; also important were hides and skins and some leather goods (Barth 1890; Ferguson 1973; Shea 1975). In the case of textiles, textile workers were found throughout the emirate, but the main centres of textile production, especially that part involving the dyeing and beating of cloth for export, were located south of the city in such places as Kura town, Bunkure, Dal, Dawakin Kudu, Garko, Dawakin Tofa, and Karaye.

All craft goods were made by hand and the level of technology was low. Some technological innovation occurred in certain crafts, notably dyeing, for which large sunken dye pits were increasingly used during the nineteenth century in response to the growing export demand for dyed cloth and clothing (Shea 1975). However, for the majority of crafts technology remained relatively static throughout the period. Increases in output were achieved through the lengthening of the working day, product specialization, the use of extra free and slave labour, and more intensive work patterns. Most craftsmen lacked the incentive or the means to make technological innovations, as they produced for a relatively stable local market of poor consumers and/or for an export market controlled by merchants and long-distance traders whose principal aim was to capture and control widely scattered markets rather than revolutionize productive techniques.

As Table 4.1 indicates, the bulk of the emirate's craft producers lived and worked outside Kano City. The city's main functions were as an entrepôt for the desert-oriented and other long-distance trade, and as a regional market centred on the city market, *Kasuwar Kurmi*. Many of the trading and commercial activities of the city were carried out in the private homes of merchants and landlords.

Although Kano City contained a wide range of craft specialists,[2] and its population increased greatly in size during the dry season through the immigration of traders and craftsmen, it was but one centre of craft production among many, with a resident population of less than 2 or 3 per cent of the emirate total (Hill 1977:3).

There was no institutional integration of craft producers into anything like a system of guilds by means of which craft workers could control the supply of raw materials, the recruitment of craft labour and the prices at which finished goods were sold. There were some city-based craft heads, notably in blacksmithing (Jaggar 1973), but these officials, rather than being independent heads of private associations, were agents of the ruling class and acted as tribute collectors and occasional organizers of communal-production groups supplying the rulers with weapons and labour for building projects. In fact, it would appear that the level and incidence of direct taxation of craft producers was low in Kano Emirate compared with other Hausa emirates. In dyeing, weaving, cloth beating, tailoring and spinning there were no craft heads who levied specific taxes on individual producers, although there was a small tax on dye pits (Fika 1978; Shea 1975). In general, the main tax revenues of the state were derived from taxes on land, crops, cattle, market transactions and traders, and from caravan tolls imposed on caravans used in the long-distance trade.

With the imposition of British colonial rule and the integration of Hausaland into the Nigerian colonial state, the economy of Kano ceased to focus on long-distance trade in the Sudan. The completion of the Lagos–Kano railway in 1912, built partly in anticipation of the growth of Kano Emirate as a major cotton-producing area linked to the British textile industry, provided a major stimulus to the export of groundnuts for the European margarine industry. Groundnuts, an indigenous but minor crop in pre-colonial Kano, formed the basis for the growth in prosperity of the emirate throughout the colonial period. From the point of view of the British colonial authorities and metropolitan commercial interests, Kano and other parts of the north were seen as potential markets for British manufactured goods, particularly textiles (Fika 1978; Helleiner 1966; Hogendorn 1978; Lubeck 1979; Shenton and Freund 1978).

TRADITIONS OF DRESS AND MODERN INTERPRETATIONS

Unlike many other peoples of Africa, the Hausa have not abandoned their traditional forms of dress for Western-style clothing. Indeed, to be identified as a Hausa depends in part upon wearing particular kinds of clothing, such as the long, flowing gown (*riga*) and the circular-shaped cap (*hula*).

The Hausa have had their own tailoring traditions for centuries. During

89

Table 4.1 *Craft workers in Kano Emirate in the early twentieth century (selected districts only)*

District or town	Weavers	Dyers	Cloth beaters	Tailors	Leather workers and boot makers	Tanners	Black-smiths	White-smiths	Builders	Wood workers	Total	Year	Reference
Kano City	227	337	80	3,450	473	122	64	204	222	n.i	5,179	1926	a
Sarkin Dawaki[1] Tsakkar Gida	2,348	1,311	174	864	93	124		266[2]	210	n.i	5,390	1909	b
Makama	5,499	4,199	650	2,700	296	563		530	42	n.i	14,479	1912	c
Dutse	4,152	1,550	261	1,665	n.i	162		172	83	n.i	8,045	1911	d
Dan Iya	3,329	833	159	1,028	55	199		115	27	115	5,860	1912	e
Barden Kereria	249	290	35	113	27	27		14	2	n.i	757	1912	f
Dan Buram	582	189	55	483	n.i	n.i	n.i	n.i	n.i	n.i	1,309	1912	g
Jaidanawa	278	38	8	142	5	90	37	n.i	n.i	3	601	1912	h
Kura town[1]	350	2,002	80	11	4	22		59	11	n.i	2,539	1909	i
Rano	1,836	501	113	442	48	36		124	n.i	119	3,219	1925	j
Kiru	8,262	1,039	446	2,801	374	n.i	417	n.i	n.i	n.i	13,339	1929	k
Tudun Wada	1,848	429	107	n.i	95	n.i	213	n.i	n.i	n.i	2,692	1926	l
Total	28,960	12,718	2,168	13,699	1,470	1,345	2,215		597	237	63,409		

Notes:

1 Refers to households or compounds and not individuals, except in the case of Kura town dyers.

2 No differentiation made between blacksmiths and whitesmiths but most likely to be blacksmiths.

Sources for Table 4.1

a National Archives, Kaduna (NAK) SOKPROF 260: Census and Reassessment of Kano City and Fagge, 1926, by Mr Hoskyns Abrahall.

b NAK SNP 7: 5570/1909: Assessing Report, Sarkin Dawaki Tsakkar Gida District, by Mr Dupigny.

c NAK SNP 7: 2793/1912: Kano Province, Makama's District Assessment Report, by Capt. Uniacke.

d NAK SNP 7: 2715/1911: Assessment Report, Dutsi District, Kano Province, 1911–12, Mr F. W. Bell.

e NAK SNP 7: 4055/1912: Kano Province, Dan Iya Sub-District, Assessment Report, Mr Webster.

f NAK SNP 7: 6969/1912: Sub-District Report on Barden Kereria, Capt. G. L. Uniacke, 1912.

g NAK SNP 7: 5785/1912: Kano Province, Dan Buram, Chiroma's District Assessment Report, Capt. Foulkes.

h NAK SNP 7: 4817/1912: Jaidanawa Sub-District Assessment Report, Capt. Foulkes.

i NAK SNP 7: 2607/1909: Kura District Assessment Report, Mr Moreton Frewen.

j NAK KANOPROF: 1523: Test Assessment, Rano District, Rano Industrial Tax, 1925–6, Mr H. L. Noble, A.D.O.

k NAK KANOPROF: 210: Kiru District Reassessment Report, 1929, Mr G. E. Watts, Cadet.

l NAK SNP 7: 2909/1925: Vol. V, Tudun Wada District Assessment Revision, 1925–6, Mr R. F. P. Orme.

N.B. As these reports were done for purposes of taxation by the British, it can be assumed that the figures represent undercounts of the true numbers. Unfortunately, there are no figures for the number of craft workers in these or any other districts during the nineteenth century.

Only a few districts are included here. In the emirate as a whole, the total for all craft workers, including certain crafts such as potting and mat making, is probably at least double that given in the table.

With the possible exception of some craftsmen in Kano City and other urban centres, the vast majority of craft workers were also farmers.

the nineteenth century the use of Hausa-style clothing spread both among Hausa and non-Hausa peoples as a consequence of the expansion of the economy of Hausaland, the political and economic incorporation of new areas into the caliphate, and the extension of trade links to regions beyond the boundaries of the caliphate's authority. In addition, as part of the civilizing mission undertaken by Muslim Hausa and Fulani clerics, many of whom were also traders and craftsmen, new converts to Islam were usually required to don Hausa-style clothing to mark their transition from the status of *arne*, or pagan, to that of *Musulmi*, or Muslim. This process of Islamization among the Hausa and among other peoples living in areas contiguous with Hausaland was particularly rapid during the nineteenth century, but it has continued into the twentieth.

Many observers have commented upon the importance of dress as a sign of civilization among the Hausa, but one quote from a study done among the Niger Republic Hausa will suffice to make the point: 'Ce costume [referring to the large Hausa *riga*] est associé à la religion musulmane à tel point qu'il est une sorte d'uniforme par lequel on reconnaît en principe les adeptes de cette religion. Une conversion religieuse se marque avant tout par une conversion vestimentaire' (Nicolas 1975:59).

The wearing of Hausa clothing as a mark of Islamic and Hausa identification has been further reinforced during the present century by the growth of Hausa cultural nationalism in the face of fears that they, the Hausa, would be dominated by other ethnic and cultural groups within the newly established state of Nigeria.

Although there have been large increases in the importation of garments into Nigeria over the past seventy years, this has had little effect on tailoring because, in the main, imported garments are made in the Western style. Thus, there are no imported substitutes for the wide variety of gowns, most of the caps, and many of the smocks and trousers made by Hausa tailors. Some imports, such as shirts, are worn by Hausa men, but they usually continue to wear the short Hausa shirts known as *yar ciki* and alternate between the two styles. Many imports, such as brassières, stockings, socks, cardigans, jerseys, pullovers, and waterproof clothing, have no traditional equivalents, and so constitute net additions to the clothing range available in the society without displacing traditional styles. Only one item of traditional clothing, the hand-woven underpants or *bante*, appears to have been displaced by imported (and domestically manufactured) substitutes. Most Nigerian clothing imports go to the non-Hausa peoples of southern Nigeria, where Westernization of dress styles has gone the furthest.

Where there is a demand for Western clothing among Hausa peoples, local tailors have responded by producing such garments themselves. In Kano, tailors who specialize in such work are located mainly outside the old city in Fagge and Sabon Gari. They make shirts, both regular and tight-fitting, trousers, including those with flared bottoms, and custom-made suits. Customers are often the young and fashion-conscious who demand a good fit, something which is more difficult to obtain if one buys 'off-the-peg'. In addition, local tailors can usually make garments more cheaply than the imported varieties. In rural areas, where most of the population lives, and where a significant proportion of tailored goods made in the city is sold, Western styles are much less important.

A further, and more important, response on the part of local tailors to changes in fashion has been the modernization of traditional styles. There has been a movement towards lighter and less bulky clothing, known as *k'aramar kaya* among the Hausa, which means that garments use up less cloth and thread, and require less labour, the net result of which has been to lower the cost of garments.

The most important factor in reducing the cost of tailored garments has been the introduction of the sewing machine, which greatly increased the speed of production, thus lowering the labour cost per unit. In pre-colonial times, all tailoring was done by hand. Today, the majority of tailors, particularly in the urban areas, use sewing machines. All machines are imported and imports have risen from a total of 8,350 machines imported during 1925 to 56,181 in 1975,[3] the major period of import expansion occurring after the second world war.

The first machines were used in Kano around the time of the first world war and were imported by European firms. Originally sold to Hausa traders, merchants, and some wealthier craftsmen, they have during the past thirty years become increasingly available to large numbers of tailors of modest means, who either purchase them through savings and the assistance of kin, or rent them. However, in the three wards studied, many tailors have been able to buy machines, and few work with rented ones. On the other hand, there are also tailors who cannot afford to buy a machine and who work as employees of others.

The speed with which tailors can produce garments has also been increased by the growing use of factory-made fabrics which come in large pieces. In the past, cloth was hand-woven into narrow strips ranging in width from half an inch to nine inches, which had then to be sewn together in order to make a piece large enough for a garment. Today, there is no need for such work, which was time-consuming and added to the cost of the garment.[4]

INDUSTRY AND COMMERCE IN URBAN KANO

The Kano Metropolitan Area (K.M.A.), which includes the old city of Kano, Waje district, and the peri-urban districts of Ungogo and Kumbotso, is the third largest urban area in Nigeria, containing an estimated population of approximately 500,000 (Frishman 1977: 45). Sixty-eight per cent of this population live in the old city and Waje and it is in these two areas that most of the industry and commerce of the K.M.A. is located. Kano is also the administrative capital of Kano State, the most populous state in the country, with an estimated population of over 10 million (Davidson 1977: 1504).[5]

Kano has always been an important commercial centre and today it is the major commercial city of the north and the second largest commercial and industrial centre in the Federation. Thus, in the early 1960's it was estimated that Metropolitan Kano accounted for 50 per cent of all trade in northern Nigeria (Trevallion *et al.* 1966: 84). The old commercial area east of the old city contains the large commercial firms engaged in the import and distribution of a wide range of imported and domestically produced commodities. Banks, insurance companies, large retail stores, many government offices and other companies are also found here (see Map 1).

Fagge ta Kudu (known locally as Kantin Kwari) is the centre for the wholesale cloth trade, and contained about 278 such enterprises in 1972 (Ministry of Trade and Industry, Kano State, 1974: 9). Largely dominated by foreign, particularly Lebanese, interests until 1972, there has been since that time a growing indigenous control of this trade as a consequence of indigenization policies pursued by the federal government.

Kurmi market, established in the fifteenth century, is the main old-city market and acts as a local and regional centre for the purchase and sale of a wide range of commodities. Textiles and clothing, plastic and enamel wares, local foods, meat, jewellery and ornaments are the main items of trade. About 2,000 traders operate from this market, of which over 200 buy and sell clothes and another 222 deal in textiles. Rimi market, also located in the city, has about 600 stalls and deals in a narrower range of goods than Kurmi.

Sabon Gari market, established by non-Hausa immigrants to Kano during the 1920's and 1930's, serves the Waje district. The main commodities traded are textiles and clothing, foodstuffs (many imported from the south), mechanical and electrical goods, and footwear. Larger than Kurmi market, it was estimated to have about 3,571 stall holders in 1963

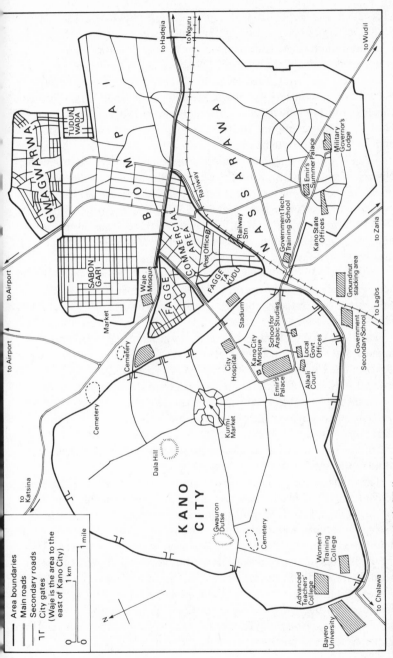

Map 1 Kano City – Waje (1974)

Area boundaries
Main roads
Secondary roads
City gates
(Waje is the area to the
east of Kano City)

0 1 km
0 1 mile

N

KANO
CITY

Dala Hill
Gwauron
Dutse

Kurmi
Market

Cemetery
Cemetery
Cemetery

Bayero
University

Advanced
Teachers'
College

Women's
Training
College

to Chalawa

to Katsina

to Airport
to Airport

GWAGWARWA

TUDUN
WADA

SABON
GARI

Market

FAGGE

Waje
Mosque

COMMERCIAL
AREA

Post Office

FAGGE
TA
KUDU

City Hospital

Kano City
Mosque

Stadium

Emir's
Palace

Alkali
Court

School for
Arabic Studies

Local
Govt
Offices

Government
Secondary School

to Hadejia

to Nguru

Railway

B O M P A I

N A S S A R A W A

Railway
Stn

Government Tech.
Training School

Kano State
Offices

Groundnut
stacking area

Emir's
Summer Palace

Military
Governor's
Lodge

to Wudil

to Zaria

to Lagos

95

(Trevallion *et al.* 1966: 137). Since the exodus of the Ibos in the mid-1960's it has become increasingly Hausa-dominated.

In addition to these large markets, there are many other market places scattered throughout the urban area. Some, such as Kasuwar K'ul-K'ul in Yalwa ward, are mainly food markets, while others, such as the night market around the Central City Mosque, deal in a wide range of non-food consumer goods. Literally hundreds of people also engage in street trading, hawking, table trading, and the sale of goods from small shops or kiosks and from within private homes.

Kano is also the major industrial and manufacturing centre for northern Nigeria. Accurate statistics for large- and medium-scale enterprises (defined in part as those having more than fifty employees) are not available. However, one 1975 estimate gives a total of 25,087 workers in 131 firms (*Nigeria Year Book* 1975: 349). The largest of these engage in the production of textiles, tanning of hides, processing of food and vegetables oils, manufacture of metal goods, brewing, and the making of sweets.

In the early 1970's there were only two industrial producers of wearing apparel using more sophisticated technology than that found in tailoring workshops. One of these produced singlets, and the other socks and stockings.[6]

The 1972 survey of smale-scale industry in Kano Metropolitan Area found 4,589 establishments employing fewer than 50 workers, most with less than 20. The total of 21,568 employees average to less than 5 per enterprise. If these data are combined with the estimate of large and medium-scale enterprises cited above, small-scale industry accounts for 46 per cent of total industrial employment, and 97 per cent of the industrial establishments. If, as I suspect, the 1972 figures are seriously underestimated, the importance of small-scale firms in the industrial structure of Kano is even greater than these figures suggest.[7]

These small-scale industries cover a diverse range of types of economic activity, not all of which involve a manufacturing component. Thus, they include grain milling, baking, blacksmithing, bicycle repair, hairdressing, dyeing, shoe making, leather working, carpentry, radio, T.V. and car repairs, photography, catering and printing. However, nearly 30 per cent (1,357) of the 4,589 small-scale establishments are engaged in tailoring. Of these 44 per cent are located in the old city and account for 37 per cent (1,098) of the total number of tailors in the Kano urban area (see Table 4.2 for a breakdown of the figures for old city tailors). The average size of the tailoring workshops is very small, only 1.8 persons per establishment, and over 60 per cent of all workshops are single-person enterprises.

Table 4.2 *Distribution of tailoring workshops by size and numbers employed: old city of Kano, 1972*

Number of persons per workshop:	Number of workshops		Total employed by workshop size:	(%)
	No.	(%)		
1	376	63	376	34
2	93	16	186	17
3	65	11	195	18
4	27	4	108	10
5 or more	37	6	233	21
Total	598	100	1,098	100

Source: Ahmadu Bello University, 1972

DIVISION OF LABOUR, MARKETS FOR TAILORED COMMODITIES AND THE ORGANIZATION OF PRODUCTION AMONG KANO CITY TAILORS

In describing the occupation of tailoring, the Hausa continue to use the term *sana'a*, which is derived from the Arabic word *san'a* meaning a craft, trade or, less commonly, guild (Baer 1964: 16). The tailor (*mad'inki*) is considered to be a *mai sana'a* (literally 'one with a craft').

However, the use of the term 'craft' or 'trade' is misleading when applied to the contemporary Kano context in so far as it implies the existence of a homogeneous body of autonomous or self-employed producers, who possess a high degree of skill based upon years of specialized training under some formally organized and highly structured system of apprenticeship, and who are able to produce a wide range of garments within a system of production which allows each producer to exert major control over what, how, and for whom garments are produced.

In fact, the tailors of Kano City are a highly differentiated category of producers. They differ in the kinds and levels of skills attained, the types of products they make, the markets they serve, the scale and types of production units within which they work, and the degree of control they have over the means of production utilized in the tailoring process. They also participate in a relatively complex division of labour, based on whether they sew by hand or machine, on type of machine used, age, skill and sex.

I will consider these[8] and other differences in more detail in order to determine the ways in which they structure the organization of tailoring

97

and the opportunities tailors have for maintaining and advancing their economic position.

The majority of the old-city tailors are Hausa and are culturally and spatially distinguished from a large proportion of their non-Hausa counterparts who live and work in the Waje district of the Kano Metropolitan Area. This distinctiveness is reinforced by an economic division of labour in that city tailors produce clothing for a predominantly Hausa market of urban and rural consumers whereas many of the tailors in the Waje district, particularly those from southern Nigeria, orient their production to non-Hausa peoples, most of whom live within this district. Cooperation between the city Hausa tailors and non-Hausa tailors is minimal or non-existent, the vast majority of city tailors working with, and trained by, other Hausa. There are Hausa tailors living and working outside the city and some city tailors who commute to work in such Waje quarters as Fagge, but the bulk of Hausa tailors live and work in the old city. It is with these latter that I am mainly concerned.

There are no special 'industrial areas' reserved for tailors, although the central city market does have a tailor's section. Work premises are either entrance rooms to private homes, special-purpose workshops, most of which are small in physical size, or, in the case of many hand sewers, any open-space where there is shade.

There are important concentrations of tailoring workshops in particular wards and clusters of wards. The major concentration runs in a band from the northeast side of the city market around the market's north and west sides and then southwards. Noted tailoring wards included within this band are Bakin Zuwo, Madabo, Makwalla, Masukwani, Duumin Arbabi, Gyaranya, Sudawa, Dandago, and Hausawa. Other concentrations are found in the Yalwa/Dogon Nama/Dala area, in a cluster of wards around the Emir's Palace, of which Soron D'inki and Kabara are the most important, and in the wards of Yakasai, Kofar Wambai, Kofar Mata and Kofar Nassarawa.

The 1972 survey of tailoring establishments showed that over 60 per cent of all workshops in the city were single-person enterprises with only 10 per cent containing 4 or more workers (Table 4.2). However, there was some ward variation in terms of size of establishment. Thus, in Soron D'inki there were 25 physically separate places of work, 80 per cent of which contained a single tailor. Those few which were larger than this contained no more than 3 persons. In Hausawa, on the other hand, out of a total of 48 workshops in the ward, only 42 per cent (20) were single-person enterprises while approximately 25 per cent (12) contained 4 or more persons. The largest workshop contained 11 persons, including the workshop

Table 4.3 *Size of tailoring workshops in three intensively studied wards*

	Per cent of tailors in workshops of:			
	1 person	2–3 people	4 or more people	N
Soron D'inki	80	20	–	(25)
Yalwa	43	40	17	(60)
Hausawa	42	33	25	(48)

head (*maigida*). Yalwa, with about 60 separate places of work, had 43 per cent (26) of workshops with a single tailor, 40 per cent with between 2 and 3, and 17 per cent with 4 or more.

Not all workshops are identical with the actual production unit. Some tailors share the same working space but do not cooperate in production. Others work alone in a particular physical location but devote part of their tailoring efforts to work which is put out to them by other tailors. For example, in Yalwa ward, one workshop head employed 5 tailors in his workshop but, during the course of a year, put out hand tailoring to approximately 30 tailors, both male and female. Workshop size also varies according to the season. In both Hausawa and Yalwa wards, larger workshop owners took on extra labour during busy times and laid it off when business was slack. These few remarks indicate that we should treat with caution the use of workshop size as an indicator of scale of operations. I shall have more to say about this later.

Across the city as a whole there are a few workshops with 20 or 30 workers. The largest visited by the author contained 14 persons. In the three wards studied, the largest single workshop in which workers were concentrated under one roof and were employed by one person contained 10 employees.

Some wards have a pre-colonial association with tailoring which has continued to the present day, others have only recently developed as major tailoring centres, while others have seen their tailoring activities decline in importance over the past seventy years. For example, Soron D'inki, which obtained its name – 'Hall of Tailoring' – from the activities of a nineteenth-century tailor who made garments for the ruling elite, later became known as a centre for the production of saddle cloths (*jalalu*, plural: *jalala*, sing.) in the later nineteenth century, but today contains few sewers who continue to do such work. Yalwa, which developed as an area of settlement for long-distance traders, their families and slaves during the nineteenth century, became noted for its Eastern-style tailoring tradition at that time, a position which it has maintained to the present. Hausawa, on the other hand, has only recently emerged as one of the main centres for the production of machine-made caps.

It should be noted that no single ward is exclusively given over to tailoring or dominated by particular tailoring families. Rather, all wards contain people pursuing a diverse range of economic and occupational activities with some having a larger proportion of tailors than others. However, certain wards are noted for their tailoring specialities and Table 4.4 provides a list of these wards and the kinds of tailoring products made there. (See Map 2 for location of these wards.)[9]

THREE KANO TAILORING WARDS: TRADITIONS AND COMPOSITION

Three very different tailoring wards were selected for intensive study. These were: Soron D'inki, located in Fuskar Kudu (south section) on the north side of the Emir's Palace; Yalwa in Fuskar Yamma (western section) but on the far northwest side of the city close to Dala Hill; and Hausawa in Fuskar Yamma.

Soron D'inki is a relatively small ward with a total area of 11.33 acres, and a total population of 987 in 1973. The ward is surrounded on 3 sides by other wards and its south side opens out onto the square of the Friday Mosque. It has seen no outward expansion over the recent past and the total population has increased (if the tax records are to be believed) by 25 per cent during the period 1945 to 1973. Of the 3 wards it has grown the least over the 1945/73 period.

The other two wards, Hausawa and Yalwa, situated as they are on the western edge of the built-up area, have grown at a much faster rate than Soron D'inki. Hausawa had a male tax-paying population of 224 in 1945 which had increased to 491 in 1973, an increase of 119 per cent. The corresponding figures for Yalwa are 323 and 572, an increase of approximately 80 per cent during the same period.

The Soron D'inki sample of 36 interviews is close to a 100-per cent sample of male tailors working in the ward in 1975/6. In the case of Hausawa, there is some under-representation of employers in workshops of more than 2 machines, although the 101 cases collected provide wide coverage. For Yalwa, however, I was unable to cover the whole ward and so certain areas have been left out. Most of the 93 interviews were taken from an area to the north of Kasuwar K'ul-K'ul, a food market in the centre of the

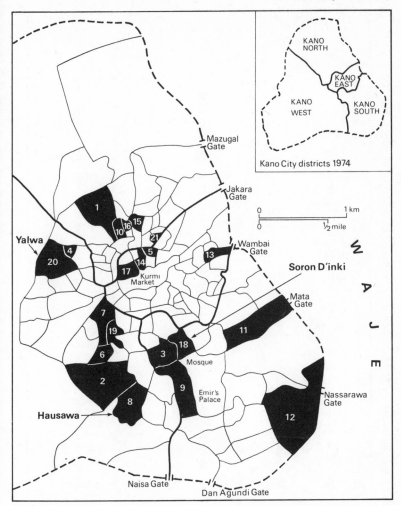

Map 2 Location of main tailoring wards in Kano City (1974)

Key (District noted: North, South, East, West)

1 Dala (N)
2 Dandago (W)
3 Daneji (S)
4 Dogon Nama (W)
5 Durumin Arbabi (E)
6 Garangamawa (W)
7 Gyaranya (W)
8 Hausawa (W)
9 Kabara (S)
10 Kangiwa (N)
11 Kofar Mata (S)
12 Kofar Nassarawa (S)
13 Kofar Wambai (E)
14 Kwarin Mabuga (E)
15 Madabo (N)
16 Makwalla (N)
17 Masukwani (E)
18 Soron D'inki (S)
19 Sudawa (W)
20 Yalwa (W)
21 Zaitawa (E)

101

Table 4.4 *Products made and the instruments of production used in selected Kano City tailoring wards, 1976*

Ward	Types of products	Instruments of production
Hausawa	Caps, gowns and smocks	Machine embroidery and assembly
Dandago	,, ,, ,,	,, ,, ,, ,,
Sudawa	Gowns, smocks and trousers	,, ,, ,, ,,
Gyaranya	,, ,, ,, ,,	,, ,, ,, ,,
Garangamawa	Caps and some gowns	,, ,, ,, ,,
Makwalla	Gowns, smocks, caps, trousers	,, ,, ,, ,,
Madabo	,, ,, ,, ,,	,, ,, ,, ,,
Karofin Kangiwa	Gowns, smocks and caps	,, ,, ,, ,,
Kwarin Mabuga	Gowns, smocks, caps, trousers	,, ,, ,, ,,
Zaitawa	,, ,, ,, ,,	,, ,, ,, ,,
Kurmi Market	Gowns, smocks and trousers	Machine assembly and some machine embroidery
Kofar Wambai	,, ,, ,,	,, ,, ,, ,,
Kofar Mata	,, ,, ,,	,, ,, ,, ,,
Kofar Nassarawa	,, ,, ,,	,, ,, ,, ,,
Yalwa	Cloaks, gowns and trousers	Much hand embroidery with growing machine embroidery
Dogon Nama	Cloaks, gowns, smocks, trousers	,, ,, ,, ,,
Dala	Gowns and smocks	Machine embroidery and assembly with some hand embroidery
Soron D'inki	Saddle covers (*jalala*), smocks and some gowns	Mainly machine assembly and embroidery with some hand embroidery
Daneji	Some saddle covers and trousers	Mainly hand embroidery
Kabara	Some saddle covers and saddle blankets (*labbati*)	Both hand and machine embroidery and machine assembly
Masukwani	Cloaks, gowns, trousers	Hand embroidery
Durumin Arbabi	Gowns and trousers	,, ,,

ward. I would estimate that this sample of 93 is about 75 per cent of the total number of tailors in that northern section of the ward.

Soron D'inki

Soron D'inki ('Room/hall of tailoring') is historically associated with the sewing of the saddle-cloth known as *jalala*. In a survey carried out in March 1975, 36 tailors were counted. Below is a breakdown of this figure according to the type of tailoring engaged in.

Table 4.5 *Types of tailor in Soron D'inki*

Type of tailor	Number
Hand *jalala* sewing	8
Hand trouser embroidery	3
Hand gown embroidery	1
Machine sewing	24
Total:	36

However, of the 8 *jalala* makers, 5 are old men who work irregularly at the craft, and 2 are part-time *jalala* makers having full-time jobs with the Local Government Authority. Of the trouser makers, 1 is a very old man who works intermittently, whereas the remaining 2 are full-time employees in one of the local Alkali's[10] courts. The single gown embroiderer works full-time at this. As can be seen from the figures, machine tailors dominate tailoring in this ward. Most do assembly and embroidery of clothing, although there are a few who specialize in machine assembly of *jalala*. Many of these machine tailors have at one time done hand sewing. For example, 2 out of 3 machine tailors in the sample were hand sewers, mainly *jalala* makers, when young.

All informants agree that in the past there were far more hand *jalala* makers than today. To some extent the sewing machine has had an impact upon the numbers doing hand sewing, but the major cause of the decline in hand *jalala* makers must be the general decline in the demand for horse decorations.[11] This made it easier for hand sewers to switch to, among other occupations, machine tailoring. Furthermore, it is not clear to what extent residents of Soron D'inki engaged in *jalala* making in pre-colonial times. The *jalala* was introduced into Hausaland and Kano by North African traders, and it is possible that up to the mid-nineteenth century most *jalalu* were imported. Elderly informants say their fathers copied *jalala* making from the Arabs, working first with bits of cloth and rags.

They say there were not a great many *jalala* makers at the turn of the century, the big increase in numbers coming with the advent of British rule and the groundnut boom. At that time farmers and others who acquired cash from the sale of groundnuts bought horses and the caparisons to go with them. This stimulated *jalala* production in the ward. However, these new consumers did not buy the traditional *jalala* made from expensive gold-and-silver braid, but a cheaper variety made with mercerized cotton. Soron D'inki specialized in producing such *jalala*, and tailors in the ward introduced many of the designs, albeit modelled on the imported variety. Informants who were young at that time say they stopped doing cap making and other craft pursuits when they saw, or were told, that *jalala* making was more profitable.

Another point is that Soron D'inki is one of the so-called Fulani wards (Paden 1973: 20), settled largely during the nineteenth century when the city expanded with the advent of Fulani rule and eclipsed Katsina as a commercial centre. Many residents of the ward in pre-colonial times were *fadawa* (courtiers) and *bayin Sarki* (slaves of the Emir) who may have found their traditional sources of livelihood drying up with the administrative reorganization which occurred during the first twenty years of British rule. Although some of these people did *jalala* making as a part-time activity in pre-colonial times, they may have come to rely upon it more and more as support from the palace was reduced. For example, one of my major informants, a machine tailor, is descended from one of the major slave officials of the nineteenth century – Dan Rimi. His grandfather was a *jakada* or court agent who was responsible for collecting taxes in the rural areas. Yet my informant's father had no experience in government, having been a tailor since childhood.

I was told that *jalala* making did not originate in Soron D'inki but in Sharfadi, an adjoining ward, and spread from there to Soron D'inki. In the past there were few master-craftsmen tailors who were skilled in a variety of tailoring techniques and who made a variety of garments. Elderly informants say it was difficult to make a living from *jalala* making alone and few had the resources to buy raw materials and employ others in a putting-out system. Some tried other jobs, such as petty trading and even long-distance trading, but found them unprofitable or were unable to maintain a supply of goods.

Yet at one time or another many residents of Soron D'inki have been *jalala* makers. For example, M. Nasiru, a machine embroiderer of expensive *jalala* made in the old style with silver braid, has a number of relatives who have been, or are, engaged in *jalala* making. He mentioned 9 close relatives who have been taught *jalala* making, although of those still living 2 no longer do *jalala* work and 5 do it on a part-time basis. One full brother of M. Nasiru does *jalala* making by hand and machine but combines this work with building and the renting out of one bicycle. A half-brother rents out bicycles, studies *ilm* (higher Muslim education) and also does both hand and machine *jalala* sewing. A parallel cousin is a hand sewer of *jalala*, combining it with whitesmithing (*'kira ta farfaru*) of buckets, bowls and rings. Another parallel cousin sews *jalala* and sells horse caparisons in the central market. M. Nasiru's father, once a *jalala* maker, now runs a Koranic school in the ward. Finally, M. Nasiru's paternal grandfather did Eastern-style sewing and sold clothes in the market. Furthermore, his father's two senior brothers are stall holders in the market and sell all types of horse gear. The history of the family in Kano and Soron D'inki goes back to pre-Fulani times when a Kanuri mallam came to Kano with his students and

4.1 The owner of a machine-tailoring workshop employing local teen-age boys. He sells the caps they make in his stall in the city market (Hausawa ward)

slaves and settled in the area. M. Nasiru says this ancestor criticized the religious laxity of the king and was expelled from the city only to return after the last *Ha'be* ruler was deposed.

In more recent times, machine tailoring played a more important role in the economic life of the ward than today. Informants report that after the second world war and in the 1950's demand for clothing increased. One of the early importers of the open-chain-stitch sewing machine was a Soron D'inki man and this brought new opportunities for machine tailors, or those with the money to buy and operate the new machines. The importer himself employed a number of tailors in the 1950's and 1960's to produce embroidered garments. Other smaller operators also set up shop and employed a few tailors to work for them. However, as more and more machines were imported and more and more people became machine tailors, the opportunities for profitable investment on a small scale in tailoring declined, and in Soron D'inki a number of tailors reduced the size of their operation. The importer no longer employs any machine tailors, relying on self-employed tailors to work for him, as needed. In any case, this man was involved in other activities besides tailoring, such as the putting out of hand-tailoring work to tailors in Jajira village, and landlordism.

During the 1950's there was an increased demand for *jalala* because of the Durbar planned for the Queen's visit in 1956. Hand tailors, already in decline, could not meet the demand and so a machine tailor in the ward hit upon the idea of producing cheap *jalala* embroidered by machine. This provided employment for some tailors, but for a very short time, although the machine embroidering of *jalala* is still done.

It is claimed by some tailors in the ward that they taught many of the younger tailors in the city how to use the embroidery machines when they were first introduced. There is a story, backed up by the tailors involved, that Alhaji Mahdi, one of the largest employers of tailors in the city during the 1950's and 1960's and regarded as a self-made man, asked for a few tailors to be sent to his workshop in Karofin Kangiwa on the north side of the market to show him how to operate the new machines. Two tailors went and instructed Alhaji Mahdi's tailors in the use of the machines.

There is a certain residual pride among some tailors in Soron D'inki that they were among the first to use the new machines, although the machines must have been used over a wide area of the city and were not channelled through one ward only. Furthermore, even today out-of-towners looking for tailoring areas of the city often come to Soron D'inki first because of its name.

Evidence for the large numbers of people who have at one time done tailoring in the ward comes partly from informants who gave me names of non-tailors with a tailoring background. For example, my chief informant told me the names of 35 people (an incomplete list, he said, which could be doubled) who had left tailoring more or less completely but who had been engaged either full- or part-time in tailoring in former times. Twenty-five of the 35 had been hand *jalala* makers, another 9 machine tailors, and one a hand cap maker. These 35 individuals are now full-time workers in other occupations. Twenty-five are in one way or another connected with the Local Government Authority, 4 are traders, 3 are in education, and the remaining few are pursuing various private economic activities.

Today there are no large workshops in the ward. The largest has 3, sometimes 4, tailors, but they are not working for a common employer; 3 are self-employed. Out of the 25 separate tailoring establishments in the ward, 12 are located in the *soro* (entrance hall or room) of a house, one is a *zaure* (a circular-shaped entrance room commonly found in rural areas today), and the remainder are *shaguna*, workshops. Out of the 36 tailors, only one rents his workshop. This man, a Fulani from Gombe, is a stranger to the ward and does not live in it. All the others are residents who work in their own homes or the homes of friends and neighbours.

Only half of the tailors in the ward consider their main occupation to be tailoring. Of the rest, the majority work part-time at tailoring while holding down relatively full-time jobs as government labourers, petty traders, horse-caparison dealers and other informal sector-type work. A minority of part-time tailors are elderly men who do only casual tailoring work, being supported mainly by kinsmen.

Yalwa

Yalwa ward, situated on the northwest side of the city, close to Dala Hill, is the centre of Eastern-style tailoring in Kano. The major period of settlement of the area which eventually became Yalwa was during the nineteenth century, particularly between the reigns of Sarkin Kano Dabo (1819–46) and his son Abdullahi Maje Karofi (1855–82). The settlement occurred partly as a consequence of the decline of Katsina as a commercial centre and the movement of long-distance traders, both Hausa and North African, to Kano. One tradition relates that the part of the ward known as K'ul-K'ul was settled by Arab and Katsina merchants under the leadership of a man named Abdullah KutKut. The Hausa, being unable to pronounce the name correctly, referred to him as K'ul-K'ul (Adamu 1968: 43) Today an important food market is held on and around the site of KutKut's original home.

107

The area is also known as Durmin K'ul-K'ul after a tree said to have been planted by him.

K'ul-K'ul is only one area within the ward of Yalwa, and traditions describing how Yalwa came to be named are different. For example, it is claimed by the descendants of a family said to be the founder of Eastern-style tailoring in Kano that the establishment of the ward is related to their own family history. The grandfather of the oldest living member of that family is said to have come to Kano on his way to Mecca. This man was a mallam who was born in Katsina and left to teach in Agades where he learnt how the sewing of clothing was done from the North African merchants who traded from there. The Emir of Kano of the time asked the man to stay in Kano and teach, giving him a house in Dukurawa ward close to the city market. After some time, Mallam Mustafa, as the man was called, complained that his house was too cramped to accommodate all his students and asked the Emir for a new compound. The Emir showed him an open area on the northwestern side of the city and said he should move here, because *ya fi yalwa*, that is, it has more space. From this the ward got its name. Today the descendants of this man still live in the area given to Mustafa, on the north side of the K'ul-K'ul market known as the street of Bulala, named after a nineteenth-century long-distance trader.[12]

Another tradition relates the naming of the ward to long-distance trading and the slave population of Kano. The Arabs who came to Kano during Dabo's time (1819-46) and later and who settled in Jingau and Dandalin Turawa, two wards to the east of Yalwa, began to look for other places to settle and some moved with their slaves to Yalwa. Families looking for places to settle with their slaves were advised: *ku kai shi yalwa* – take him to the open space. In this way the ward got its name. The former *maiunguwa* of the ward gave me a similar story to this, saying that long-distance traders would buy slaves in Sokoto and other towns after selling their own goods and bring them back to Kano and settle them in Yalwa. These slaves would work for their masters doing domestic tasks such as firewood selling and farming. Over the years the slave population of the ward grew and the area became known as *Yalwar Bayi* – the area abundant with slaves.

It is clear that the ward took shape in the nineteenth century, and a major period of expansion is connected with the movement of merchants and long-distance traders from Katsina to Kano. However, Yalwa, like the other wards discussed, was part of a larger administrative unit and was not given specific administrative identity until the 1930's. It is likely that the tailoring of Eastern-style clothing came with the influx of Katsina traders.

All informants agree that up to the time of Dabo and Maje Karofi clothing of this style was imported by North African and Hausa merchants. However, Mustafa is said to have taught his sons how to tailor in this fashion and from this the tradition of work in the ward grew. In fact, informants say Mustafa was secretive about how the work was done and did not display the clothing he and his sons made. Such clothing was produced for the aristocratic and business elite of the time and was not sold in quantity. As far as is known, there were few restrictions on who could wear what type of outfit,[13] the major limiting factor here being the general poverty of the population.

During the time of Mustafa's sons, other people learned how to tailor in this style and eventually the occupation became open to anyone. However, today the majority of Eastern-style tailors are still working in Yalwa and the surrounding wards of Madigawa and Dogon Nama. Of course, with the introduction of the sewing machine these styles are now made by machine, but the best work is still hand done.

Out of 93 tailors interviewed, 54 were exclusively hand sewers, 29 did machine sewing, and the remaining 10 did both hand and machine work. Many of these men came from non-tailoring backgrounds, if measured by father's and paternal grandfather's primary occupation. In fact, only 15 per cent had both fathers and paternal grandfathers who did tailoring as a primary occupation. Accurate information on tailoring background was difficult to get as many younger tailors did not know the kind of work their grandfathers did. However, overall, 42 cases (45 per cent of those interviewed) had either a father, a paternal grandfather or both who were tailors. This figure would probably be higher if occupation of paternal grandfather were known in all cases.

If secondary occupations are taken into account, only 26 of the 93 tailors (28 per cent) had no background whatsoever in tailoring. The vast majority of the sample of tailors in Yalwa have at the minimum a father or paternal grandfather who did *some* tailoring, either as a primary or secondary occupation. Furthermore, the majority of those fathers and grandfathers were hand tailors, although not all of them specialists in Eastern-style clothing. There were 25 cases where the father and/or grandfather did old-style sewing (see page 115). Of these, however, only 4 had both father and grandfather doing such work full-time as a primary occupation.

It should be noted that these figures say nothing about the tailoring experience of other members of the respondent's family and it may well be that brothers or cousins of the fathers and grandfathers of those interviewed were tailors.

R. J. Pokrant

Long-distance trade in kola nuts, cattle, or clothing was the other frequently mentioned primary occupation of fathers and paternal grandfathers of the Yalwa tailors. Nine fathers and 4 grandfathers were reported to have combined these two occupations. However, several informants did not know the primary occupation of their paternal grandfather, and others may have been unaware of the full range of his activities.

Table 4.6 *Primary occupations of fathers and paternal grandfathers: Yalwa. Total sample*

	Father was:		Paternal grandfather was:	
	Number	Per cent	Number	Per cent
Tailor	30	32	12	13
Long-distance trader	20	21.5	32	34.5
Market trader	21	22.5	1	1
Muslim priest	8	9	16	17
Other craft	4	4.5	5	5.5
Government	1	1	1	1
Farmer	5	5.5	10	11
Labourer	1	1	0	
Teacher	1	1	0	
No information	2	2	16	17
	93	100	93	100

Table 4.6 shows the primary occupations of fathers and paternal grandfathers. A feature of this table is the drop in occurrence of long-distance trading between the two generations. Over the past seventy years long-distance trading, particularly in kola nuts, has declined sharply, so that fewer and fewer of the sons and grandsons of long-distance traders have been able to continue in this occupation. As a consequence of this, there has been a shift into other occupations, of which tailoring is one of the most important.

Hausawa

Some traditions date the origins of Hausawa from the time of the Fulani Jihad in 1806. Yusufu, one of the Alkali, became Magajin Mallam, and was responsible for answering all letters from the Sultan of Sokoto to the Emir of Kano. From this activity he became known as *Amsawa*. Through mispronunciation, this became *Hausawa*. A similar tradition states that the people living in the area of Hausawa at the time of the Jihad supported the Fulani call to arms and aided Usman dan Fodio in the war. They are said to have answered the call – *amsawa* – and from this the ward became known as *Hausawa*.

Chamberlin argues (Chamberlin 1975: 72–4) that the Hausawa of Hausawa ward are the descendants of followers of Abdullahi Suka, an important local mallam in Kano in the sixteenth or seventeenth century. Suka was driven out by the Kano rulers for promoting Islam too zealously. When the Fulani took over Kano in the early nineteenth century they referred to the residents of this area as 'Hausawa' which means Hausa people, as a mark of distinction given to the residents, presumably because of their support of the Jihad forces and the ideals for which it stood. In fact, it may have covered a wider area in those days, as other people in sur-rounding wards also supported the Jihad.

Whatever its origins, the ward today is a major centre of the machine production of caps, with and without embroidery. Out of the 48 tailoring establishments counted in March 1975, 25 (over half) specialized in cap-making alone, with a further 3 doing both cap and gown work. Eighteen establishments specialized in gown making, and the remaining 2 workshops were unspecialized. Another count done in December of the same year showed that the number of establishments doing both cap and gown work rose from 3 to 10, largely at the expense of those workshops specializing in gown making. However, shifts of this nature should not be seen as per-manent, but as a reflection of variations in demand. Thus, although most gown workshops can maintain a certain minimum level of production throughout the year, at certain times demand rises both for caps and gowns and new workers may be taken on to satisfy it. Most of the workshops, and certainly all of those specializing in cap making, are producing for a wide market and not personal customers.

The mean size of workshop, measured by the number of sewing machines found in each, was 3.7, and the distribution of machines per workshop was as shown in Table 4.7.

Table 4.7 *Hausawa: number of sewing machines per workshop*[14]

											Total
Number of sewing machines	1	2	3	4	5	6	7	8	9	10	177
Number of workshops	10	9	7	7	4	6	0	2	2	1	48
Per cent of workshops	21	19	15	15	8	12	0	4	4	2	100%

There is no significant tendency for the larger workshops to be either cap or gown specialists. For example, only 3 out of 18 gown workshops had more than 5 machines in them, compared with 5 out of 25 cap workshops. The largest workshop specialized in gown making, but only at one time during the year. In the re-survey it was shown that this particular workshop had started to do some cap making. In any case, not all sewing machines found in one workshop are necessarily owned by the owner or renter of that workshop.

The vast majority of tailors in Hausawa are machine tailors. Amongst the 101 tailors interviewed there were no hand tailors at all. Indeed, there are very few hand sewers in the ward, and those who are are usually part-time hand sewers holding down full-time jobs elsewhere. None of my informants think the ward was traditionally associated with hand sewing, although like every ward in the city there were hand sewers resident there in the past. Furthermore, the ward is linked with Fulani rule and some part of the population has been involved in emirate government. Weaving was one occupation which had some importance in the past and there is one area within Hausawa known as Masa'ka, the Hausa word for weavers. Another part of the ward acted as a resting place for visitors to Kano, and many Kanuri settled there. Some were traders but the immigrants did a variety of jobs. Farming was of major importance to residents of the area and it is said Hausawa farmers were very skilled. One part of the ward is known as Hori from *mahora'kato* or 'those who train or educate well'. Finally, the area around the mosque is known among the residents as Hausawa, the mosque having been built on the instructions of the then Sultan of Sokoto, Muhammed Bello, who wished to reward the people of Hausawa for their support to the Jihadi forces. The office of Magajin Mallam was created as a vehicle for expressing the views of the ward, and one of the office's functions until the civil war of 1893–4 was to advise the Emir. One of my tailoring informants whose ancestors were connected with affairs of the palace told me that, because of the refusal of the people of Hausawa to take sides in that dynastic conflict, they suffered afterwards through being deprived of patronage at court and many turned to cap making as a means of earning a livelihood. It is interesting to note that Nadel in his work on Nupe makes a similar observation (Nadel 1969: 286). Apparently, cap making is regarded among the Nupe as an occupation for aristocrats who have fallen on hard times. The added complication of British conquest must have intensified this restriction on access to royal and aristocratic favour through a further tightening of purse strings and the removal of the officials from residence in the city to their areas of jurisdiction, thus forcing many of their followers to look for alternative sources of support.

Turning to the material on Hausawa tailors, one finds only 8 per cent of the respondents have both fathers and grandfathers who were full-time tailors. Table 4.8 shows the occupational characteristics of the fathers and

Table 4.8 *Hausawa: primary occupations of fathers and paternal grandfathers. Total sample*

	Father was:	Paternal grandfather was:
Tailor	24	13
Trader*	31	9
Muslim priest	15	18
Other craft	6	5
Government official (Fulani)	3	14
Government employee (colonial/ post colonial)	6	2
Farmer	16	26
Occupation not known	–	14
Total	101	101

* Includes local market and petty traders as well as long-distance traders.

paternal grandfathers of Hausawa tailors. Over 60 per cent of the sample have no history of tailoring in their background, as measured by father's and paternal grandfather's primary occupation. Some 14 per cent of all respondents did not know their paternal grandfather's occupation. However, even if all these paternal grandfathers were tailors (an unlikely event), this would still leave 50 per cent of respondents whose fathers or paternal grandfathers were not primarily tailors. Furthermore, only 4 of the sons of the 14 paternal grandfathers for whom there is no information on primary occupation were tailors. Assuming that in these 4 cases the paternal grandfathers were themselves tailors, this would only increase the proportion of tailors with fathers *and* paternal grandfathers who were also tailors to 12 per cent.

SPECIALIZATION AND THE DIVISION OF LABOUR

Kano city-tailors produce a wide range of garments. The largest range of clothing is made for adult men whose basic wardrobe consists of caps, gowns, smocks and trousers. The major items of women's dress include the wrapper, head kerchief and shawl. Children's clothes are, in the main, copies of adult styles. Horse caparisons made by tailors include the saddle cover and a range of blankets placed under the saddle and referred to generically as *mashimfud'i*. Probably only 5 per cent of Kano tailors make saddle covers and horse blankets.

Each of the above-mentioned types of garments can be further differentiated into many different styles distinguished by shape, cut, and the type and amount of embroidery. Male clothing is the most varied, ranging from plain work smocks (*yar shara*) to elaborately embroidered gowns, such as the *aska biyu* or *malum-malum*, which can take up to 15 yards of cloth to make. These latter types of gowns can sell for as little as 8 to 10 Naira and as much as 80 to 100 Naira,[15] depending upon the amount and type of cloth used, the quality of the embroidery thread, the amount and density of the embroidery, the care taken in cutting cloth and doing the sewing, and whether the sewing is done by hand or by machine. I have witnessed transactions in which 90 Naira was charged for hand embroidery alone. For many tailors that constitutes 3 months' earnings.

The most expensive garments are purchased by members of the elite, including aristocrats, members of the various royal families in Kano and other emirates, civil servants and wealthy merchants. However, the bulk of clothing produced by city tailors is sold to less well-off consumers working as wage employees in industry, commerce and government, to the large numbers of people in the informal sector, and to poor rural consumers. Some city-made garments are sold in other northern states and in the Niger Republic. There is very little trade with the southern parts of the country. The total market for Kano city-made clothing probably consists of between 10 and 15 million people, most of whom reside in Kano State and adjoining states. The vast majority of these consumers possess limited purchasing power.

The bulk of clothing produced for this market is machine made. Machine tailors (*mad'inkan keke*) constitute a majority of male tailors in the city and probably outnumber their hand-sewing (*mad'inkan hannu*) counterparts by a ratio of at least 5 to 1. However, the majority of female tailors are hand sewers.

The ratio of machine to hand tailors varies from ward to ward. Thus, in Soron D'inki, 33 per cent of a sample of 36 tailors do hand sewing. In Hausawa, out of a sample of 101 tailors, none are hand sewers, although a few men do cap making as a secondary occupation. Of the three wards, Yalwa contains the largest number of hand tailors, with 58 per cent (54) of a sample of 93 tailors doing this kind of work.

114

Hand sewing: All hand sewers, with a few exceptions, are embroiderers, the assembly of clothing having been taken over by machine tailors. Hand embroiderers are further differentiated into two main types. There are those trained within the tradition of tailoring known as *D'inkin gargajiya* (old-style tailors), and those trained as *D'inkin gabas* (Eastern-style) tailors. Clothing styles made within these two traditions are distinguished by the cut of garments, stitching techniques, and embroidery designs. In the past, the two traditions were distinguished by the kinds of cloth and thread used, old-style tailors using locally woven cloth and hand-spun thread made from cotton or silk, and Eastern-style tailors making much greater use of imported velvet, satin, serge or flannel, and various types of silk thread, but today most hand embroiderers work with Nigerian and imported factory-made cloth and thread.

Old-style hand embroiderers are scattered across the city, there being no particular wards containing large concentrations of tailors working within

4.2 This self-employed machine-embroiderer is working on an old-style gown commissioned by a personal customer. He owns his own machine, and works (rent-free) in a corner of a relative's workshop (Sudawa ward)

this tradition. On the other hand, Eastern-style hand embroiderers are found mainly in the wards of Yalwa, Masukwani, and Durmin Arbabi, with Yalwa containing the largest number.

These two types of hand embroiderers work mainly on gowns, smocks, and trousers. In addition, there are a few specialized trouser embroiderers working in the Soron D'inki/Daneji area. Hand-*jalala* and other horse-caparison makers are mainly confined to the wards of Soron D'inki, Sharfad'i and Kabara. As with specialized hand embroiderers of trousers, there are a few of these and the majority are either elderly men or men with other full-time occupations.

The city also contains large numbers of male embroiderers of caps, the majority of whom are Koranic students who pursue cap making in order to earn a little money to support them in their studies. A very high proportion of female tailors also hand embroider caps.

Apart from these city-resident hand embroiderers, the Close Settled Zone around the city contains many hand embroiderers of gowns and caps. Some work at home while others commute to the city, although all divide their time between tailoring and farming. There is a particularly close rela-tionship between the farmer–embroiderers of Jajira village area, located to the northwest of the urban area, and the city.

Machine sewing: Machine tailors are of three kinds. The largest pro-portion of machine tailors use straight-stitch sewing machines; their basic function is the assembly of clothing. There are several reasons for the large number of such tailors: (1) the relatively low cost of straight-stitch machines, which sell for anywhere between 60 or 70 Naira up to 200 Naira, or roughly half to one third the price of the next most costly range of sewing machines; (2) the relative ease with which such machines can be obtained, either new or second-hand, and the ease of repair; (3) the high demand for clothing without embroidery; (4) the fact that all garments, be they plain or embroidered, require the services of a straight-stitch machin-ist at least for assembly.

The next most commonly found type is the open-chain-stitch machine. Tailors using this can produce machine copies of old-style hand embroidery work as well as styles for which there are no hand-sewn equivalents. New open-chain-stitch machines cost around 300 to 400 Naira, depending upon the make, while second-hand ones sell for between 150 and 200 Naira. The relatively high cost of these machines, coupled with the more specialized kinds of tailoring they are capable of performing, limits their attractiveness to many tailors. They are usually found in larger workshops where they are used in conjunction with single-stitch machines.

116

The third, and least common, kind is the zig-zag machine. This produces unique embroidery designs as well as machine copies of hand-sewn Eastern-style embroidery designs. Zig-zag embroidery is particularly popular among women and the few zig-zag machinists (all men) rely to a great extent on the female market to stay in business. However, like open-chain-stitch machinists, they produce a specialized product for a market which is even narrower than that of other embroidery machinists. These machines are very costly to purchase new, some selling for up to 1,000 Naira. They are difficult to obtain, liable to frequent breakdown, and often noisy and tiring to operate. For these reasons, there are relatively few zig-zag machinists in the city, the bulk of machine embroidery being done on the open-chain-stitch type.

Machine tailoring is generally regarded as more lucrative than hand sewing and many hand sewers have shifted into machine tailoring over the years. Thus, two thirds of machine tailors in both Soron D'inki and Yalwa wards were once hand sewers. However, like the Hausawa tailors, the greater proportion of city machinists have no hand-tailoring experience.

I have concentrated so far upon describing the wide range of products made by city tailors, the spatial distribution of tailoring activities, the traditions of tailoring within which tailors are trained, and the instruments of production used in the tailoring process. There remains the question of the ways in which tailors organize their productive activities and the relationship between the forms of organization and the markets which tailors serve.

THE ORGANIZATION OF PRODUCTION

Artisan tailors

Many city tailors are artisans who produce clothing to the direct order of personal customers who will wear it themselves. Artisans engage directly in production, either working alone or with the assistance of family members and/or unrelated apprentices. Artisan workshops are usually small in size and the amount of capital invested in such workshops consists of little more than a sewing machine, sewing thread, scissors, tape measure and work bench. The single most important item of capital investment is the sewing machine. The majority of machine-tailoring artisans possess one machine which they either own or rent. In the three wards studied, of those artisans who used a sewing machine, over 85 per cent owned their own sewing machines which they had purchased through savings and/or through cash provided by parents and kinsmen.

Artisan hand sewers require no major items of capital equipment, their

117

major investment being the time involved in acquiring the skills necessary to sew a range of tailored garments. Few artisans carry stocks of cloth, as customers are expected to provide their own cloth when they place an order with the tailor.

The market for artisan-made clothing is largely local, with artisans supplying customers drawn from the neighbourhoods and wards in which they live and work, from other parts of the city and people from rural areas who come into the city to get clothes.

Less than half of the tailors in the three wards studied were artisans. In Soron D'inki artisans comprised 47 per cent of tailors; 37 per cent (34) of those in Yalwa were artisans and 8 per cent (8) of tailors in Hausawa were artisans.

Types of artisan tailors: The most commonly found is the neighbourhood all-purpose tailor who makes a wide variety of garments by machine and who does alterations and repairs. Smaller numbers of hand embroiderers and machine embroiderers provide a more specialized embroidering service which ranges from the embroidery of elaborate designs on gowns, smocks and trousers to more modest pieces of work such as the *kwad'o da linzami* (frog and bridle) motif found on the necks of most old-style gowns.

In Soron D'inki and Hausawa wards, the majority of artisans make clothing by machine, with a few hand and machine embroiderers of old-style gowns for men, blouses for women, embroidered trousers and saddle covers. In Yalwa, many hand and machine artisan tailors do the specialized embroidery work of the Eastern style, which consists of stitching a cord-like thread into motifs on the body of garments. This unique kind of embroidery is very popular among middle- and upper-income consumers and it is this demand which sustains many of the embroiderers in Yalwa. In addition to these Eastern-style embroiderers, there are four old-style hand embroiderers, two of whom are religious teachers and one a former ward head, who continue to make elaborately embroidered garments for a declining market. One of these four men produces highly creative and novel embroidery designs and has been the subject of a paper written by an art historian (Heathcote 1972). Formerly, there were more tailors of this type, but they have either died or shifted into other kinds of work, including Eastern-style tailoring. Those who remain are all elderly men.

Strategies of competition used by artisan tailors

The reliance of artisans on a local market – a high proportion of which consists of low-income earners whose demand for clothing is irregular –

and the large number of tailors who compete for the work available set limits on the extent to which they can, as artisans, expand their productive activities. However, there are a number of strategies pursued by artisan tailors by which they attempt to ensure for themselves a certain share of the market.

First, some make themselves visible to customers by working in the city market, where they can catch trade from visitors to the market, especially farmers who come to Kano to purchase various commodities for domestic consumption. Others work along the main roads and around the city gates where people pass by in large numbers. Others rely more upon attracting a neighbourhood clientele built up over a number of years. By becoming known to their customers, they hope to establish reputations for reliability and good-quality work. These ward-based artisans often look down on city-market tailors who they consider produce poor-quality clothing for unsophisticated rural people.

Another way of attracting customers is for the artisan to enter into informal cooperative relations with other artisans specializing in different aspects of garment production. Thus, machine assemblers will refer customers to a hand or machine embroiderer of their acquaintance in the expectation that customers will be referred to them on future occasions.

A further means of attracting customers involves the artisan in being able to produce a wide variety of garments in response to the differing tastes of consumers and thereby reduce the risks inherent in specialization. This option works best for machine assemblers whose services are required on all artisan-produced garments. Some artisans, including embroiderers, do seek to attract customers by their reputation for expertise in producing particular styles. However, by developing skills as all-purpose tailors, machine assemblers are in a better position to adapt quickly to changes in fashion than they would be if they relied upon a particular specialization.

Another strategy is that of price cutting. However, most artisans, especially machine assemblers, regard this as undesirable. They argue that, because of the high degree of competition among them, their prices are already so low they can just about meet their costs. Among artisan machine assemblers in the three wards, I found little variation in the prices they charged on a wide variety of garments. Bargaining over price does take place, and younger and less experienced tailors who were just starting out on their tailoring careers often charged less than the going rate in order to get business, but the range of variation between the asking and accepted price is limited, no more than 5 to 10 per cent. In some cases, artisans will charge poorer customers less than wealthier ones for the same garment, but

R. J. Pokrant

they will take special care with garments for the better-off so as to ensure that these customers continue to patronize them.

Indeed, one way of attracting business is to concentrate upon supplying custom-made garments to wealthier members of the community. By the very nature of this market, few tailors can hope to rely upon it for the bulk of their business. The best examples of elite-market-oriented artisans I came across were highly skilled hand embroiderers with a known reputation based upon years of training under a master craftsman, from whom they were able to obtain the right kinds of customer connections. For example, two hand embroiderers living in Yalwa and Dogon Nama wards were trained by two members of one of the oldest Eastern-style tailoring families in the area. Through their association with these master craftsmen they had built up a clientele which included former politicians, wealthy merchants, civil servants and other government officials, and members of

4.3 A mounted nobleman (?) at a Salla festival in Kano City wears a hand-woven, indigo-dyed gown closely covered with hand embroidery. His turban is of the famous beaten, indigo-dyed cloth, known as *D'an Kura*

120

various royal families in the emirates of Katsina, Kano, Hadejia and Daura. One of the two tailors had, in fact, 'inherited' the informal position of tailor to the Emir of Kano and obtained large amounts of work through this connection. As his business grew he put out more and more work to specially selected expert hand embroiderers he knew, thereby becoming a regular employer of tailoring labour. However, to this day he continues to embroider some garments himself in the entrance room to his home.

These two men represent success stories, but it should be noted that a number of other embroiderers taught by this same family fared less well. In general, few artisans can rely upon supplying an elite market and most must draw their custom from middle- and low-income earners.

Cost-reducing strategies and relations of production

Not only is the market for artisans' services local, it is also periodic and seasonal. Thus, there are busy times of the year, such as the harvest season and during religious festivals (especially Ramadan), when families purchase new wardrobes, and when pilgrims return from Mecca bringing with them cloth purchased there. These are followed by periods of little activity. To cope with this periodic demand, artisans adopt a number of cost-reducing strategies.

First, the artisan exploits to the full his one major asset, personal labour-power, by working long hours at a very intensive pace during busy periods, thereby reducing his need to employ extra labour. During Ramadan, for example, I observed many artisan workshops in which the tailors worked 15 to 20 hours a day in order to meet orders before the end of the fasting period.[16]

However, artisans do need extra labour at certain times, and they usually draw upon family members, unrelated workers who are apprenticed to them, and other tailors who are finding it difficult to attract customers. Family members utilized include wives, the artisan's own children and those of kinsmen and relatives. Unrelated apprentices are usually unmarried boys who are the children of friends, neighbours and other local people known personally to the artisans. Apprentices are usually unpaid, receiving instead food, clothing, and occasional pocket or food money. Unrelated apprentices sometimes live with their master, but many do not as they are often drawn from the local neighbourhood and return home at the end of each day.

Apprenticeship: Hausa apprenticeship is a relatively casual and informal system of instruction. Apprentices do not pay to be taught, nor are there

121

any official ceremonies which mark the entry of a boy into the occupation or his successful completion of an apprenticeship. They act as menial labour performing household tasks, running errands, sweeping out the workshop and other odd jobs. Sewing tasks are given at the discretion of the master. The length of an apprenticeship depends, in part, upon the type of tailoring the apprentice is learning. An apprentice to a highly skilled hand embroiderer may take five to ten years whereas an apprentice to a machine assembler may be quite proficient after a couple of years.[17] The point at which the apprentice starts to receive payment for work done depends upon his own ability, how keen the master is to instruct his apprentice, how much access he allows him to a sewing machine, and how prosperous the master's business is.

Not all artisans can either obtain or retain apprentices. In particular, those in types of sewing which are in decline find it very difficult to attract people to work under them. The old-style hand embroiderers of Yalwa and the hand sewers of *jalala* in Soron D'inki are good examples of this. Even artisans whose product is still in demand have difficulties in retaining the services of an apprentice. Thus, in Yalwa ward, some hand embroiderers of Eastern-style garments complained about the lack of shame (*kunya*) and respect (*ladabi*) of young boys of today, who wanted to learn a few skills quickly and be paid for what they produced. A major reason for this situation was the fact that in this and adjacent wards there were larger workshop owners who produced garments in bulk and were willing to pay young boys for performing relatively simple tailoring tasks after a short period of training. Thus, young boys sometimes learned a few skills at the workshop of an artisan and then left to work for others. In many cases, boys acquired their tailoring skills by sitting with other teenagers in the ward and watching what they did, thus removing the need to be apprenticed at all. These young boys saw no reason to submit themselves to long years of training when quicker monetary returns were available elsewhere. Another instance of the de-skilling of the labour process was observed in Hausawa ward, where workshops producing cheap caps and other garments for a wide market subdivided the tailoring tasks so that workers specialized narrowly.

In Soron D'inki, artisan tailors relied more upon family helpers in their tailoring work. They neither wanted nor could attract unrelated apprentices because their business prospects were so poor. Furthermore, these artisans were teaching their children not because they expected them to become full-time tailors but in order to provide them with a skill which they could fall back on if no other, more lucrative, kinds of employment were available.

Thus, although apprenticeship is, in general, a means of obtaining cheap labour, such labour is not always available nor is it always wanted. Those in the best position to attract apprentices are the more successful workshops, which are often not organized along artisanal lines.

Forms of cooperation among artisan tailors

In a few cases, artisan tailors put out excess work they obtain to other artisans who have fallen on hard times, the putting-out tailor paying the artisan a piece-rate less than he himself would receive for the same work. The advantage of this arrangement to the putter-out is that he has no obligation to continue providing the poorer tailor with work after a specific order is completed. Neither does he have to spend time training the tailor, nor, in the case of machine tailoring, provide the tailor with a sewing machine. However, this type of arrangement is more common among tailors producing for a wider market, particularly larger workshop owners.

Another way of reducing costs is for artisans to share work premises. If rent is paid for a workshop, the cooperating tailor pays less rent than he

4.4 Two hand embroiderers of Eastern-style gowns working in the entrance hall of a relative who is a hand embroiderer and thread salesman. The elderly man on the right has come to pass the time with them. (Border between Yalwa and Madigawa wards)

would if he worked alone. However, in the three wards intensively studied, joint-renting of premises is unusual, it being more common for tailors to work rent-free either in the entrance rooms to their homes, in the entrance rooms of friends and relatives and neighbours, and at the workshops of non-artisan tailors who are not fully using their premises. The ability to operate in this manner is made possible by the fact that the majority of artisans are either born in the wards in which they work or have been long-term residents there.

Sharing of tools also provides a means of reducing costs, but this is usually an *ad hoc* arrangement and often consists of little more than sharing of tape measures and scissors. Joint purchase of raw materials is rare, as most artisans are too poor to be able to raise enough money to invest in expensive items such as cloth. Indeed, the majority of artisans expect their customers to provide their own cloth, which is, in fact, one way of reducing costs of production and the risks involved in carrying stocks of raw materials. A number of artisans point out that even if they did have a small stock of cloth on hand, they could not provide the variety which is available to the customer at the many retail cloth outlets in the city. Nor could they provide cloth at competitive prices unless they purchased in bulk.

These forms of cooperation usually take place among small groups of friends or relatives. Larger-scale cooperation among strangers is much more rare. Artisans do see the advantages of such cooperation, not only in the bulk purchase of cloth but in the sharing of customers, agreements to set prices at a higher level, and in the marketing of finished products. But there is great scepticism about the possibilities of such forms of cooperation succeeding. Among the reasons given by artisans for such scepticism are the following.

Constraints on cooperation: First, artisans are widely dispersed across the city, are differentiated according to the types of products they make, the instruments of production they use, and the kinds of customers upon whom they rely for their work. Thus, a skilled hand embroiderer in Yalwa who specializes in producing high-quality gowns for wealthy customers sees no affinity between his work situation and that of a machine assembler in Yakasai or Soron D'inki who produces custom-made, but low-quality, garments for neighbourhood customers of limited means.

Second, as most artisans have little capital, they are fearful of handing over what they have to an organization which may become remote from them and misuse funds.

Third, given the limited means of most artisans, funds to establish a cooperative must come from other sources. If they come from wealthier tailors, who in the majority of cases are not artisans, or from other persons, there is a general fear that these better-off persons will simply use the funds to finance their own activities or those of their friends. A number of artisans pointed to attempts in the past to organize a city-wide association of tailors, which failed, so it is said, because of corruption and mismanagement at the top by the association's leaders, who built up relations with cloth suppliers and government officials only to use them to their own advantage.

Most artisans prefer cooperative arrangements to be on a small scale, and consider the government to be in the best position to assist. However, none of the artisans interviewed had ever approached the government on this matter nor had they heard of any attempts by government to institute such a scheme. In fact, during the fieldwork period there was established a government scheme to assist craft workers, including tailors, but only two groups of tailors, one in Yakasai and one from Gyadi-Gyadi outside the city, had approached the government officer in charge. Officials interviewed reinforced the views expressed by artisans by pointing out that few tailors were willing to commit any resources to a cooperative, a requirement set by the scheme's organizers. In the case of the Yakasai tailors, the fear was expressed that it was only a front for a big man who was willing to supply the tailors part of the cash in order to secure for himself a large government grant on easy terms. Under this arrangement, the cooperating tailors would have become quasi-employees of the financier, thus defeating the object of the cooperative.

Supplementary occupations

Another way of coping with the uncertainties of the market for artisan-made clothing is to supplement earnings from tailoring by obtaining wage-paying jobs, doing some farming, or engaging in various small-scale income-generating activities. A quarter of the artisans in Soron D'inki and Hausawa were, in fact, wage-earners working as government labourers, gate-keepers, builders' labourers, and guards for private companies. Tailoring had become a secondary activity for them, something which helped boost their more regular income as wage earners. A few artisans in Hausawa and Yalwa did farming during the wet season on farms owned either by themselves or members of their households, and crops grown were used for domestic consumption. Other informal ways of generating a small income included fencing stolen goods such as radios and cloth and acting as brokers in the disposal of hand-made caps, gowns and other consumer goods. For married artisans, another source of income came from work done by wives, who made caps, prepared and sold foodstuffs, and engaged in petty trading. Money earned in these ways, although controlled by the women themselves, did relieve the artisans of the necessity of meeting certain household expenses.

The high degree of competition among artisan tailors, their reliance on a local and irregular market of personal clients and the generally low incomes of most of those who employ their services, combine to make it difficult for the majority of artisans to earn more than just enough to subsist. Some leave tailoring altogether, others combine artisanal work in tailoring with employment in wage-paying jobs outside tailoring, while others are pushed into quasi-employee relationships with bigger tailors, merchants and business men who have access to sources of work and outlets for tailored garments not available to the artisan.

Market-oriented tailors

There is another type of tailoring unit, which, unlike the artisan, is oriented to the production of garments for a wider market of customers with whom the producers have no direct contact. The marketing of their garments is mediated by specialized clothes dealers, itinerant traders, government contractors, merchants and other types of middlemen.

As with artisan tailors, market-oriented workshops are found throughout the old city. However there is greater concentration in certain wards, of which Hausawa is an example. There the bulk of production is of caps and, to a lesser extent, gowns and smocks. Market-oriented tailors do produce a wide range of garments, and some workshops make elaborately embroidered gowns, though of a poorer quality than those made by highly skilled artisan embroiderers. There is much less individual styling in garments made for sale in the market and generally embroidery is standardized. The emphasis is on bulk output rather than quality or personal service.

Most market workshops are based on machine sewing. A high proportion of their output is for sale through the city market where there are nearly 200 specialized clothes dealers about equally divided between cap sellers and those who deal in all other garments. There is also a small section of dealers selling accoutrements for horses: saddle covers, horse blankets, saddles, bridles, bits and harnesses. There too are specialized cloth sellers from whom many market tailors purchase the cloth they use.

While most artisan workshops are small, there is greater variation among those who produce for sale in the market. Many work alone with occasional help from young boys in quasi-apprenticeship roles. However, the range of garment styles such boys learn to sew is narrower than with artisans' apprentices since the market-oriented tailors themselves tend to specialize. At the other extreme, the largest workshop in Hausawa contained 11 tailors, including the workshop head. In the smaller workshops, those with fewer than 4 workers, the workshop head owns the sewing machines and is himself also active in production. In the larger ones employees work on sewing machines provided by the head, who does not himself tailor, but organizes production, cuts cloth, buys raw materials, and sells the finished products. Taking the whole of the city, there is a tiny minority of larger workshops with as many as 20 or 25 employees.

In the three wards studied, Hausawa contains the largest number of market-oriented workshops – a total of 40 out of 48 workshops in the ward. One quarter of these market workshops contain 4 or more employees (known locally as *direbobi*), the remainder less than 4. In Yalwa there is a smaller proportion of larger workshops than in Hausawa, although one or two bigger tailors put out considerable amounts of work to local hand embroiderers. Many of the hand embroiderers in this ward combine artisanal work with that of work for other tailors. There were two full-time market-oriented workshops in Soron D'inki, one producing cheap saddle cloths, the other making plain smocks for sale in the market.

Many small-scale market-oriented tailors are in a similar position to artisans in that they have little capital and operate on a day-to-day basis by purchasing small amounts of cloth, making a few caps or other garments, and selling them at the market.

The bigger market producers in Yalwa and Hausawa wards are, in the main, older than smaller operators. In Hausawa, in particular, most have been tailors for at least twenty years or more. Their businesses have been built up over a long period of time through saving and help from kinsmen and relatives. All have been apprentices of other tailors at some point. Indeed, it is very rare to find any tailoring-workshop owners who have not had any previous experience in tailoring.

The advantages larger workshop owners have over smaller operators include their ability to produce large quantities of garments, their greater knowledge of market conditions, the long-standing trading and, in some cases, credit relations they have with clothes dealers, cloth sellers, visiting traders, and merchants, and their ability to diversify production strategies to meet changing conditions of demand. In some instances, they engage in off-season tailoring when many employees are without work and can be hired at lower piece-rates than those prevailing during the busy season. In this way, stocks of garments are stored and then sold off at peak periods when prices rise.

However, even in the largest workshops there are periods of little activity when employers cannot get fresh orders or dispose of garments already made. Those who sell their products through the city market are the most vulnerable in this respect.

All market-oriented tailoring employers, large or small, employ workers on a piece-rate basis. As well as saving them money, it reduces their need to supervise the work force as the employee has a built-in incentive to produce as much as possible. Highest rates are paid to embroiderers, but they vary according to the quality of the work required. In general, they are about half the rates an embroiderer would charge if he worked for himself using his own sewing machine. Profits on embroidered garments are the highest in tailoring, but a tailor can produce more plain garments in a given time period.

The lowest rates of pay are found in machine cap making, as the return on the sale of caps is very low. Thus, many older tailoring employees shun such work, regarding it as the work of children and unmarried youths. Indeed, a high proportion of employees in the ward are unmarried and young. They circulate around the ward seeking cap-machining work in order to earn a little pocket money. Most of them have little or no intention of becoming tailors. A similar situation prevails in Yalwa ward, where many children do the hand sewing of the inside seams of garments.

Workshop owners recruit both kin and non-kin. In a majority of cases observed in Hausawa, and to a lesser extent in Yalwa, tailoring employees were unrelated to those for whom they worked. However, most labour is recruited locally.

The organization of labour within a large workshop

This is best indicated by an example. This workshop consists of 5 machines, 4 machine tailors and the workshop head. Three of the employees are relatives of the workshop head. One, a brother, owns his own machine and so is strictly speaking not an employee; he does work both for himself and for the workshop head. Others work exclusively as employees. They make up gowns for sale to the city market, for private customers, and for sale through a long-distance trader who visits Maiduguri every month. Work is also sold through a textile merchant in the Syrian quarter. All garments are embroidered and most embroidery is put out to hand embroiderers in the ward.

A gown is made in the following sequence of operations:

(1) The cloth is cut by the workshop head into the body, front and back, and arms.

(2) The parts to be embroidered are taken by an employee or young boy to a retired hand sewer who stamps an outline of the embroidery design.

(3) The embroidery work is distributed to different hand embroiderers. One man may get the sleeves to do, another the neck. When the work is finished it is returned to the workshop.

(4) The parts are sewn together by machine in the workshop.

(5) The complete garment is taken to the ironer.

(6) The inside seams are sewn by young boys working along the street or elsewhere in the ward; sometimes this work is given to women in the workshop head's household, to kinswomen or other women.

(7) The workshop head goes off to sell the garment. If it is to be sold to the Maiduguri trader, he expects payment before the man leaves, although credit may be grudgingly given.

The self-employed brother of the workshop head does assembly and machine embroidery by stitching cord-like thread into patterns on gowns. Private customers are measured by the workshop head, but the measurement is not very precise. Garments made for sale through intermediaries are more standardized.

Cloth is bought from the city market and also from a local factory. Thread is also bought from the local factory or from thread dealers in the ward who organize gangs of boys to spin single-ply thread into cords. Formerly this work was done by the tailors themselves, but with the increase in demand for this style of decoration specialized thread spinners have emerged.

All the tailors who do work for the workshop head are personally known to him, including the hand tailors who work at home or in another workshop. Few are ever asked to do complete embroidery work on a gown. Efficiency and speed in production are important so there is pressure for hand embroiderers to become proficient at particular motifs. This is a clear example of specialization on detail work, as they may never be asked to do more than one or two designs for a narrow range of garments.

Of all those employed by the workshop head, only the three machinists who sew in his workshop work exclusively for him. His younger brother also works on his own account; the hand embroiderers and young boys who do the inside seams take work from anyone who offers it, as well as doing artisan tailoring when they have the opportunity. The man who stamps designs on cloth works for many workshops; the thread dealers and those who work for them supply many local tailors. This workshop is currently prospering and so is able to provide work for many different people. But even a successful workshop cannot provide the same amount of work throughout the year. Even for a successful workshop demand is irregular. All work is paid for by the piece, which makes up somewhat for the fact that it is not possible to supervise work that is put out. Although this workshop head makes use of male hand embroiderers and boys and women outside his own shop, his steady labour comes from his own employees. Even they are not always available, as they are young boys working for pocket money and not strongly committed to learning the trade.[18] They said that they felt a family obligation to work for their uncle 'until something better came along', but they didn't want to remain tailors if they could avoid it.

This reluctance to make a permanent commitment to tailoring is not uncommon. The workshop head himself wanted to leave tailoring eventually and become a cloth merchant. He bought his own cloth from a man who had in a sense become his patron, and whom he hoped would help him get a place in the textile market in Kantin Kwari. However, he hadn't yet saved enough for the necessary stock. Although he had started out intending to build up a tailoring workshop, this had become a means to a more appealing goal.

CONCLUSIONS

The high value traditionally placed on clothing in Hausa culture is reflected in the prominence of tailors as artisans and as market-oriented producers. Perhaps the most striking feature of the organization of Kano tailoring is its openness. Apprenticeship is informal and for some bypassed entirely. At any one time many tailors are artisans, either working alone or in occasional informal cooperation. But such an artisan may previously have employed two or three tailors in a small market-oriented workshop. Some of the older machine tailors in Soron D'inki reflect this pattern, having expanded their operations during periods of rising demand and then contracted when other producers entered the market. Or the artisan may be saving and planning to establish such a workshop. A man working as a cloth trader today may have begun as a tailor, but this is becoming increasingly difficult to do because of the large numbers already involved in cloth retailing or because the capital required to establish oneself as a wholesaler is beyond the reach of most producers. What is more common is for the producer to carry on other occupations, either during the day or when demand for clothing is slack. A self-employed artisan may also take in detail sewing for a workshop which, in some instances, results in the undermining of the artisan's autonomy as a producer. The uncertainty of the market situation of tailors often means that apprentices, who appear to be the mainstay of many workshops, are only marking time until something better turns up.

The flexibility which characterizes tailoring in contemporary Kano is, moreover, not a recent response to 'modernization'. The traditions of the three wards studied intensively describe more long-term change. Soron D'inki was first known as a centre for elaborately embroidered gowns and horse caparisons made by a small number of tailors for court dignitaries. The *jalala* for which the ward is now famous became a major product only in the second half of the nineteenth century; in the early colonial period and during the present century there has been a shift from hand-made to machine-made saddle cloths. Yalwa was first a centre for long-distance traders, among whose imports were Eastern-style gowns. The technique of making Eastern-style gowns was first introduced during the nineteenth century, and at first was a carefully guarded secret, spreading outside the family of the original tailor only slowly.

The machine workshops of Hausawa are seen as a recent innovation dating back to the 1920's and 1930's with the major period of expansion occurring after the second world war. During this century there has been an effective adoption of a succession of three different kinds of sewing machine, the first of which has entirely replaced hand sewing (at least, in the old city) in the making up of garments. The more complex machines make possible machine embroidery at a fraction of the cost of hand work. Over the same period there has been an overwhelming shift from narrow-strip locally woven cloth to factory-produced textiles. The growth of productivity with the use of sewing machines (all imported) and manufactured cloth has been reinforced by the introduction of machine workshops. The most productive workshops are those where a single employer, owning a number of machines, can concentrate his productive efforts and split the process of production among his employees, each one concentrating on a particular task. This is especially important where production is for a wide market of poor consumers and where emphasis is placed on producing many garments at low cost.

131

Although tailors are found throughout the rural areas of Kano State, it is in the city that the tailoring division of labour reaches its most developed form. City tailors are close to a concentrated market of urban consumers; raw materials and instruments of production are readily available from specialized suppliers; tailoring labour is easy to obtain; and, in the case of Kano, the city is the commercial centre for a wide regional market and is located within an area of dense rural settlement known as the Kano Close Settled Zone. Tailors can dispose of their products through specialized clothes dealers operating from the various urban market places (who, in turn, sell to visiting rural traders), through merchants and other intermediaries, as well as by selling to rural customers who come to Kano to work and to buy various commodities for domestic consumption.

Yet, despite the huge market, ready adoption of new technology and materials, and a complex and flexible division of labour, there appears to be a ceiling on the size of workshops. Perhaps the high degree of competition among tailors and the fact that much of the distribution of tailored commodities is in the hands of specialized intermediaries who provide a link between producers and the large but scattered market makes it difficult for producers to expand beyond a certain size. There are some tailors who combine production of clothing with the selling of finished products through their own retail outlets, but they are few. The ability to do this depends upon the tailor's scale of operations having already reached such a size that they are able to withdraw from production and divide their time between retailing and workshop supervision.

Furthermore, a successful workshop owner tends to move out of production into dealing in cloth, or into an entirely different occupation, rather than further expanding and rationalizing his tailoring business. These conditions of workshop organization, together with other features of the market situation of tailors, perhaps limit the extent to which workshops can serve as models for industrial factory production.

5 Production and control in the Indian garment export industry

D. A. Swallow

INTRODUCTION

In the early summer of 1979 one of India's large and successful garment manufacturing and exporting companies closed down its modern factory on Bombay's Worli district seafront. This company, Paville Fashions Pvt. Ltd,[1] which had grown from a thirty-machine operation in 1967 to an operation which at the height of its production in 1976 exported 35,746,644 rupees' worth of goods, in January 1977 was producing over 100,000 garments a month and in the mid-1970's won a series of export awards. Despite this success, in 1979 it became impracticable to continue large-scale manufacturing.

The closure was not quite as dramatic as at first it seemed. In fact the company was changing its production strategy. Instead of depending on a large-scale unit for all its production, it turned to another system and started to subcontract much of its work to smaller units.

Throughout its short history the Indian garment export industry has been closely connected with the handloom industry. Even manufacturers with large-scale garment factories have depended on supplies of handloom cloth from an industry which continues to depend on various putting-out and subcontracting systems. To the historian of the handloom export trade, Paville's story would strike a familiar chord. During the history of the handloom cloth industry there have been various attempts to centralize production, and to replace a system of indirect control with one of direct control. But there too large-scale centralized production has rarely proved to be economical or practicable from the point of view of the capitalist merchants.

The recurrence of the same pattern in the garment industry raises questions about the reasons for the failure of centralized production and the persistence of small-scale productive operations. To what extent is this pattern a function of the relatively low capital equipment costs of both industries? To what extent is it exacerbated by the garment industry's heavy

133

involvement in the export trade, and to what extent is it a result of India's severe unemployment and underemployment problems?

These questions are explored in the following way. First I look at the effects centuries of involvement in long-distance trade have had on the organization of the handloom cloth industry in southern India, tracing the pattern of its response to fluctuations in trade and the way government has become increasingly involved in the industry. Against this background I then look at the history of Cannanore, a major weaving centre in Kerala, which became particularly involved in the production of cloth for the garment industry in the early 1970's, and examine the way its trade history and recent fluctuations in the garment export industry have affected the local organization of production. Finally, I return to the industry that is now a major purchaser of handloom cloth, and to the company that is the focus of this paper – a company which itself bought large quantities of cloth in Cannanore – examining the reasons for its changing fortunes and its final 'closure' against the background of the international trading system in which it had to operate. In conclusion, I summarize the themes which run like a persistent thread through the general and specific accounts, and suggest reasons for their interconnection.

THE SOUTH INDIAN HANDLOOM INDUSTRY

Cotton cloth was being produced throughout the Indian subcontinent when the British East India Company started its trading operations at the turn of the seventeenth century, but like their European competitors the British bought primarily in regions (Punjab, Gujarat, Bengal and the Coromandel coast) well accustomed to production for export (Chaudhuri 1974: 136). The system of cloth procurement was complex, and factors faced endless difficulties in their dealings with the long chain of intermediaries through whom orders were transmitted to the weavers who actually produced the cloth (Irwin 1955:11–12).

Weaving was largely household-based and weavers were dispersed throughout the towns and villages of exporting regions. Although in all cotton-growing areas coarse cloth would have been produced locally for village clients (Fischer and Shah 1970:169) from yarn spun by their womenfolk from their own cotton in exchange for grain or yarn (Kessinger 1974:57–8), many weavers were involved in specialist production for a complicated inter- and intra-regional trade in cloth for the Indian market. They would then be dependent on traders who could hold and control stocks and give information about the state of the market (Chaudhuri

1974:147ff). When producing for the overseas export market the weaver's dependency on the trader was even greater.

The production of finished cloth involves a series of intricate processes: cotton is cultivated, harvested, ginned and cleaned and spun into yarn; yarn is woven into cloth and cloth finished by dyeing or bleaching. All these operations were performed by different specialist groups. All were separately financed. Each set of artisans produced and sold its product against cash advances, and the entrepreneurial groups linking the stages of the process were distinct from each other (*ibid.*: 151, 157, 175). Theoretically the artisan still retained a measure of economic freedom. At times of export demand he could work for the export market, and at other times he could work for the local market on his own account (*ibid.*: 147). In addition, in an economy in which land was still an abundant resource, many weavers would combine their trade with part-time farming, and could move right out of the industry if it declined radically (*ibid.*: 170).

The British were particularly concerned with two aspects of this system, both of which were related to the question of control over production. One was the physical dispersion of the industry, particularly in South India, and the other was the system of indirect financing (*ibid.*: 152–7). The first signs of a developing putting-out system appeared in the 1670's, but it was only in the next century, and mainly as a result of increasing political instability and large-scale movements of weavers, that trends towards physical centralization appeared in the south and that merchants increased their control over workers (*ibid.*: 145, 157, 159). A recent account of the South Indian handloom industry in the nineteenth and early twentieth centuries (Baker, forthcoming) analyses the further development of these tendencies.

Accounts of nineteenth-century Indian history paint a picture of the handloom industry collapsing under the pressure of competition as the tide of trade turned and British exports captured the Indian market. But though this may have been true of parts of North India, in South India, despite gloomy reports (e.g. Thurston 1906: 520ff), a quick review of employment figures gives the opposite impression. The number of people actually employed in the industry rose during the nineteenth century. Baker (forthcoming: chap. 3) shows, however, that the situation was complex. The growth in the industry was not a result of a large increase in domestic consumption, as this stood steady during the period and failed to match the overall population increase. Instead it depended on periodic increases in demand from the export market. South India, unlike North India, had never lost its export trade. Its traditional markets in southeast Asia remained important throughout the period, and at the end of the nineteenth century new markets opened up in the African colonies.

Exports in handloom-piece goods continued to grow in the twentieth century, increasing fivefold between the 1880's and the 1950's, but there were serious fluctuations in trade during this later period, as India became more and more involved in the world economy, and dealt with export markets whose unpredictability was on a scale hitherto unknown to the Indian merchant-manufacturer. The industry was confronted with a series of economic crises, and at times its fragility became only too evident when large numbers of weavers were put out of work (*ibid.*).

It is not then surprising to find that the capitalist merchant-manufacturers developed tactics to deal with the uncertainties of the situation. During the nineteenth and twentieth centuries a classic putting-out system really developed. The merchant supplied the weaver with working capital, now usually in the form of materials, specified the type and design of cloth, took back the woven cloth, sometimes organized its finishing, transported it to market and arranged its sale. The merchant's prime concern was to control processes of production sufficiently to generate supplies when the market was good and to avoid tying up his capital in useless stocks of finished cloth when the market was bad (*ibid.*). It was the indirect putting-out system which allowed him to do this. He had no obligation to a fixed labour force and so could stop production simply by refusing to advance more yarn or other working capital. But he also needed always to be able to draw on large numbers of weavers when demand was good. In part this was achieved by keeping large numbers of weavers in debt, but in part it was made possible by other characteristics of the industry.

Throughout the nineteenth and early twentieth centuries, the textile industry in South India was the second largest source of employment after agriculture in the rural areas (Richards 1918: vol. I, 263; Cox 1894: vol. II, 159; Hemingway 1907: 157), and it was also the largest single urban occupation. Baker (forthcoming) argues that weaving was an easy occupation to enter. Although it involved some manual dexterity, the techniques for the production of medium- or coarse-quality cloths were not difficult to learn, and there was no need for an arduous apprenticeship. Fixed capital, in the form of the loom and other equipment, was low[2] and a weaver moving into the industry could seek working capital from a merchant. In fact, weaving was an occupation to which both lower-middle service classes and labouring classes could turn, especially in the towns.

During the first half of the twentieth century the particularly variable nature of the cloth trade had a number of significant effects on the structure of financing and production. As Baker (*ibid.*) shows, it is possible to make an analytical distinction between two types of weavers. The weavers specializing in finer quality cloths, which demanded considerable skill and were destined for export, were to be found mainly in the port towns and their hinterlands, and were mostly from traditional weaving castes, such as the Devangas in Madras City and the Sengundars in Chingleput.[3] By contrast weavers in the inland districts tended to produce coarser goods for local and regional markets. Weaving communities were likely to be mixed and contained a number of different weaving castes and people from other communities (Nicholson 1898: vol. II, 160; Brackenbury 1915: 109). The organizational modes of the two types also tended to differ. In the former case many weavers were likely to be independent or working under small-scale master weavers. Weaver, master weaver and yarn merchant frequently came from the same caste, and the local caste organization was somewhat like a caste guild. In the latter case weavers were less likely to be independent, and more likely to be organized in groups of several hundred to several thousand under master weavers or yarn-merchant capitalists. Significantly, after each export crisis, it was the proportion of looms producing fine cloths that declined, as weavers who had turned to the production of coarse cloth 'temporarily' found that they could not return to their former skilled work. At the same time, as the number of looms grew, each weaver's share of the market grew smaller. Finance became more difficult, and only men with established capital resources could take advantage of temporary upward swings in the market, with the result that control of the industry gradually became concentrated in the hands of relatively small numbers of capitalists,[4] and the smaller guild-like units gave way more and more to larger and more loosely organized units.

Another result of the state of the trade was a gradual tendency towards urban centralization in the industry (Baker, *ibid.*). The face of South India was changing steadily during the nineteenth and early twentieth centuries as railways and roads were constructed, and towns developed on the new routes along the uplands as the centres of new agriculturally based industries and the collection points for the developing trade in agricultural commodities. The numbers of weavers in both the old court and temple towns of the valleys, and in these new upland towns, increased. In times of trouble, outlying weavers were likely neither to get orders nor to get the little welfare that the government provided. In addition, the controlling capitalists had some interest in this movement. Some of the ancillary processes could be rationalized and more of the production centralized. However, the move to the towns did not herald a general movement from a household to a factory-and-production-line system of organization, and a putting-out system was still the basic form of organization. In some of the newer weaving centres though, weaving capitalists did develop larger-scale factory-like production units, some of which survived the further series of crises which hit the industry immediately after the second world war. Few have survived today as privately owned units, and the history of their abandonment or takeover reflects the continuity of capitalist response to the vagaries of the market right through to the late 1970's.

In the immediate post-independence period the handloom industry suffered severe yarn shortages. Many of undivided India's northern and western cotton fields now belonged to Pakistan. The Indian mill industry, no longer producing large quantities of cloth for the armed forces, was beginning to compete seriously for the domestic market and some of India's traditional southeast-Asian and African markets were developing their own mill industries and instituted protective legislation against Indian imports. The newly independent Indian government was caught in a cleft stick. Eager to promote its own mill industry, it was also irrevocably committed to a policy of support for the handloom industry.[5]

The industry staggered through the 1950's with declining exports but by the end of the decade the government made concerted efforts to promote exports in new markets, and set up the Handloom Export Promotion Council. During the 1960's exports of handloom cloth to new markets in Europe and America began to increase, and from the middle of the decade demand for handloom cloth from a nascent garment export industry also burgeoned. After the turn of the decade the industry escalated and particular cloths were in sudden heavy demand, causing a series of localized booms in the South Indian cloth-producing areas.[6]

One such locality was the town of Cannanore in northern Kerala, one of the new weaving centres of the late nineteenth century, and one whose fortunes in recent years have been intimately connected with the fortunes of the garment export industry. It was here that the garment-manufacturing company, whose story provides the focus for this paper, bought as much as 90 per cent of its cloth at certain points in the mid-1970's. Cannanore provides a good example of the pattern of capitalist response in the post-independence period.

Cannanore

Kerala, unlike Tamilnad, is not particularly renowned as a centre of handloom cloth production. At present, handloom cloth is woven throughout the state, but the majority of the 90,030 looms are to be found in the three coastal districts of Trivandrum (much of which corresponds to the former Travancore State and which has 19,234 looms), Kozhikode and Cannanore (both of which were in the old Malabar area of the Madras Presidency and have 14,318 and 40,144 looms respectively) (Govt of Kerala 1977: 53).

Traditionally this southwestern coastal area was not a big cloth export region. In the eighteenth century the Dutch toyed with and gave up the idea of trading in cloth in the region (Das Gupta 1967: 78ff). In the early nineteenth century Francis Buchanan (1807: vol. II, 360, 421, 450, 475–6, 509) and at the end of the century Mateer (1883: 239) noted the import-ance of cloth imports into the southwest coastal kingdoms from other parts of the Madras Presidency.[7]

There were, though, traditional centres of cloth production and a com-plex local and regional trade in cloth. A number of centres in southern Travancore, many of which are now in Tirunelveli district of Tamilnad, were famous for their fine men's lower cloths, and in the north, around the present Cannanore, weavers were famous for a particular type of towel cloth which was used in the region by both men and women as a towel and loose upper garment. The better-known centres in both north and south (Mateer 1883: 240) were populated by caste weavers called Chaliyans. There were also Tamil Devanga Chettis and Kaikolans (Logan 1887: vol. I, 115; Innes 1951: vol. I, 253), but much of the weaving was done by people of other castes – Chettis (merchants), barbers, Muslims and especially the Izhavas, a numerous low caste, most of whose members found employment as agricultural labourers.[8] In all of these centres weaving was done on the simple and cheap pit loom that is found throughout South India.

The exact history of the traditional Chaliyan weaving communities in the northern Cannanore area is obscure, but it seems likely that the Chaliyans were immigrants from eastern Tamilnad (Thurston 1909: vol. II, 11) who were encouraged into the area by the local rajas, and who later adopted Malayalam as their mother tongue. Like the established weaving settlements of southern Travancore, the villages are organized along single straight streets, at the centre of which are usually temples to the god Ganapati, the elephant god and son of Siva. This settlement is in striking contrast to the typical dispersed pattern of most Kerala villages.

Up till the end of the nineteenth century the northern communities were only involved in the production of cheap, rather coarse cloths which were sold within the region to the middle and lower castes (Innes 1951: vol. 1, 253). Higher-quality cloths were mostly imported from Tamilnad or

D. A. Swallow

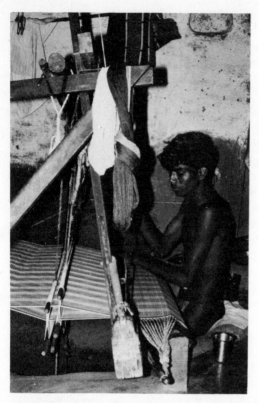

5.1 Village weaver using pit loom with flying shuttle (Tamilnad)

south Travancore. At the end of the nineteenth century a very different
weaving industry began to develop. The Basel German Evangelical Mission,[9]
which had been active in Malabar since 1839, had set up a weaving establishment in the town (Innes 1908: vol. I, 212 and 252) and, in an attempt to
provide an occupation for their low-caste converts, set up its factory with
European-style upright-frame looms fitted with fly shuttles, and jacquard
looms. The mission's potential congregation seems to have been more
interested in weaving than bible stories, and very shortly a number of
enterprising men from the Thiyya (Tiyar, Tiyya) caste – the northern
equivalent of the Izhavas – responded to new opportunities, ignored the
proselytizing and followed the Christian example only to the extent of
learning to weave on the new efficient frame looms. Soon a number of
them had set up several looms and established their own small units.

140

Cannanore's industry has continued to expand, despite massive fluctuations in trade. In the early years of the century the units made sheets, towels and tablecloths and heavy cloths for what are known in India as 'men's suitings', and exported them to the hill regions of South India and to the colder winter climes of North India (Innes 1951: vol. I, 253). Traditionally there had been virtually no cloth dyeing in the area, but now newly available German imported dyes made production of dark winter colours possible (Thurston 1897: 21). The factories used mill yarn from Madura, Tinnevelly and Kallayi, or imported yarn, mostly from England. By the 1930's the town's cloth merchants had started to export cloth to Ceylon – one of South India's long-established export marts – sending cloth made from mercerized-cotton yarn imported from Japan. This market collapsed just before the second world war.

The war and post-war periods were troublesome ones, as Cannanore manufacturers, competing with a mill industry totally dependent on Indian cotton, were now faced with the problem of severe yarn shortages. Here, as in the rest of South India, when yarn prices were high, manufacturers would simply stop production, waiting for prices to drop, and so minimize their own financial risk. At times, though, they did speculate, and the history of the Cannanore textile industry is scattered with the casualties of such speculations. In the later 1940's, for example, a number of Cannanore manufacturers thought that they could make up for the deficiencies in cotton yarn by weaving cloth from synthetic viscose yarn, but the cloth proved unpopular and hundreds of yards of cloth, stockpiled in anticipation of a market situation in which it would compete favourably, deteriorated rapidly in storage. In the 1950's the pattern of production changed again. Since the war, Cannanore manufacturers had been making cloth for 'men's shirtings', but in the later 1950's they also began to manufacture furnishing fabrics for the Indian market, later exporting some of these to northern Europe, especially Scandinavia. This trade grew steadily during the 1960's along with the production of cloth for men's shirts, but at the end of the decade Cannanore suddenly prospered and enjoyed an unexpected boom. The account of the boom has become something of a legend in the town and has all the oversimplification of such legends.

It appears that a Scandinavian shirt importer, exploring the cloth-production centres of South India in the winter of 1969, asked one of the Cannanore manufacturers if he could reproduce the effect of a crinkly crepe bandage as a shirt material. Cannanore had had its own spinning mills since 1945 (Dalal & Co. 1964: 83). One of the most inventive of the manufacturer's weaving masters discovered how to produce the effect by

141

weaving cloth with specially prepared high-twist yarn of 20s count and then washing it in caustic soda. The result was the crepe or cheese-cloth that swamped American and European markets throughout the early 1970's. The manufacturer managed to guard his precious secret for one season, but the demand increased dramatically; by the next season the Cannanore Spinning and Weaving Mills was producing the high-twist yarn in quantity and Cannanore's boom began.

Overall control of the Cannanore industry has remained with a relatively small number of capitalists from an early period. Some of the first Thiyya families to start weaving expanded their operations into very large enterprises.[10] But, in addition, amongst the longest established manufacturers were a Christian whose grandfather had started the enterprise as an individual weaver, a Punjabi and a Gujarati trading family. As the industry grew, these capitalists increased both the number of looms under their control and the size of their factories. Between the two world wars a number of factories, housing as many as 200 looms or more, were built in both Cannanore and its suburban villages. In these factories the magnates employed wage labour, paid at piece-rates, and centralized all the stages in the production process from the dyeing and bleaching of yarn to the piece dyeing of cloth. But this still represented only a small proportion of the area's loom capacity and much of the work was still being put out to individual households. Although at first the Thiyya community predominated in the industry, other castes – particularly Muslims and other lower castes – took to weaving and the traditional Chaliyan weaving communities started to work for the developing industry.

Initially it was in the factories that the new upright-frame looms with fly shuttles were concentrated, but gradually these looms replaced the simpler and lighter pit looms with thrown shuttle in the individual household units. However, when in the 1950's some of the manufacturers started to produce furnishing fabrics and very wide frame looms and jacquard attachments were needed for the large size and complicated cloths, only the factories were large enough to house them and only the bigger manufacturers able to afford the capital outlay.[11]

Inevitably it was the same merchant manufacturers, who had plentiful capital resources, who benefited from the crepe boom as well. Their factory space was of course totally inadequate for the quantity of cloth needed, and the very large looms unsuitable for this kind of work. Moreover the cloth was extremely easy to weave. So the bulk of work was put out, some of it directly to weaving householders but much to a growing class of small middlemen who had begun to build their own small factories,

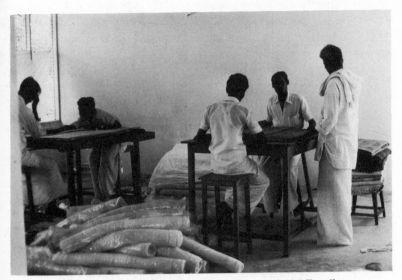

5.2 Checking cloth brought in from outworkers – Alagiri Textiles (Tamilnad)

housing between 6 and 30 looms. Many of the big manufacturers had begun to reduce their establishment costs during the 1960's by setting up some of their own supervisors as 'master weavers',[12] in some cases initially renting or selling them looms (usually on credit) from their own establishments, and by putting out more and more work to them. When in 1974 the Kerala State government became more rigorous in its application of Factory Act rules[13] and introduced minimum wages (Varkey 1968: 32) for hand-loom weavers, this pattern had intensified.

The boom when it came had not deceived most of the merchant manufacturers, many of whom had already experienced similar rises and their subsequent collapse. These manufacturers either kept their factory space for the safe production of furnishing fabrics, putting out all their work for the garment export industry, and/or kept a very small central sampling and dyeing unit, sometimes leaving the unused parts of the factory buildings to gather dust, sometimes converting them to other purposes, and sometimes selling them.

So when in the later 1970's the youth of the West tired of cheese-cloth and Cannanore faced increasing competition from the power looms of Tamilnad, it was the smaller 'middlemen' master weavers and those they employed directly who begun to suffer first. By 1978 many a small factory was lying closed or operating at quarter capacity.

Alongside the privately organized industry in Kerala is a growing handloom cooperative movement. Cannanore itself boasts the first Indian handloom cooperative society, established in 1942, although when the movement began to develop in the 1950's its growth in Cannanore was slower than in south Kerala where village weaving centres now have several primary cooperative societies and where the few large private factories were very early taken over as 'industrial' cooperative societies. In 1976 Mrs Gandhi, continuing the Congress government's policy of support for the handloom industry, made a grant to the handloom sector. This heralded a programme of expansion which was continued by the Janata government, and in 1978 a number of Cannanore's large factories, abandoned by their capitalist owners, were in the process of being purchased by the government for use as 'industrial' cooperatives.

To describe the organization of production in an area like Cannanore is not an easy matter. The production of cotton cloth entails a series of operations. Cotton has to be grown, cleaned, ginned and spun into yarn. Yarn in turn may need to be bleached or dyed before being wound on the bobbins for the preparation of the warp or on to perns to be placed in the shuttle for the weft thread of the cloth. The warp has to be prepared and set, the cloth woven, cut from the loom, checked, bleached, dyed or washed before being dried on racks or the ground, brushed clear of dust, packaged and dispatched.

Nowadays all the yarn used in the handloom industry in Cannanore is mill spun, either locally at the Cannanore Spinning and Weaving Mills, or in other Tamilnad centres such as Coimbatore, Salem or Madurai, and is purchased usually through dealers in the town. Virtually all cloth for the garment export industry is produced to order, in both the private and the cooperative sectors. The manufacturer or cooperative chairman or secretary may keep samples of types of cloth his weavers can produce, and may develop ideas in his own sampling unit, but often the garment manufacturer will give the handloom manufacturer a sample, or representation of a design, of the cloth to be developed.[14]

The private merchant-manufacturer usually dyes the yarn for a bulk order in his own dyeing units in order to maintain colour consistency throughout an order, and the prepared yarn is then collected by or delivered to the master weaver/manufacturers or household weavers who are directly responsible for the manufacture of the cloth. Yarn is usually supplied on credit, and on receipt of the finished product the merchant-manufacturer pays for the cloth less the cost of the yarn, but at times a subcontracting manufacturer will be responsible for the buying and dyeing of the yarn himself.

In both large and small private factories the remaining processes are often centralized. Yarn is wound on to bobbins and perns, the warp is set on to the loom and the cloth woven. Workers are simply paid piece-rates. But the owners of both large and small factories may also put work out to individual households. Households may take yarn on credit and manage all the remaining operations, using either family or hired labour. Alternatively, they may in turn put out the warping work to another unit, or may receive prepared warps initially. The small factories may also put out yarn to individual households to be wound, taking it back to be woven in the factory, or to be put out to different households for weaving.

Variations in the organization of production seem at first sight to be simpler in the cooperative sector. A cooperative society, whether consisting of household-based members or organized as a factory (an 'industrial' cooperative), may sell its products through its own depots, but more often nowadays it will take orders from an agent operating for the cooperatives

5.3 Women winding thread in one of the larger weaving factories in Cannanore. This factory produces furnishing fabric for both domestic use and export

D. A. Swallow

or from the cooperative marketing society, Apex. In the large factory-organized 'industrial' cooperatives, which operate rather like the large-scale private factories, most of the functions are centralized.[15] Here, all the employees are shareholders in a society which owns all the materials, buildings, equipment and finished products. By contrast, in the cottage-based weavers' cooperative societies, dyed yarn is supplied on credit to members who wind, set the warp and weave the cloth in their own households on their own looms, bringing back the fabric to the society to be marketed. However, householder cooperative members sometimes expand their operations, employing hired labour and investing in warping frames – and preparing warps for other households at a charge.

The village of Azhikode, on the outskirts of Cannanore and one of the two largest weaving centres in the Cannanore subdivision of Cannanore district, illustrates the complex way these various organizations intermesh on the ground. More than 2,200 (1977 figure) out of a population which was 30,439 in 1971 (see Table 5.1 on page 149) are employed in one or other capacity in the industry. Azhikode has one large factory, and one primary weaving cooperative society, which gives out work to household-production units. Additionally there are a considerable number of smaller businesses. According to a recent census,[16] approximately a third of Azhikode's handloom workers are employed in household units and two-thirds in larger units. However it is not easy to make a clear distinction either between the private and the public sector or between the 'household units' and the 'businesses'. Household units in the Cannanore region employ a higher proportion of non-household members than do similar units in the south of the state. In practice there exists a complex pattern of stratification within which individual households move up and down as their economic circumstances change.

The units range from the proprietary business which takes orders, dyes yarn and sometimes prepares warps, giving them out to other households or smaller businesses to wind and weave; the proprietary business which controls all the operations in its own sheds attached or adjacent to the owner's house, employing most of the labour and providing supervision from household members or close kin; to the household unit which provides some of its own labour but also employs some help and takes orders from larger units; to the household unit which just weaves on its own account, employing no extra help, and working either for a larger private unit or directly for a primary weaving cooperative society, in the first case receiving prepared warps from the unit, in the second paying another larger unit for the preparation of the warp; to the household which has no

146

looms but which receives winding work from others and/or provides labour for larger units, either in Azhikode or elsewhere in the Cannanore subdivision.

The division of labour by age and sex in Cannanore differs from that found in the southern part of the state and in Tamilnad. Here weaving is done only by men. The work of winding on to bobbins and perns is done by women and girls over school age, and only occasionally by young girls or children. Children, when not in school, have the task of fetching and carrying empty perns and bobbins and hanks of cotton yarn between household and household, along with other fetching-and-carrying tasks. Young boys do the work of twisting a new warp on to remnants of the old one on the loom, and men do all the warp preparation and dyeing.

The weaving establishments of Azhikode are almost totally dependent on the export industry for work. It is not then surprising that the cooperative sector has grown more slowly here than in the south of Kerala where more of the production is for the domestic Indian market. The private sector can respond much faster to the ever-changing demands of the garment export industry, and garment manufacturers, like the company studied, find that they can deal with the private manufacturers much more satisfactorily than with the cooperatives. Although some cooperatives do work for the export market, they suffer certain disadvantages. They are burdened with a cumbersome administration. They are bound by established rates of pay and so cannot play with prices at times of slack demand as easily as the private manufacturers. The latter can reduce prices to get work, sometimes cutting their own profits, but more often passing the loss down the line of intermediaries to the artisans themselves. If the market collapses completely they simply stop putting out work and wait for it to pick up again.

In the private sector, it is at times of high demand, when they know that they are in a strong bargaining position, that the weavers can insist on full rates of pay effectively. Rates of pay are higher in Kerala than in Tamilnad, and it is well known that Cannanore weavers, like their brethren in other industries and occupations in the state, are well organized by comparison with their counterparts in Tamilnad. The weavers and the production units are physically concentrated and this means not only that news can travel fast, but also that the weaver who hires out his labour can and does shift from one place of work to another as opportunities change, and that the man who weaves on his own loom can seek work from a range of merchant-manufacturers. But at times of slack demand the Cannanore weavers are as vulnerable as their Tamil counterparts.

147

D. A. Swallow

Cannanore in the 1970's continues to demonstrate the principles that have characterized the handloom industry for generations. Cannanore's recent boom certainly resulted from the creation of a new demand from within the garment export industry, but it depended crucially on the existence of a large potential work force, hitherto unemployed or underemployed, which could move into the industry. It was shown above that weaving was never totally the preserve of the so-called weaving castes, that there has always been mobility into and out of the handloom industry. At the turn of the nineteenth and twentieth centuries, the total numbers of people employed in the industry in many parts of the Madras Presidency was greater than the total number of the weaving castes (Nicholson 1898: vol. II, 160; Richards 1918: vol. I, 1, 263). Weaving has often been an alternative or part-time occupation for agriculturalists, since, although skilled weaving has usually been the preserve of specific weaving castes, the weaving of coarse cloth has never required great skill and at times of export boom extra weavers would be sought. The situation is much the same today, despite the fact that the form and direction of exports have changed. Although some of the new demand for cloth for the garment industry has demanded skilled work, much of the cloth and especially the crepe cloth produced in the Cannanore region has been very easy to produce. It is not then surprising that the majority of the weavers in Cannanore are not from weaving castes, or that, unlike many of the caste weavers in Tamilnad, most of them think of their job not as skilled work as do many of the Devengas and Sengundars of Tamilnad, but simply as an occupation when no better is available.

The attitude is significant. It reflects the realities of the employment situation in northern Kerala. Coastal Kerala has one of the highest population densities (Cannanore district in 1971 had 664 persons per square mile) in a densely populated subcontinent, and substantially fewer of Kerala's work force (in 1961 38.30 per cent and 1971 48.63 per cent) fall into the categories of cultivator and agricultural labourer than the national average (in 1961 69.49 per cent and in 1971 68.63 per cent) (Chandra Sekhar 1971: 62–3). This has been the pattern in Malabar since the turn of the century, when it was noted that Malabar's agricultural work force was lower than that for the Madras Presidency as a whole, and that fishing, the timber industry, and the manufacture of palm products (toddy drawing, oil pressing, rope making etc.) were extremely important sources of employment in the area (Innes 1908: vol. I, 248). However, the proportion of agricultural labourers to the whole work force, which increased significantly at an all-India level in the decade 1961–71 (16.71 per cent – 25.76

148

Table 5.1 *Occupational structure in Cannanore district, Kerala, 1971*

	Cannanore district		Cannanore subdivision		Azhikode	
	Male	Female	Male	Female	Male	Female
Total population	1,172,338	1,192,826	247,461	254,305	15,180	15,259
Total workers	538,887	175,706	112,175	31,309	7,179	1,067
I. Cultivators	112,905	17,973	7,287	3,118	172	45
II. Agricultural labourers	134,264	108,119	13,214	16,818	263	278
III. Livestock, forestry, fishing, hunting, plantations	32,339	5,483	4,578	183	512	6
IV. Mining and quarrying	4,870	129	1,083	25	39	–
Va. Household industry	17,518	10,396	4,499	2,154	182	50
Vb. Other than household industry	80,370	8,876	40,575	3,281	3,868	357
VI. Construction	9,850	337	2,401	112	162	12
VII. Trade and commerce	67,479	3,455	18,043	368	890	42
VIII. Transport, storage, communications	19,179	2,009	6,395	631	547	61
IX. Other services	60,113	18,929	14,100	4,619	544	216
Non-workers	633,451	1,017,120	135,286	222,996	8,001	14,192

Source: Census of India 1971, Series 9, Kerala, part XB, pp. 112–13.

per cent), grew even faster in Kerala (17.38 per cent – 30.68 per cent). In Cannanore district in 1971 agricultural labourers represented 33.96 per cent of the work force (see Table 5.1), and it is probable that this proportion has increased further over the past ten years.

In the immediate vicinity of Cannanore, the town's three main manufacturing industries – weaving, *beedi*-cigarette making,[17] and spinning in the mills – and in the wider locality the timber, brick and tile industries offer men the best alternative occupations to agricultural labour. Although virtually all the weavers I interviewed in Cannanore subdivision owned their own houseplots, they rarely had more than a tenth of an acre of surrounding garden land, on which they grew coconut trees, and other fruit or vegetables, but very few had rice paddy land. Some weavers did do agricultural labouring work at peak seasons, but it was from just that sort of under-employment that most wished to escape. Other recognized alternatives included general labouring ('coolie' work) – for example in the construction industry – or small-scale trading and shop keeping, or emigration to the cities of Northern India: more recently emigration has extended to the Persian Gulf. For women, who in Cannanore subdivision provide more than half the agricultural labour, the choice of employment is even more restricted. Both men and women I talked to recognized the desperate insecurity of the weaving industry and the difficulties of some of the alternatives. All of them hoped for better things for their children. Many wished them to stay at school, to matriculate, and to qualify themselves for clerical and government jobs which would carry some security. It was the same concern for security that led those who could to seek employment at the industrial cooperatives, as these did have a better chance of getting work for the subsidized domestic market, and were a channel through which weavers could express grievances to the government.

The pattern described by Baker (forthcoming: chap. 3) for the Madras Presidency during the first four decades of the twentieth century – when the number of weavers and looms grew at times of general economic depression, and urban working- and lower-middle-class and service communities turned to weaving when there were no other possible occupations – also fits the situation in Cannanore in this decade.

THE INDIAN GARMENT EXPORT INDUSTRY

There are striking parallels between the traditional handloom export industry and trade and the present garment export industry. Many of the garment manufacturers depend on the handloom industry for the bulk of their cloth supplies. The system of cloth production and procurement has not changed substantially. As in the days of the East India Company, fashion demands determine the designs of the cloth being produced. Garment companies' agents still have to shift their orders from centre to centre as fashion demands change, and different centres are still skilled in the production of particular types and weights of cloth. Today a garment manufacturer wanting fine cloth will order through a Coimbatore or Madurai 'manufacturer'. One wanting crepe will order through either Cannanore or Erode in Tamilnad; one wanting heavier autumn-weight fabrics through Karur; and one wanting middle-weight 'Madras' checks will place his orders through Madras dealers. Although there has been a pattern of increasing concentration over the past 150 years, much of the production in South India is still dispersed in villages as much as 200 miles from the urban centres where the merchants negotiate with their clients. The example of one of the most concentrated centres has shown that, from the manufacturer's point of view, the disadvantages of centralization and direct control of production are greater than their advantages. Centralization increases overheads and entails regular responsibility to a large work force which could prove difficult to manage, while a putting-out system is well suited to a variable export market. The manufacturer can quickly amass large quantities of cloth at times of high demand, and draw in his horns and reduce his capital outlay when demand is slack or the market seems unprofitable. The situation for the garment manufacturer is no different. The organized Indian garment industry has grown up largely as an export industry, and the garment exporter, like his counterpart in the handloom industry, is at the mercy of highly variable markets and is competing in a highly competitive international trading system.

A ready-made-garment industry was almost non-existent in India at the beginning of the second world war. Domestic demand for sewn clothes – and the majority of the traditional forms of clothing demand folded but not sewn cloth – has always been and is still mainly satisfied by individual tailors sewing to order on cloth provided by their client. It was not to meet domestic demand that a semi-organized industry developed in India, but to meet the demand for standard types of military uniforms in a period of war. As the industry was not initially geared to a domestic civilian market, it foundered at the end of the war, and made little headway in the 1950's when the production of clothing and made-up garments was increasing at a rapid rate on a world scale (Narayanaswami and Sri Ram 1972: 27). It was not until the second half of the 1960's that the industry began to develop its export potential.

The main reasons for its growth at this point were the introduction of an attractive export scheme in 1959, which was fully implemented by 1962, and the spectacular success of a particular type of handloom cloth, known as 'bleeding Madras', on U.S. markets in the mid-1960's, some of which was processed into garments in India. In addition, increasing urban growth in the 1950's and 1960's led to the assumption that domestic demand for ready-made clothing would gradually increase (*ibid*.: 27). These domestic and export possibilities meant that the number of production units began to increase. Whereas the industry had previously been primarily cottage based, big business houses and established textile mills now began to set up garment subsidiaries, often in existing under-utilized factory space. Smaller private companies began to sprout, initially setting up small numbers of machines in a variety of types of building (*ibid*.: 35ff).

Since the turn of the decade it has been the dramatic growth in exports (from Rupees 150 million worth in 1971 to 2,450 million in 1976) which has shaped the industry.[18] The domestic market has grown steadily in major urban centres, but, despite continuing over-optimistic estimates, it has shown few signs of matching the rate of the increase in the export market, and actually declined between 1974 and 1976. Throughout the last two decades it has been cheaper to have clothes made up by a local tailor (*ibid*.: 95). Women's clothes offer little scope for standardization as the sari is a folded, unsewn garment, and clothing habits show little tendency to change. But perhaps the major stumbling block which inhibits even the sale of men's and children's wear is the lack of an organized retail system extending beyond the major urban centres (*ibid*.: 96).

By the later 1970's the vulnerability of an industry dependent on exports became evident. By 1976 over 90 per cent of India's garment exports were going to Western Europe and North America, and about 80 per cent were fashion or casual clothing rather than standard garments, children's wear or institutional clothing (Govt of Maharashtra 1977: 36–8). The bulk was restricted to cotton garments and summer-weight clothing, to particular types of cloth, especially particular types of handloom cloth, and to particular types of garment – women's shirts and blouses. Manufacturers and government too late recognized the danger of the specialization and the risk of the buying countries' adverse reactions. Internal difficulties inhibited diversification and the market reached crisis point in 1977. The pattern of response to this situation can be well illustrated by the history of a single company, Paville Fashions, the Bombay company introduced above.

The case of Paville Fashions

Paville Fashions is a private limited company, whose shareholders are all members of a single family. The family, surprisingly, is not from an established business caste or community such as the Marwaris, the Gujarati Hindu or Jain Banias, the Bohra Muslims or the Parsees, but is of mixed Kashmiri Pandit and Konkani Saraswat Brahmin origins, with traditions of government service under both Indian rulers and the British (Conlon 1977; Dobbin 1972: 3-6; Rama Rau 1978). The company was started by Mrs Wagle, who in 1962 began to export silk handloom fabrics to Western Europe. In 1967 the family went into partnership with the heads of a leading textile mill and an established garment-manufacturing house in Bombay, and production started on thirty sewing machines in a corner of the garment manufacturer's premises. At first production was restricted to high-quality silk women's garments which sold in expensive boutiques and stores in London and New York, and Mrs Wagle herself, working with a designer, a master tailor, a fabric officer and a shipping manager, supervised the whole design and production operation. She also acted as her own salesman, despite the fact that she had no formal training in business, textile technology or design. Within the year the Wagle family bought out the two partners, soon shifted to new premises and began to expand.

In 1970, after working for a year in London with the Samuel Sherman fashion group, the son of the family joined the business and the company began to move into the mass market. By 1972 they had established a close relationship with a leading Los Angeles shirt firm and with one of the major New York importers, and from 1974-6 they concentrated their production on shirts for these importers though they still took small orders for the higher-priced market from designers such as the London-based Jean Muir. In 1976 Mrs Wagle's husband, who had moved from a career in the Indian Civil Service to one in private industry, retired from his position as managing director and chairman of a major heavy-engineering company and became actively involved in the business.[19]

In 1974 the company had taken the capital risk of constructing a garment factory of its own, and by 1976 it employed a work force of over 1,200 in Bombay – in its factory, in its original rented premises, in a storage warehouse and at its central city offices. Tailors, helpers, sorters, pressers and packers were working a two-shift, six-day week, supervised by a small, tightly knit, management group directed by the three family members.

The family that owns Paville Fashions comes from Bombay's highly

153

Westernized elite, but the middle management that worked under it in 1978 came from the range of communities that make up Bombay's widening middle class. The seven officers (i.e. departmental heads) came from a variety of backgrounds. The designer and finance officer were both Parsees, the sales manager a Sindhi, the production manager a Punjabi Mohyal Brahmin, the labour officer a Maratha, the shipping manager a north-Kerala Thiyya, and the fabric-development officer a Kerala Tamil Iyer Brahmin. The larger body of clerical and secretarial staff, totalling 55, came from similar kinds of background. There were Parsees, Marathas, Christians from Kerala, Goa and the area around Bombay, Rajputs, Jats and Bohra Muslims.

Most of the managerial staff and virtually all the secretarial and clerical staff came from backgrounds which had had at least one generation's experience of city life. All the departmental heads had had college education to bachelor-degree standards, and several had higher degrees. All spoke English with ease and all the men wore Western dress, as, for much of the time, did the Parsee and Christian girls.

The five-storey factory building was designed by an American-trained Indian architect and measured up to any international standards. It was light and airy and designed to catch the cross ventilation of the sea breezes in the hottest weather. The basement served as storage for newly arrived cloth, and at times for the temporary storage of finished and packaged goods waiting for shipment, though for much of the period of study both the receipt and checking of cloth and final packing were done in the rented warehouse at some distance from the factory. Three floors were devoted to stitching and were equipped with imported German (Pfaff) industrial electric sewing machines, button-holing and button-stitching machines. The fourth floor was the main cutting floor, equipped with high-powered cutting machines and a small number of machines used solely for the production of sample garments to be approved by buyers and used by road salesmen. On this floor also were the offices of the factory manager, the supervisory staff and the welfare officer, and the telex room. The top (fifth) floor housed the main showroom, served as an informal office for the senior management and was often used for major management meetings. The offices of the designer and the fabric-procurement officer were also on the top floor. Production was highly systematized, the flow being directed from pattern design on the top floor, to cutting and sampling on the fourth, sewing on the lower floors and pressing before packing on the ground floor.

Within each sewing floor, sets of small production units operated, a single shirt passing through a number of machinists' hands for the different stages of manufacture. Each operation was separately assessed to establish standard production rates; a full record was kept of each machinist's daily and monthly production rates; and production rates and quality were checked by group supervisors and floor supervisors, most of whom had moved up from the floor and so stood in an ambiguous position between management and workers. The workers themselves were fully organized. All were members of the Bombay Labour Union, a union which at the time of the study had strong Janata Party connections, and their affairs in the factory were represented by a factory labour union committee.

In early December 1977 the total number of employees on the company books stood at 1,005, a little lower than its 1976 peak. This number included the officers, shift supervisor, 10 floor supervisors, 26 group supervisors, 44 clerks, 14 cutters, 530 tailors, 305 helpers, 27 ironers, 14 checkers, 5 maintenance staff, 12 sweepers (cleaners), 4 peons (messengers, orderlies), and 6 general staff. Tailors were those who actually operated the high-speed electric sewing machines. The category 'helper' included packers, sorters, thread cutters and those who worked on buttonhole- and button-stitching machinery. A helper could be promoted to the status of tailor, and there was also a promotion path from tailor to checker or group supervisor and thence to floor supervisor.

The tailors and helpers, the two largest groups of workers, were recruited in waves as the company expanded. The first wave were men, who came mainly from a number of districts around Hyderabad in Andhra Pradesh. They came from traditional weaving castes (mostly the Padma Sale caste), and from other castes associated with the textile industry, and also from the Telegu Komati trading caste. All of them were simply referred to by non-Telegu speakers as 'Telengis', in reference to Telengana, the part of Andhra Pradesh from which most of them came. Many of the tailors came from families which had already sent one generation of workers to the Bombay mills or to small tailoring establishments in the city, keeping their families in the village.

The next major wave of tailors and helpers came from a different area. Virtually all were from the state of Maharashtra, from the districts of Ratnagiri, Kohlapur and Colaba, which have supplied a large proportion of the Bombay labour force (Joshi and Joshi 1976: 18). The majority called themselves Marathas, the largest caste category in Maharashtra (see Carter 1974: 53), though some admitted to hailing from the Bhandari caste. From 1974 onwards both men and women were recruited, though preference was given to women in the hope that they would be less disruptive than men. The majority of these tailors came from families which were

originally peasant farmers. Over 60 per cent of an interviewed sample[20] of
the Maharashtrian tailors and helpers came from families which still held
land in their villages, but almost 50 per cent of them were the second generation of their families to move into the city for work, their fathers having
been employed either in the mills or 'in service' in small industries or
businesses. There was also a handful of tailors from other parts of India –
from Goa, from Kerala, from Gujarat and from the northern parts of
Karnataka (cf. Joshi and Joshi 1976: 18). The ironers and sweepers by
contrast all came from Uttar Pradesh.

The pattern of employment looks a little like that in the handloom
industry. At first the nascent organized industry tends to draw employees
from groups traditionally engaged in the production or processing of cloth,
who for generations have been practising the manual skills needed. As the
industry expands, the skill is seen as one which can be acquired by anyone.
This pattern is also reflected in the methods by which the tailors had
learned their craft. The average work force was very young – with the
average age under 30, although actual ages of the whole work force ranged
from 18 to 52. Ninety-five per cent of the interviewed sample of tailors and
helpers were literate and had had formal education at least up to the end
of primary school. After finishing their schooling they had learned tailoring in one of two ways. The men had usually learned their trade by
'apprenticing' themselves to small tailoring establishments, often moving
from there to small factories before gaining employment at this company.
The women, who formed a large part of the second wave of tailors, had, by
contrast, usually attended one of the many government or privately funded
training institutes or home-based private tailoring classes which have sprung
up in Bombay.

The whole work force was paid monthly salaries, and employees worked
an eight-hour, six-day week. The tailors' and helpers' salaries ranged
between Rupees 250 and Rupees 680 a month, with the possibility of
attendance and production bonuses of up Rupees 150 each month. In
addition employees were protected with life-insurance policies, had two
weeks of paid annual leave, and were entitled to sickness benefits. The
method of payment was somewhat exceptional, as most garment
companies – and even the larger ones – continued to pay their workers at
piece-rates, as did the majority of the textile mills. The workers were thus
secured a minimum wage, provided that they achieved agreed productivity
norms. This wage stood at the top end of the scale found in the garment
industry in Maharashtra, although on a day-to-day measurement more
undoubtedly could be earned in a small sweat shop where work was paid
by piece-rate.[21]

However, despite this security, the relationship between management and workers was far from happy, and a series of disputes in 1977 led to a temporary closure at the end of the year – a closure which proved to be a forewarning of worse to come. Interestingly, the disputes were not over rates of pay as such, but were a reaction to stricter productivity demands. The disputes and the subsequent history of the company can be understood only in the context of the wider pattern of events on the world market which were outside the control of both workers and management.

International trade, national policies and local disputes

In March 1977, without warning, Britain and France imposed an embargo on any further shirt imports into their countries from India. The reasons behind this move were complex. Recession had hit the countries of the European Economic Community and Scandinavia, and they were unable to stem the tide of garment imports. Up till this point it had suited the developed world to allow the free import of fabrics into their countries, as they assumed that their own processing and converting industries were safe, and that the bulk of the imports were grey cloth. The garment-exporting industries of the developing world had, however, been expanding. In 1973–4 there was a large increase in the number of garments exported from the developing world. For a time this was assumed to be a flash in the pan, caused by current currency problems and blamed partially on Japan. But in the subsequent years these exports continued to grow, and the Western economic situation got worse rather than better. There were continuing currency problems, huge rises in oil prices which affected the costs of many industries, and the contingent general rise in prices. From 1975 to 1977 the inflationary spiral could not be stopped. Many of the textile-converting industries are labour intensive, and inflation in price and thus wage structure meant that it was impossible for domestic industries to bring their prices down to compete on an equal footing with the imported goods, which, because of much lower labour costs in the manufacturing countries, were undercutting them and threatening their viability.

The United States had thought ahead, and back in 1970 and 1971 had negotiated with their major importing countries – Hong Kong, South Korea and Taiwan – setting quotas on garment imports. India was still too insignificant to be included in these agreements, but in 1974, as her exports to the U.S.A. began to increase dramatically, India was called in for negotiations. Europe by contrast had not thought far enough ahead. Quotas for India had been established and revised under the United Nations General Agreement on Tariffs and Trade (G.A.T.T.), but as the tide of imports

157

surged several countries panicked, responded suddenly to the pressures of their domestic industries, and unilaterally banned the imports of Indian shirts and blouses, although established quotas for handloom shirts and blouses had not been reached for the year.[22]

The result was that many of the garments were redirected and found a market at very reduced prices in the U.S.A. In addition it was a very late spring and summer throughout most of the U.S.A. and the cold weather meant that demand for cottons was very slow moving. Paville's American orders fell dramatically and the company was eventually reduced to laying off 150 'temporary' workers.[23] This was a cause of bitterness although the permanent work force was kept on, but in fact the company only had sufficient work during the following six months for the remaining tailors to work at half capacity.

In September, with a new winter-season's demands, new orders flooded in, but productivity remained sluggish, and it soon became obvious that a number of tailors were effectively organizing a go-slow and were intimidating any other members of the work force who tried to respond to the management's demands. At the same time the factory's union committee began to make a series of demands – for a full meal in the canteen; for uniforms for the lift operator; and, more importantly, for a change from the system of group component production to a one-man-one-shirt system; and for the reinstatement of the 150 dismissed temporary workers.

Groups of workers began to obstruct the transport of finished goods between the factory and airport or docks, and cloth between the dyers and factory. One of the tailors was beaten up by two others, who were immediately suspended. Some of the management were involved in physical confrontations, and events culminated in an unresolved dispute between workers and management which resulted in a lock-out and the factory's closure for five weeks. Immediately after the closure, 150 of the permanent work force were sent charge sheets reprimanding them for unruly behaviour deliberately intended to disrupt the smooth functioning of the factory's production. Many of the same workers were also sent official warnings that their productivity was below agreed levels and that they were in danger of being sacked.

The situation was bad for the workers, but it was also bad for the management, now in the unhappy position of having large orders which it could not manufacture and of holding large quantities of cloth and trimmings for which payment would very shortly be demanded. While negotiations between the company's management, the Labour Commissioner, representatives of the Bombay Labour Union and the factory's union committee continued, a new strategy was being developed. The company began to subcontract as much work as it could to other companies and to smaller units with machine space and time. This obviously meant that quality supervision was more difficult, and ten new checkers were temporarily employed. At the height of the trouble the company was using twenty-four different subcontractors, supplying them with all materials and paying a manufacturing fee per piece.

Official negotiations made little headway, but after five weeks the management simply began to reopen the factory floor by floor, arguing that they had had to close because production had been made impossible, and that now it was once again possible they were reopening. Many of the dismissal notices that had been sent out at the height of the dispute were waived, but the company succeeded in getting rid of the really troublesome elements in the work force.

However, discontent on the factory floor did not disappear. Productivity remained low and the company sought professional advice. After consultation with the Bombay Labour Union, the company wrote to the Labour Research Institute in Bombay which then made a study of the situation and submitted a report, and a legal agreement was made between

5.4 Male tailors in one of the units to which Paville put out work during the strike (Bombay)

union and management. But the agreement itself then became a source of conflict. Management and union interpreted the crucial phrase 'norms of production' in different ways. The union took the dispute to court and the management lost its case. However, separate negotiations continued out of court both for the duration of the hearing and afterwards. The court decision had not provided a practical solution to the problem and the two parties eventually agreed on a mutually acceptable formula.

This series of crises presaged things to come and the management had sufficient foresight to plan ahead. They decided to reopen their old premises, as a new company, and to start production there again, so that they could avoid having their production brought to a complete halt again by industrial dispute, and they set up a highly skilled sampling unit to which the mother company could subcontract all its sampling work.

The company's fears were well founded. In 1978 came a crop of disasters. In April 1978 the U.S.A. had also restricted imports. Additionally there was increasing uncertainty and indecision within India over the allocation of garment export quotas.

Since the introduction of fixed quotas for the import of garments into the U.S.A. and the E.E.C. countries, Indian garment manufacturers had awaited with some trepidation the annual rulings on quota allocations by the Indian government. In December 1977 new G.A.T.T. treaties had been drawn up. The new Multi Fibre Agreement affected India on two counts. No longer was any distinction made between mill-made and handloom garments, and no longer were the quotas fixed in terms of the value of exports. Instead, the quotas specified the numbers of garments allowed in each category. These changes had important repercussions. In order to gain the best return on their exports the Indian government fixed quota allocations which gave an advantage to 'high price realization' garments. This policy obviously favoured the manufacturers in the higher-price market, but other manufacturers were badly hit. Simply to raise prices would have meant that products were no longer competitive. In addition the South Indian manufacturers, many of whom were also handloom-cloth merchants and all of whom produced only handloom garments, felt that they were being done down by a clique of Bombay and Delhi manufacturers who were less closely tied to the handloom industry and who would increase their use of higher-price mill cloth. The handloom merchants' lobby, riding on the band-wagon of the Janata Party's support of small-scale industry in general and of the handloom industry in particular, won a fixed allocation for handloom garments.

The increasingly complex system of allocation fostered internal compe-

160

tition between manufacturers, and tension built up in anticipation of the announcement of the 1979 quota allocations. On the expected date, 20 December 1978, no announcement was made. The delay was due to the fact that a number of small manufacturers[24] had sued the government and questioned its legal right to determine allocations in the way it did. Finally, on 1 January, a series of highly complex allocations was announced along with a statement which put the industry into further disarray. The government announced that it was, forthwith, ceasing to grant any export incentives at all to the industry, but was to give both the handloom and mill-cloth export industry a 10-per-cent export incentive subsidy. The rationale was that the garment industry was well established, that there were three times as many potential exports as quota places, and that cloth exports were running well below quota allocations from importing countries. From the government point of view this was logical, but for the manufacturers, who had already committed themselves to prices on the basis of an incentive subsidy promised until April 1979, this was another disaster. And for many the disaster was compounded by the announcement the following day that 124 exporters were to be taken off the registered list of exporters for failing to export quota allocations they had been granted in the previous year.

Many of the latest decisions about quota allocations were ostensibly geared to the advantage of small-scale units. The larger manufacturers, such as the company under study, which had large permanent work forces, and which provided good working conditions and facilities, vigorously demanded that they should have a fixed allocation. Their lobby in turn was successful. On Friday 5 January it was announced that 5 per cent of the total quota would go to established manufacturers.

After hectic efforts over the next few days the company managed to negotiate a large enough quota allocation to cover its orders for the next three to four months, but it was rapidly becoming clear to the management that its present vulnerability was intolerable. It depended almost totally on the U.S. market, and manufactured only women's blouses and men's shirts – the two most competitive categories in the business. It had too little flexibility in its markets to adapt as the pattern of international trading veered and the Indian government made sudden panic decisions in response. It could not transfer its production to the domestic market where there was little demand for its products.[25] But above all it had too little flexibility in its productive organization. Unlike very small-scale units which could avoid factory act legislation, it was legally bound to its workers.

161

There were several possible answers to the problem. The company could diversify its markets and the range of products it manufactured in order to spread its risk. It could close down its manufacturing unit and, as others had already done, set up production overseas in countries like Sri Lanka or Kenya, and export to them subsidized handloom cloth, re-exporting made-up garments. Alternatively it could simply close down the main production unit and operate for a time on a much smaller scale from the newly established daughter company, using the factory premises for other purposes or renting them out. In the event, by the summer of 1979 the owners of the company, who had prided themselves on their enlightened outlook, their rationally organized system of production, and their sense of responsibility to their employees, admitted defeat, and closed the factory down in favour of the persuasive advantages of a subcontracting system.

In many ways the company had been something of an anomaly in the Indian garment industry. It had built itself up solely as a full-scale export-ing company specializing in fashion garments; it did not have any other trading operations and, unlike companies run by families from well-established trading communities, it had no experience of trade in other commodities; and the growth of its garment unit was not, as it was in many other exporting companies, a sideline which it saw as a temporary money-spinner while the export boom lasted. In fact the pattern of its operation ran counter to the general one.

The general pattern is similar to that found in the handloom cloth trade. Like the handloom textile industry, the garment industry is, relatively speaking, very low capital intensive. For the average garment manufacturer, Paville's beautiful new factory and its very efficient imported machines would seem unnecessarily excessive overheads. The majority of the Indian garment manufacturers and particularly the large-scale exporters have maintained a position of much more limited liability. Many of the 'big' manufacturers and exporters in fact operate through a network of units to which they subcontract or put out work, season by season. The bulk of the productive industry remains small-scale although much of the export trade is in the hands of large-scale traders. In Delhi much of the industry is cot-tage based still and in Bombay the typical productive unit is small and is housed in rented premises, with Indian-made electric machines crowded together. For such small manufacturers, as for the handloom weaver, the biggest risk would lie in any independent outlay on working materials while producing for a notoriously uncertain export market. In fact the situation is even more circumscribed. The small-scale producer working in the export field is totally dependent on getting orders from a registered exporter. He has the knowledge of the market and its rapid changes, and only he can deal with the vagaries of the international and national trading regulations. Only he can negotiate with the buying agents of importing companies and only he speaks the language of fashion. So smaller-scale manufacturers take orders, material and finishings from a larger-scale exporter, and their labour force, to whom they remain uncommitted, increases and decreases as the state of their order book changes. The tailor himself, like the urban weaver, will move from unit to unit as and when work is available, at times joining the small workshop of a tailor or a small unit producing for the domestic market and at times taking up other forms of employment, on some occasions working very little and depending on kin, at others working all hours of the day and night.

CONCLUSIONS

The case of Paville remains of great interest. The company tried to set up a 'rationalized' system of production, on the model of organized industry, with a system of direct control over its labour, and a fully organized method of discussion and negotiation between work force and management. But the attempt failed and the company began to operate a system better understood by many of its local competitors. What is even more striking is the marked similarity between the garment export industry and the handloom export industry in this respect. The British East India Company agents talked hopefully of centralizing the production of hand-loom cloths in the eighteenth century, but, except for times of actual disturbance when weavers sought protection inside the walls of their forts, this wish never came about. In the middle decades of the twentieth century in some of the small towns of South India, larger factories for the production of handloom cloth did spring up, but now many lie in total or near-total disuse, while some are the homes of heavily subsidized weaving cooperative societies.

The similarity in pattern reflects common features in both systems – in particular their dependence on a highly volatile export market. The handloom industry's share of the domestic market is gradually but steadily declining, despite gallant efforts to sustain it, and as a result its dependence on the export market increases. Although the industry is still cottage based in many parts of South India, few weavers weave on their own account, even when they own their own looms. Most are totally dependent on capitalist merchants. The export market gets yearly more volatile, and at the same time the traditional alternative sources of employment – cloth production for the domestic market, and part-time work on the land – become either more scarce or less profitable. Yet the industry seems to attract an increasing number of weavers, winders, twisters and dyers, who each get smaller and smaller shares of the market.

The garment industry is also dependent on the export market, but in this case it developed essentially as an export industry, and the domestic market in ready-made garments has expanded too slowly to counteract the shock of a series of crises in the export market.[26] The industry has grown dramatically over the past fifteen years for several reasons. Like the handloom industry it is able to utilize the considerable manual skill and manpower resources of the subcontinent. Indian garments first became popular because they were made from handloom cloth which came in a wide range of textures and infinitely varied designs. As in the handloom industry, costs remain low and prices are competitive in the international market. Capital investment in machinery and housing can be kept low, and labour is cheap and plentiful, while government incentives for garments and subsidies in the handloom industry have till recently further reduced the costs of production. Production units remain small and few manufacturers take on the burden of a large permanent work force.

Not surprisingly, the recent series of crises in the export market, the increase in costs with the end of subsidies, and increasing hostility from importing countries' domestic industries will reinforce these tendencies. Manufacturers will keep their units small-scale, and those running larger units may well tend to revert to smaller-scale systems of production, reducing their risk by subcontracting work to sweat shops.

However, the persistence of small-scale production more generally cannot simply be explained in terms of the exigencies of a particular export-trading situation. The importance of exports is clearly a dominant cause in this particular case, but the predominance of small-scale production in India's garment industry has many parallels. The garment industry has depended on sweat-shop production throughout the world during its early history, and is still dependent on sweat-shop labour and putting-out systems in many parts of the Western world. Europe and the U.S.A. have been notorious for these conditions, and the histories of their garment industries provide a good example of the way nineteenth-century industrial capitalism threw up numerous small-scale, labour-intensive operations alongside the more obvious large firms and factories (Samuel 1977: 15). India now has a massively burgeoning population, increasing pressure on land, large-scale labour migration into the towns and inadequate employment (Joshi and Joshi 1976; Mehta 1976: 111). In such a situation small-scale, labour-intensive industries such as these, controlled indirectly by merchants and traders, though liable to severe and frequent crises, will continue to draw worker and capitalist alike.

6 Harris Tweed: construction, retention and representation of a cottage industry

Judith Ennew

INTRODUCTION

The durable luxury textile called Harris Tweed is produced exclusively on the Scottish offshore islands known as the Outer Hebrides or Western Isles. This string of islands, some thirty miles to the west of mainland Scotland, has been regarded as a problem area since its incorporation into the United Kingdom, along with the rest of Scotland, in 1707. The history of the 'Hebridean Problem' is similar to that of the 'Irish Problem', at least with respect to the nineteenth century. In the 1830's, 40's and 50's, potato famines and unrest about land reform brought the poverty of the High-landers and Hebrideans, as well as that of their Irish neighbours, to the attention of the national conscience. The difference between the Irish and Hebridean views of the situation at the time is reflected in the different histories of the two areas since 1880. The Irish Land League, which was the chief organ of protest in Ireland, was vociferous in its calls for national self-determination and land reform. The latter was envisaged as, at the least, returning the land to the people, at the most, leading to national-ization of land. Although the Highland Land League was affiliated to its Irish counterpart, it exhibited a greater divergence between nationalist and socialist philosophies. The roots of both the Labour Party in Scotland and the Scottish Nationalist Party can be traced back to the Highland Land League (Hunter 1974; Kellas 1966). Differences in attitude to land reform were even more important. Highland Land Leaguers made repeated pleas for land reform, but this did not refer to the abolition of landlord–tenant relationships in favour of small-farm ownership, let alone the nationaliz-ation of land. What the majority of Highland land reformers desired was simply the reform of land tenure. Before 1886, small tenants, known by then as 'crofters', held their land at will from lairds, whose main interests

166

were sheep farms and deer parks. The small tenants demanded that more land should be made available to existing tenants and landless Highlanders and also that all tenants should have security of tenure.

The main reason why crofting tenants did not have security of tenure at this time is not that crofting is an ancient landholding system based in traditional custom, but rather that it is the relatively recent product of social change and disruption in the eighteenth and early nineteenth centuries. As Hunter has documented in a recent book, *The Making of the Crofting Community* (1976), social change in the Highlands and Islands in this period proceeded at a rapid rate. The previous 'traditional' landholding system was one by which agricultural tenancies were held by a mixture of kinship ties with, and military obligations to, a clan chief. But after the Act of Union and the subsequent military suppression of Scotland, clan chiefs increasingly became landowning lairds, intent upon improving their land and obtaining a cash income. The agricultural population became subject to being moved, or 'cleared', from its holdings in order to make room for larger and more profitable sheep farms and, later, deer parks. New villages and townships were formed as the result of wholesale, and often brutal, evictions and the tenants, besides being forced to farm poorer land, were also obliged to seek wage labour in non-agricultural work in order to pay rents in cash rather than by labour or goods, as had previously been the case.

The 1886 Crofters (Scotland) Act established, in the seven Crofting Counties of northwestern Scotland (including the Hebrides, Shetlands and Orkneys) that form of land tenure which has dominated these areas ever since.[1] The croft is a small agricultural holding, consisting of arable infield and a share in moorland grazings, which last are administered on a township or village basis. Although the croft is held under tenure, the tenancy can be, and usually is, inherited. A state-appointed body, the Crofters Commission, regulates such inheritance and any other changes of tenant.

The crofting system is thus a recent, legal construction, which is the product of social change rather than a traditional form which has resisted social change. This is an important point, as will be seen later in this paper when the status of the 'cottage' in the cottage industry is discussed. With respect to the development of the Harris Tweed industry, a further important characteristic of crofting tenure is that few crofts have, or have ever had, the resources for self-sufficiency. Prior to the Act of Union in 1707, the small landholders of the Highlands and Islands combined subsistence agriculture with a variety of other activities, including raising cattle for trade with the south of Scotland and even England. From the eighteenth century onwards, it became increasingly important to obtain some form of additional income from wage labour. The most usual sources of this income were west-coast and foreign fishing, whaling, kelp manufacture,[2] seasonal employment on the mainland, construction and some small manufacturing industries. Thus the population of the Hebrides, prior to the passing of the 1886 Crofting Act, was already incorporated into the development of capitalism in the United Kingdom as a whole, and can for some purpose be regarded as a proletariat (Ennew 1980a: chap. 3). Yet, as we shall see, the production of tweed during this period was almost wholly limited to domestic use.

A critical factor in the development of this domestic occupation into the present Harris Tweed industry is the attitude of the British state towards problem areas such as the Highlands and Islands of Scotland. The conceptualization of an area as a problem area tends to change alongside economic and political development. Thus, in the eighteenth century, the Scottish, and later the British, crown found the Hebrides difficult to administer, because of their wild and remote location; and a problem, because of the refuge they offered to invading military forces. The solution was military intervention and economic colonization.[3] During the nineteenth century, as we have seen, a problem of poverty and famine was recognized by state and philanthropic organizations. Much of the misery was the direct result of landlords improving the resources of their land through clearances and kelp manufacture (Hunter 1976; Prebble 1969). Mass emigration of the 'redundant' population of the area was advocated and encouraged, on the model established in the nineteenth-century Poor Laws of both England and Scotland (Select Committee on Emigration 1841: 62, 82). According to these laws, the pauper was an indigent, a tax upon the ratepayers of a parish. One major aim of the legislation was to relieve the ratepayers of responsibility for the welfare of the pauper. Enforced migration to the colonies was one solution to the problem, as was the regulation of the poor, and their morals, within the workhouse system (Gilbert 1970: 51).

By the increased franchise allowed in the 1882 Franchise Act, legislative attitudes towards poverty and problem areas were radically altered. Universal male suffrage entailed that parliamentary power passed from the monopoly control of land- and property-holding classes. It was, for instance, as a direct consequence of this act that six 'crofter' members of parliament were elected in 1883, and crofting reform became possible (Hunter 1974). The problem of the Highlands and Hebrides gradually came to be seen as one of 'unemployment'; a word which appears in Hansard, the daily record of parliamentary debate, only after the Boer War (Gilbert 1970: 51f). The

168

solution to the unemployment problem at first followed the pattern of the Poor Laws in moving people into areas of employment by, for instance, establishing Labour Exchanges in 1905. But, since the 1920's the state has increasingly intervened by encouraging industry to move into areas of high unemployment in order to increase job opportunities. It is against this background that the development of the Harris Tweed industry must be examined (Ennew 1978a: chaps. 2 and 3).

One of the largest schemes of United Kingdom state intervention to ameliorate the unemployment of any problem area was the establishing in 1965 of the Highlands and Islands Development Board. The area which the Board has responsibility to develop coincides with the seven Crofting Counties. Its original remit was described as being 'a merchant bank with a social purpose' (Gilchrist 1971: 3), and the H.I.D.B. is unique in being the only government body with direct power to invest in private enterprise. In these roles, the H.I.D.B. has been involved in the recent history of the Harris Tweed industry. But, as we shall see, development in the early stages was brought about by a mixture of state intervention, private entrepreneurship and philanthropic concern. It was the attention of local land- and property-holding agencies which brought the first Harris Tweeds into the national market place. But the development of the industry was encouraged principally by state agencies: the Congested Districts Board and the Highland Home Industries Board. The latter, in particular, sought to encourage industrial growth from indigenous crafts through the development of cottage industries, along the lines established in the 'industrial revolution' of the south of the United Kingdom. In reports submitted to parliament in 1902 and again in 1914, all manner of indigenous crafts, or suggested possible crafts, were examined and, as a result, many attempts were made by the Board (monitored largely by the Congested Districts Board) to artificially stimulate the growth of these into large- or small-scale industrial enterprises (*Brand Report* 1902; *Scott Report* 1914).

One of the few success stories in the chequered history of this type of state intervention into industrial growth in the Highland region has been the Harris Tweed industry. The production of Harris Tweed has been limited to the Outer Hebrides by successive legislation or legislative acts. But the paradox is that this legislation has been protective, rather than specifically directed towards industrial development. The success of this state intervention depends not upon encouraging industrial development from craft, through cottage industry, to capitalist industrial enterprise, but upon the retention of certain cottage-industry elements. The very definition of Harris Tweed, in law, depends upon the production of the cloth within a

Judith Ennew

'cottage industry'. But this is not the cottage industry of the 'industrial revolution'. The Harris Tweed industry's conception of cottage industry is twofold, developed from and defined by legislation and the advertising industry. Both differ from the definition proposed in the introduction to this book, as they differ from other academic constructions. Market forces, legislation and academia have different motivations. But the consequences of these constructions for the worker within the Harris Tweed industry make it a particularly interesting subject for more than academic analysis.

THE COTTAGE INDUSTRY ACCORDING TO THE LAW

In legal terms, the Harris Tweed Certification Mark – or Orb Mark (Figure 6.1) – is the absolute property of the Harris Tweed Association. This body was formed in 1909 to protect the industry from mainland competition, and began actually stamping tweed in 1911. The Orb Mark is applied to each tweed by inspectors, who ascertain that each piece contains the requisite number of warp and weft threads. Each tweed is accompanied by a declaration form, signed by the weaver, which certifies that the cloth has been hand woven at home, and the inspectors tour the islands regularly to check that power looms are not used. If the inspector is satisfied that all the requirements of the Association have been complied with, the Orb Mark is applied, by means of a hot iron and transfer, at intervals of approximately three yards.

Fig. 6.1 The Orb Mark: registered trade mark of the Harris Tweed Association

170

The use of the Orb Mark is a hard-won privilege. In 1934, the legal definition was rephrased, after arguments about the use of mill-spun yarn. The new definition, which was upheld again in 1964, after the longest recorded judgement in the Scottish Court of Session, now reads that *Harris Tweed means a tweed made from pure virgin wool produced in Scotland, spun, dyed and finished in the Outer Hebrides and handwoven by islanders at their own homes in the Islands of Lewis, Harris, Uist, Barra and their several purtenances and all known as the Outer Hebrides.*

The statement that hand weaving takes place at the home of the weaver is designed to ensure that Harris Tweed remains, legally speaking, a cottage industry, despite the use of factory-produced yarn. This legal definition is the means by which the Certification Mark is recognized by the Board of Trade and also brings certain advantages in exports to the United States, where import tariffs are lower for 'cottage-industry' products. The necessity for appearing as a cottage industry also relates to the socio-economic and geographical circumstances of the Hebrides. Because of the unemployment problem, employment opportunities in the islands are, where possible, protected by the state. Harris Tweed has become an important source of employment. But transport over the thirty-mile stretch of water between the islands and the mainland adds enormously to the cost of any goods exported. One solution to this problem is to produce highly priced 'luxury' goods, which do not compete in the same market as, for instance, cheaper textiles produced in bulk in more accessible areas. Harris Tweed is a high-quality, durable textile with considerable aesthetic appeal. But these characteristics are not functions of the fact that it is produced in the Outer Hebrides. Other textiles of similar quality were produced on the mainland before 1934 and marketed as Harris Tweed, without the Certification Mark. The Mark is not simply a sign of quality; it is the mark of a protected industry, and the unique features which it can guarantee on the market, over the above quality of workmanship and materials used, are the location of production and the manner of production. The Outer Hebrides and the Harris Tweed weavers thus became the focus of legislative intervention.

THE COTTAGE INDUSTRY ACCORDING TO THE MEDIA

The marketing of Harris Tweed takes place within a particular complex of ideas about the Hebrides which I have called elsewhere the 'Hebridean Myth' (Ennew 1978a; 1980b). This is related in media usage to the construction of the Celtic Fringe, which is formed from those areas of the United Kingdom which have been mythologized as wild and natural since the eighteenth century, when they served as the location of much of the material used by the Scottish Enlightenment philosophers for developmental notions of society (Meek 1967). More recently, Chapman has suggested that these areas serve as a foil for the definition of the industrial and Anglo-Saxon areas of the United Kingdom. In an investigation of the function served by the Celtic Myth in the production of English identity, Chapman points out that the romantically conceived Celtic regions are represented as a picture of the departing 'tradition', with which the modernity of urban, industrial existence is perpetually contrasted. Since the eighteenth century, these areas 'have posed for the urban intellectual as a location of the wild, the creative and the insecure' (Chapman 1978: 18).

It is helpful at this point to examine one example of this mythologizing process, as it affects Harris Tweed in the media. In 1976, the BBC television series *Nationwide* produced a series of programmes on the Hebrides. Magazine programmes such as this, which are screened at the early-evening, peak, family-viewing times, frequently show similar series, under the rubric of discovering little-known, or remote areas of the United Kingdom (or, as it is invariably referred to in this context, the British Isles). The emphasis is always upon the ancient as opposed to the modern, the traditional as opposed to the industrial, the folk as opposed to mass society. In this way, the media draw upon, and reinforce, the Celtic Myth.

The subject of one programme in the 1976 series was the Harris Tweed industry. This was described as producing a unique textile, using handweaving methods, which competes with the techniques and production processes of mass production, in industrial parts of the United Kingdom and the rest of the developed world. The programme was made shortly after a vital controversy over the proposed restructuring of the Harris Tweed industry through the introduction of a power-driven, double-width loom. According to the programme's English presenter, these proposals were the result of the twentieth century finally 'catching up with' the Harris Tweed weavers, who were now 'facing the Industrial Revolution' albeit somewhat late in the day. The programme ended with the presenter himself slipping on a jacket made of Harris Tweed and surmising, as he fingered the lapels, that the garment could eventually become one of the 'museum pieces of the last, true cottage industry' (*Nationwide* 9 Nov. 1976; presenter James Fox).

In the *Nationwide* programme, the Harris Tweed worker who was chosen to represent the industry was a Mrs MacDonald of Harris, who actually engages in the entire process of production of the textile which she markets. She shears the sheep, spins and dyes the wool and finally hand weaves the tweeds. In fact, Mrs MacDonald's textile is probably the only cloth which can be described as 'Harris Tweed', in that it is entirely manufactured in Harris. But this textile does not bear the Orb Mark. At the time at which the programme was made, there were only three weavers of Orb Marked tweed in Harris; the remainder came from Lewis and all other production operations took place on the northern island.[4] Mrs MacDonald would not in any case be eligible for weaver status within the Harris Tweed industry because, as will be explained below, she is not a member of the Transport and General Workers' Union.

The television programme did admit that not all weavers can spin. This is an understatement. I doubt if any of today's Harris Tweed weavers can spin. But it did claim that all weavers work in barns or sheds, next to their traditional crofting homes. As has been pointed out, production in or near the home is crucial to the status of Harris Tweed in law, as it is one of the legal requirements which guarantee the textile as 'genuine' Harris Tweed. As far as the media are concerned, this home is the 'traditional crofting home', and is therefore a type of housing known as a 'black house'. Films about the Hebrides tend to feature this type of building, as if it were still the type of home inhabited by the majority of Hebrideans. The tendency is so marked that, when I visited Lewis in 1979 with a television producer, several Hebrideans expressed the desire that there should be 'no more films about black houses'. Yet for the media, as for the advertising industry, the cottage itself is one of the most important components of the cottage industry.

The way in which television and film are concerned with the Celtic and Hebridean Myths is part of a complex of media ideas in which literature, and to a certain extent academia, collaborate (Ennew 1980b). The misty Hebrides of 'tradition' is evoked even in the standard work on the Harris Tweed industry, which is published in a series of books about the offshore islands of the United Kingdom, which are essentially guides for the discerning tourist (Thompson 1969). This book shows photographs of traditional processing: spinning wheels, hand carding, and the finishing processes carried out at a communal work feast, known in Gaelic as *luadh* or waulking. Many of the photographs date back to the early years of this century and the book also contains details of early dyeing procedures using Hebridean flora; records Gaelic terms now seldom in use; and sets down some Gaelic waulking songs which are now likely to be heard only at singing competitions during a *Mod* or Gaelic festival. This would be no problem if the book made it clear that this is part of the history of Harris Tweed, but (as is usually the case with the production of the Hebridean or

173

any other Myth) chronology is collapsed, and past and present production processes are not clearly distinguished.

THE COTTAGE INDUSTRY ACCORDING TO THE ADVERTISING INDUSTRY

Literature promoting Harris Tweed in the international market is produced under the auspices of the Harris Tweed Association. This advertising material is structured around the elusive but unique quality of 'authenticity' which Harris Tweed offers in addition to its more concrete advantages: those of a well-made, durable textile. The latter qualities perhaps justify its status on the market as an expensive commodity, but it is 'authenticity' which converts expense into 'luxury'. Thus:

> Harris Tweed has a world wide reputation for quality and versatility. Nowhere else do natural environment and traditional skills combine to produce hand woven fabric of such excellence.

> It has survived in a world of falling standards and mass production because it has been developed and adapted to provide styles and colours of the present day without sacrificing its origins and authenticity; and the authenticity – symbolised and protected by the Orb Mark.

> . . . It is a unique textile which unmistakably mirrors the beauty, and the resilience and the magic of its Scottish island origins . . . (*Harris Tweed Handbook* 1975: p. 4 of unpaginated pages)

It is interesting to note the way in which this advertisement evokes and utilizes the Celtic Myth, by equating mass-production processes and modernity with 'falling standards' and contrasting this with authentic, traditional origins. Then the image of the good life is reinforced with words like 'beauty', 'resilience' and even 'magic'.

The representations of the advertising industry, like those of the media, imply that Harris tweed is a hand-woven textile, that traditional processes are used in its manufacture and that the industry is not yet involved in capitalist relations of production. The individual weaver, like Mrs MacDonald of Harris, who is involved in all production processes, is almost invariably evoked by the media representations. The advertising image is similar to this, emphasizing that the industry has 'flourished in competition with larger, highly mechanized textile producers' on the foundation of the

self-employed weaver (*ibid.*; one-page insert, produced in four languages):
'At home, in his own workshop, often helped by his wife, the Hebridean
weaver is his own manager, foreman and craftsman weaver.' Thus one of
the qualities by which the textile is marketed refers to the production process. The cloth is marketed as the product of an individual worker, whose
labour is not bound by the forces of machinofacture and mass production.
His work is thus implied to be creative and non-alienative, for these are the
good (authentic) qualities of the cottage industry and its products. These
are contrasted with the 'falling standards' of industrial labour; as the advertising industry makes use of the dichotomies produced in the Celtic Myth.

Even within the advertising material, the paradoxes of the situation of
the Harris Tweed industry are not entirely concealed. I have noted elsewhere the contradiction in which the H.I.D.B. is caught by the dual remit
in which it is obliged to encourage industrial growth at the same time as
preserving the 'crofting way of life', which in this context is conceived as
pre-industrial (Ennew 1980a: 54). The Harris Tweed industry is in a similar situation. The image which must be 'sold' is that of the craft worker in
a cottage industry; but even the *Harris Tweed Handbook* cannot fail to
mention the activities of the spinning mills, from which the weavers
receive the already-warped yarn and to which they return the woven
tweeds to be finished and marketed. The realities of this production process will be examined in more detail later in this paper, but it is important
to note that Harris Tweed production takes place in a context of industrial
capital and that, however *isolated* the weaver may be geographically from
other producers and other parts of the production process, he is not *independent* either of capital or of industrial labour in the mills.

The role of mill workers is glossed over in advertising material in such a
way that it appears that little or no machinery is used, even in the mills.
Emphasis is laid upon those parts of the production process which are performed by hand, such as warping and darning. In a reference to the latter
process the *Handbook* states 'The pieces of tweed also pass through the
skilled hands of the mending department' (*ibid.*); yet this 'skill' is relatively
easily acquired.

Further problems arise over the origins of the materials used in the production process. As we have seen, the media prefer to show Mrs MacDonald
shearing her own sheep. The standard work on Harris Tweed discusses traditional dyes made from mosses and other natural products (Thompson
1969). The *Harris Tweed Handbook* starts its four-language insert, 'The
Story of Harris', with a picture of a Blackfaced sheep. But even the *Handbook* has to admit to the use of modern dyes within the spinning mills, and

knowledge of naturally ocurring dyestuffs is now almost entirely the province of antiquarians and historians. But the most interesting contradiction concerns the sheep. The Orb Mark definition merely stresses the use of '100 per cent Scottish wool' and the *Handbook* states that most of the wool used in Harris Tweed production comes from mainland Scotland. The Hebridean wool clip is too small and, in general, of too poor a quality to supply the industry. In any case, United Kingdom legislation requires that all wool produced for other than domestic consumption should be marketed through central Wool Marketing Boards.[5] But, despite making this admission regarding the origin of the wool, the *Handbook* still goes on to imply that the wool used for Harris Tweed is produced in a pre-industrial, community-based, traditional agricultural process. Having just mentioned the fact that most of the wool comes from mainland Scotland (where sheep farms tend to be large, and run as businesses), the *Handbook* switches to a spurious evocation of the pre-industrial good life: 'In the early summer, the island communities join together to round up and shear the local Black-faced sheep. This is a social occasion, and the women of the islands share work equally with the men.' In the next sentence, the wool is 'taken to the factories' so that, by elision and omission, mainland wool, its manner of production and the Wool Marketing Board, are excluded from the image of the 'cottage industry'.

Part of the evocation of the pre-industrial good life is the cottage, the home in which the legal definition requires handweaving to take place. The *Harris Tweed Handbook* prints a picture of a 'crofthouse'; a 'stone and thatch building' which it does admit is 'fast disappearing as the weavers replace them with more modern homes'. The photograph shows a 'black house' of the type featured so frequently in the media presentations which offend many younger Hebrideans. To write that these houses are 'fast disappearing' is an understatement. The black house can scarcely ever be seen on the islands, except as ruins besides new houses, in use as barns, or, in the village of Arnol on the west coast of Lewis, restored as a national monument for tourists to view.

The campaign to eradicate this type of housing began in 1830, when the laird of Lewis, Lord Seaforth, ordered that his tenants should build a partition in the one-roomed dwellings which people shared with animals. After 1879, the new proprietor, Sir James Matheson, offered improving leases to encourage people to implement this and other sanitary measures. Improvements were further expedited by the terms of the 1886 Crofting Act (*Brand Report* 1902: lxxv, lxxxvii, lxxxviii). Even the term 'black house' which is often applied to 'traditional housing' is not in itself tra-

6.1 Weaving sheds on a Stornoway council-housing estate

ditional. Originally, the Gaelic word for this housing was *tigh* (house); the addition of the word *dubh* (black) came only after new houses, satisfying the sanitary authorities (*tigh geal*: white house), were built in the islands after the 1880's (Fenton 1978: 35).

Today the most usual type of rural Lewis dwelling is a single-storey chalet-type house, often with an extra room added in a gable roof. In many cases, these houses are adjoined by the remains of the low, thatched, doubled-walled 'black house', which is now used as a byre, a storehouse or perhaps a weaving shed. If a weaver does combine this activity with crofting agriculture, the tweed will indeed be woven on the croft, within hailing distance of the house. But many weavers live in council houses in Stornoway, the main town of the Hebrides, and are fully employed weavers without crofting status. The combination of crofting and weaving is not, strictly speaking, traditional and is an uneasy marriage of poorly suited economic forms.

THE ORIGINS, 'SURVIVAL' AND 'AUTHENTICITY' OF THE COTTAGE INDUSTRY

It is interesting to examine the history of tweed production and to see how much of the present industry is a 'survival' of 'tradition' in the face of

Judith Ennew

pressures to industrialize. It will be seen that the industry is, in part, the product of state intervention and development schemes. It will also be seen that state intervention has been successful only because of capitalist intervention.

There are some reports that plaiding was exported from the Hebrides before the seventeenth century (*Scott Report* 1914: 2-5). But this trade died as the southern cloth industry grew, and, until the 1840's, weaving was not an economic activity in the Outer Hebrides at anything other than the household or domestic level. In the rent rolls for Lewis of 1718, one reads that some rents were paid in kind, in the form of bolls of meal, stirks, chickens, pounds of butter and, very occasionally, wool. Few sheep were kept by small tenants. It was landlords and tenants of large farms who kept flocks, which supplied wool to southern markets. Crofters on Lewis did not use wool or tweed for barter at this time. None of the early nineteenth-century extant rent rolls for Lewis mention rents paid in wool or tweed. This differs from St Kilda, one of the Hebridean outlying islands, from which tweed was the main article of export, paid as rent to the Harris factor (Steel 1975: 88-9). One of the fishing reports on the West Highlands and Islands, made in 1786, stated that the people of the area had no manufactures and emphasized that fish were the main potential source of wealth. All the crafts mentioned in this report have to do with fishing: coopering, net making, sail making and so forth. The sole exception is a manufacturing house, set up at Rodil in Harris, for spinning wool and linen thread, as well as twine for herring nets (Knox 1787: 5, 26-7, 38, 158). Most of the suggestions made then, and later, about the possibility of developing manufacture in the Hebrides, emphasize the use of hemp and flax rather than wool; one even mentions spinning lint from moss (Headrick 1800).

The fact that threads other than wool are mentioned can be understood by examining the list of exports from Lewis in 1855. Of the total value of £88,093, approximately 80 per cent was due to the fishing industry and less than 5 per cent was accounted for by wool (*Encyclopaedia Britannica* 1857: 9-10). This is hardly surprising, as it was not until the 1850's that the Lewis clearances resulted in farms large enough for the production of fleece in any quantity. The indigenous, small-tenant population did not depend upon sheep as a major factor in their mixed economy until the early twentieth century. Until then, crofter fishermen kept cattle and poultry, grew crops of barley and oats, and bitterly resented the sheep which roamed over the areas they had once farmed (Minutes 1895: 1059). A few sheep were kept by crofters, and the fleece spun for home consump-

178

tion. Mitchell, writing in 1883, described the people of Lewis wearing clothes of their own woollen manufacture, but these were hardly the heather-mixture patterns which are now sold as Harris Tweed. The people Mitchell saw were wearing plain clothing, the men dressed in browns and greys and the women in striped or coloured patterns (Mitchell 1883: 233). The Reverend W. A. Smith, who lived on Lewis for many years, in the mid-nineteenth century, stated that wool for domestic use was more often imported. Local wool was often left in natural colours and made into stockings because it was softer than the imported variety. Indigo blue dye (a relatively expensive import) was in frequent use, and crotal, a local moss, was used for dark brown dyes. But Smith reported that extensive knowledge of the use of natural materials for dyes was not common, and that commercially manufactured, purchased dyes were often used (W. A. Smith 1875: 61).

Some cloth was produced for local markets, particularly for the larger settlements of Stornoway, in Lewis, and Tarbert, in Harris. In 1844, the Earl of Dunmore directed some Harris weavers to copy his tartan in tweed, and used the cloth for his gillies. The cloth was so warm and waterproof that its qualities became well-known among the deer-stalking landowners. Lady Dunmore and a Mrs Thomas marketed some Harris-produced cloth in London between 1857 and 1888. The first Lewis-produced cloth is reported to have been sold in 1881 (*Scott Report* 1914: 33–4).

Evidence of the organization of production for the purely domestic sphere can be obtained from the older generation in Lewis and Harris. Many homes still contain spinning wheels and carding implements, and it is still possible to find examples of the original, ponderous wooden looms with hand-thrown shuttles which have not yet been taken away to mainland folk museums. Older women can describe how they clipped the wool from their family sheep, although written sources mention plucking rather than clipping (W. A. Smith 1875: 60). The fleece were carded, spun and dyed, using substances such as mosses from the moor in a large pot over the fire; all the women in the family took part in these operations. Frequently some of the processes did not take place in the home, and the washed wool would be sent to a carding mill in Tarbert or Stornoway, or to be spun on the mainland. Weaving was done in the long winter evenings and was usually, but not always, a female occupation. The woven tweed would be finished by groups of six women working together, singing rhythmic waulking songs in Gaelic.

Once the raw materials like indigo were imported and the product was offered for sale on the market, new forms of organization appeared. The

179

small producers for domestic use became rapidly enmeshed in the development of merchant and interest-bearing capital. The link with merchants frequently began because of a shortage of wool, which resulted from the small numbers of sheep actually kept by crofters. But a further factor was that a class of landless cottars and squatters had been produced by the clearances. These families had little or no access to the means of agricultural subsistence. Cottars lived in dwellings on the infield holdings, usually those of crofting kin. Squatters had an even more precarious existence on the common land. Cottars and squatters seem to have been more heavily involved in both indigenous fishing activities and the wage-earning opportunities presented by foreign fishing operations than the crofters. They were also quickly absorbed into weaving activities, as the demand grew from the external market. Thus, even from this early stage in its history, Harris Tweed production was not well integrated with crofting agriculture. Although tweed production was the mainstay of the cottar population, and provided opportunities for the crofters to earn cash to pay money rents, they were obliged to purchase wool from Glasgow and Leith. Local merchants provided the capital and received the profits of this trade (*Napier Report* 1884: 1039–40). In the Lochs district of Lewis in 1892, for instance, one village contained a total of twenty houses on twelve or thirteen holdings. Six or seven households were engaged in production of tweed for the market. But, as they had no grazings even for their very few sheep, they were obliged to buy wool from outside. The cloth was sold to a Stornoway merchant, who always paid in kind: sometimes food, sometimes more wool. To see the households through the production process, subsistence goods would probably be supplied on credit at high interest rates, for this was the case in the fishing industry in which the same merchants dealt (Ennew 1980a: 32). Raw material was usually also provided on credit against the finished product. Thus the producer was inevitably deeply in debt to the merchant. In the village of Ballallan in 1892, weaving was found to be on the decrease, because merchants were oversupplied and debts rapidly mounting. One crofter stated in evidence to the Royal Commission (Highlands and Islands) in 1892 that tweed was definitely not a growing industry on the island, because the crofters could not keep themselves supplied with home-produced wool. It was stated that unless cottars were given land, and crofters given more land, it would not be possible to graze more sheep or produce tweed at a rate profitable to the direct producers (Minutes 1895: 1008, 1067).

In addition to not having control over the raw materials, many weavers did not own their own looms. Frequently the loom was supplied, on credit, ɔy merchants; so the saying arose that one produced one tweed for oneself and another for the loom. In order to try to break the merchant hold on weavers, Mrs Stewart Mackenzie, whose family had once been lairds of Lewis, set up a selling agency, known as the Crofters Agency, in 1890. But this was ineffectual and the first relief for the weavers came with state intervention when the Scottish Home Industries Association was established as a limited company in 1896, and the truck, or barter, system for paying for completed tweeds in kind was eradicated. The *Scott Report* on the working of the Highland Home Industries Association states:

> It was found that some of the people who dealt at the depot at Tarbert in Harris were so poor that they were often in want of wool or necessaries between the time they began to make a web of cloth and the finishing of it and it was judged necessary to advance such commodities which comprised wool, dyes, meal, sugar. (*Scott Report* 1914:45)

Newspaper reports of the time show how bitterly merchants resented this interference in their activities (e.g. *Highland News* 1901-3: letter columns, various dates). But they compensated by setting up carding mills, as this operation was one of the production bottle-necks. The second mill to be set up was built in Stornoway by Aeneas Mackenzie in 1903.[6] This was seen as a great relief by the Commissioners for the Congested Districts Board of 1904:

> ... the poor people ... formerly sent their wool south, and after weeks of idle waiting very often got back some inferior stuff in place of their own good wool. Now they can come and see their wool carded, and return home the same evening. (*Congested Districts (Scotland) Sixth Report* 1904: Appendix C-33)

It is possible to gain some idea of the nature of the merchant class by gleaning details of the life of Aeneas Mackenzie from local newspaper reports. In copies of the *Highland News* (Western Edition) 1892-4, Aeneas Mackenzie was first described as a salvage contractor. His commercial activities included offering to sell cement to the Stornoway Pier and Harbour Commission and dealing in the import and sale of slates. He was involved in providing capital for tweed production, besides being the owner of the carding mill mentioned above. In addition he had considerable property in the town of Stornoway and he built and owned ships. His involvement in import and export of goods must have rested in part upon his access to this transport. Although there is no direct evidence that he owned fishing boats, he took an interest in fishing matters and was a prominent speaker at many heated public meetings on the proposed closed fishing season in the Minch. There seems little doubt that he was engaged in fish-curing activities, which usually entailed money lending, and it is clear from the evidence of at least one Sheriff's Court bankruptcy case that he was involved in lending money, at interest, to small fish curers. His position within Stornoway was of high standing. He was a Noble Grand of the Odd-fellows Brothers and a President of the Stornoway Athletic Club. His wife was a prominent member of the British Wives' Temperence Movement and Aeneas himself was described in one report as the 'head centre of Lewis Toryism' (*Highland News* 24 June 1893; 2 Dec. 1893; 16 Jan. 1894; 3 Feb. 1894; 17 Mar. 1894; 7 April 1894; 9 June 1894).

By 1906 there were two carding mills in Stornoway, and it was at about this time that the main focus of production moved from Harris to Lewis. Spinning also proved to be a bottle-neck, and with increased demand for the cloth during and after the first world war, it became difficult for the crofter-weaver to carry out all operations within the household. Mills on the islands, and on the mainland, took an increasing interest in both carding and spinning. The weaver gradually ceased to control the whole of the production process. There were also problems of quality control, which were related to the type of loom then in use, and to the limited ability of weavers who had previously been producing solely for domestic purposes. The selling organization required consistent quality of textile and con-tinuity of pattern in order to fill market demands. The various interested agencies took steps to control quality and improve skills, thus ensuring that Harris Tweed is not simply a survivor of folk skills and craft which have been passed down from generation to generation.

One changing factor is the traditional loom. The *bearst-bheag* (small loom) was in use until the end of the last century. In this model, the shuttle was thrown by hand and the yarn was wound on sheep-trotter bones, which were used as bobbins. The *bearst-mhor* (big loom) was introduced in 1900 and was based on the same principle, except that there was a box to receive the hand-operated shuttle. The Congested Districts Board encour-aged the use of this loom, and offered interest-free loans for improvement and purchase. This was part of a programme to make tweed more market-able. On the small loom it was only possible to produce narrow webs of tweed of limited use. Moreover, the colours produced by dyeing on dom-estic premises were irregular, because of the small pots used. Large boilers were supplied to weavers for this purpose. The Board's second report states that:

The people as a rule were accessible and glad to receive instruction and advice, although in some cases the instructor found on a second visit, that the workers reverted to their own more antiquated system, because it was less troublesome than the methods advanced (*Congested Districts (Scotland) Second Report* 1899–1900: Appendix IX, 22)

The next major change in the production process was to the Hattersley domestic loom. The first example of the Hattersley appeared on the islands in 1912, but it is only since the 1920's, when the island's proprietor encouraged the use of this loom, that this model, which is capable of weaving more intricate patterns, has been in general use.

The most important feature of the Hattersley is that it is not, strictly speaking, a handloom. The weaver simply provides the motive power for the treadle with his feet. This works the automatic shuttle devices. His skill is limited to tying in the broken threads and setting up and tying off

6.2 Weaver pedalling a Hattersley loom; note that the hands are not used

tweeds which arrive, already warped, from the mills. There is thus very little difference in skill between the operator of the single-width Hattersley, which produces cloth 29 in wide, and the operator of a double-width, fully mechanized loom. The real difference lies in the fact that the Hattersley worker is the source of power *as well as* machine minder.

THE WEAVERS IN TODAY'S COTTAGE INDUSTRY

In 1976, the Harris Tweed weavers of Lewis and Harris numbered just over 500, of whom only a handful lived in Harris (Figure 6.2). Only 20 were women. The average age was 55, and few men encouraged their sons to enter the trade. This may give the false impression that old skills are dying out, but it is usual for young men to migrate temporarily to the mainland in search of employment and to return and inherit the family croft in middle age, when they may well take up weaving. The reality of Harris Tweed production belies the rural myth of advertising literature. As already pointed out, textiles woven on a Hattersley loom are not hand woven but foot woven. The weaver does not touch the textile, except to tie in the warp, fill the shuttles and tie in the broken threads, as is done by a factory worker. Far from getting any creative pleasure from producing the cloth, many weavers loathe the work, seeing it only as an instrumental means to

6.3 Weaver tying threads

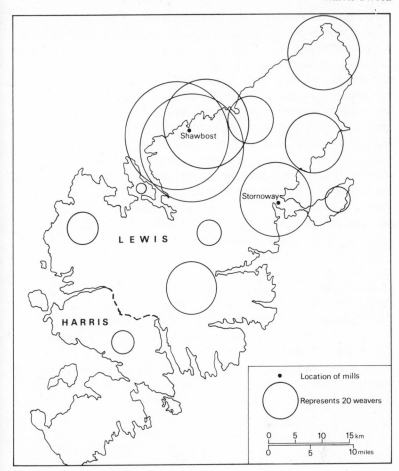

Fig. 6.2 Distribution of weavers by local district in 1976. *Source*: mills'
official issuing list

producing a cash income. Isolated in small huts, half deafened by the inces-
sant clatter of the loom, with eyes trained (often in poor light) upon repe-
titive patterns like herringbone, watching for broken threads, many find
the job monotonous. As one weaver stated, 'I put cotton wool in my ears
and count the coin as I do it.' One Lewis man recently put his loom sym-
bolically outside the house and swore that 'even if tweeds were paid £100
a time', he would never return to the work. Another described the hard
work of keeping the treadle in motion, as 'like cycling uphill all day long'.

Judith Ennew

As Figure 6.2 shows, weaving activities are fairly evenly distributed around Lewis, even though transport difficulties and the centralization of the industry have prevented the more southerly islands from continuing to take part in production. Yet, as one Lewis weaver said, 'It does spread the coin around the island.' Without the tweed industry, rural areas would provide little employment and more men would be compelled to commute to Stornoway or emigrate to the mainland for work. Certainly, Harris Tweed was the mainstay of the Lewis economy in the 1930's when the fisheries failed. The boom years of the 1960's raised hopes of a new prosperity (Figure 6.3), and some weavers do seem to enjoy the work, like the man who said: 'Harris Tweed has been good to me. I left being an electrician 21 years ago to start. I like to be free. You can please yourself. When you are working as a weaver, you are working and being paid by results and we have produced something for everyone's benefit. There's monotony in every job, but I'd hate to work in a factory.'

The attributes most frequently mentioned as making a good weaver are intelligence, alertness and conscientiousness. In addition, weavers need mechanical aptitude in order to keep the loom maintained. The loom is in the possession and control of the weaver, who also owns his own shed and electrically-driven, bobbin-winding machine, which is often operated by his wife and children. Under the terms of the Orb Mark, the shed should be sited within 250 yards of the weaver's home. The advertising literature states, or implies, that this is a croft house, even when it is not a black house. But there are rows of weaving huts situated in the middle of a Stornoway council estate. The Stornoway weavers are virtually full-time

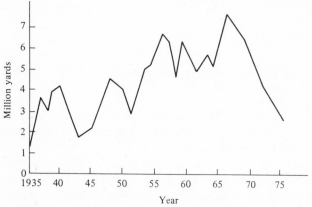

Fig. 6.3 Graph showing tweed production from 1935 to 1975. (Figures supplied by Harris Tweed Association)

186

workers and have no croft holdings. During good periods in 1976, their income could rise to £66 a week. They tend to work regular hours and to take coffee or tea breaks at set intervals. They can also be heard to be critical of 'part-time' rural weavers.

Weaving in rural areas used to take place in the winter months and, as long as this continued, it represented a perfect compromise between crofting agriculture and modern industry. But, because of market demands, (which have come about because the Harris Tweed industry has entered the fashion market), the most profitable time of year for weaving is from April to July; in other words, just that period of the year when crofters will wish to spend time in agricultural tasks. Thus it is not unusual for a man to spend three days a week during June out on the moor 'at the peats' and the remaining three pedalling in a small shed for ten to twelve hours a day. Earnings of £66 a week may drop to as little as £20 spread over three weeks during the winter; and when the mills close for three weeks in the summer there is no work at all. But at busy times, town weavers, who have no agricultural responsibilities, may suddenly have to weave a tweed in a hurry, so that the mills can complete a vital order; for the tweed may have been left unwoven for a month by a weaver in a remote rural area, while he planted his potatoes and cut his peats.

The official, government status of the weaver is 'self-employed', but this is a constant source of problems and ambiguities for the weaver and mills alike. None of the bodies with vested interests in Harris Tweed (the Transport and General Workers' Union, Spinners Federation, Harris Tweed Association, Highlands and Islands Development Board) have been able to solve this difficulty, despite the fact that a special case was made out for the weavers prior to the National Insurance Acts of the 1940's. The weavers resent paying a full National Insurance contribution, and many wrongly believe that if they were employees the full contribution would be met by the employer.[7] Because of their self-employed status, they are unable to claim benefits, such as sickness pay, when the mills are closed during the summer. They are of course eligible to apply for social security benefits during this time, but here again many labour under misconceptions. Some feel reluctant to apply for benefits, for, whereas unemployment and sick pay are considered a 'right', they regard social security as a 'charity'. This is not an uncommon attitude to social security within the United Kingdom, particularly among older people, who have memories of the harsh application of the 'means test' in the 1930's recession. Many object to the amount of information about their finances which they have to supply in order to apply for social security, and fear that they will be found 'in the wrong' by official bureaucracy. Many others simply fail to understand the bureaucratic process altogether. One otherwise progressive weaver grumbled that 'You could go on social security, but they send someone asking. If you are on social security *all* the time, then they don't ask. *They* get away with it.' Another complained, 'I filled in the forms one year, but they want you to do it every year. It isn't worth the trouble.'

The main difficulty lies in the relationship which self-employed status constructs between the weaver and the mills. Although the weaver is portrayed as an independent producer in the advertising literature, he is in effect an employee of the mill. Weavers do not belong to the anomalous Union of the Self Employed, but are members of the large and powerful Transport and General Workers' Union. Unless they have a T.G.W.U. card, they cannot get on the list which the mills use to distribute tweeds to weavers. This paradox is joined by another: weaver membership of the T.G.W.U. does not guarantee regular employment or wages. Union membership is thus useful for the mills' control of the scattered force of outworkers. Yet for the weavers it is primarily a negotiating structure for setting the piece-work rate for each tweed.

The difference between Harris Tweed production and textile production in, for example, a Lancashire mill, is that the tweed mill loses partial control over the production process while the tweeds travel back and forth across the island to the outworkers. This degree of mobility, which is required by the protective legislation incorporated in the Orb Mark, greatly increases the proportion of productive capital required by this stage of the production. The manifest increase in cost of this part of the process is taken up with transport costs, but the loss of mill control which it entails brings further, less obvious, costs. The mills are unable to monitor either quality of weaving or time spent in weaving. An entire order for fifty tweeds may be held up because one weaver leaves his tweeds to attend to his peats, or to go to a funeral. The mill is still able to exert some influence upon the process, partly through the distribution system, and partly through the system of fines, which are levied for mistakes in weaving. This could result in a weaver having to buy back from the mill an entire tweed, at a cost in 1976 of £23. Weavers referred to this as a 'fair system', and it is controlled by the Union. Moreover, the weaver is given four days of grace to come to the mill to assess the mistake for himself, before the fine is levied.

Like the employees directly employed by the mills in spinning, warping and finishing, the weaver depends upon the mills for a cash income. This dependence is directly experienced. During the winter, a weaver may often remark that he is 'grateful' for the few tweeds he is sent. From the weavers' point of view the tweeds arrive with no apparent regularity. The van delivering the tweeds is eagerly awaited and is the source of much gossip in rural areas. Within each small rural area, deliveries appear random and capricious, because the mills operate the distribution list on an island-wide basis. The weavers' list, negotiated by the T.G.W.U. in order to create a fair distribution of tweeds, is a crucial factor in weaver/mill relationships.

The principle of the T.G.W.U. list in 1976 was that mills agreed to send tweeds to weavers in strict rotation, with all mills working from the same standard list. The negotiations had begun because of animosity between rural and urban weavers. Country-based weavers claimed that those working in or near the town were able to visit the mills and collect extra tweeds. Men from the areas immediately adjacent to Stornoway were the objects of much suspicion from those in remote 'West Side' areas. It was supposed that they had friends or relatives working for the mills, who would ensure that the tweeds were sent. The system was changed again in 1977, because these suspicions were still being voiced. But distribution is bound to be unequal because of the differing abilities of the weavers. The skill necessary for producing the more complex patterns have often been mastered only by younger men, a fact which emphasizes that this industry does not avail itself of traditional skills which have been passed down through the generations. The Master List classifies weavers as A, B and C grade according to the patterns they can produce. Newer patterns require a certain amount of mechanical skill in setting up the tappets, even though the warp arrives already wound by the mill workers. The number of tweeds sent to a particular weaver depends partly upon his skill at tappet work, something which can be learnt from another weaver, but which is likely to have been learnt in the first instance from a course at the Lewis Castle Technical College in Stornoway. Special short courses were run at various times during the boom years of the 1960's, but many weavers did not trouble to take the course at the time because 'easy' tweeds were in abundant supply. These weavers are now graded low on the list. It has also been claimed that some weavers are low graded, because they claimed poor eyesight during the boom years; this was in order to ensure that only 'easy' tweeds were sent to them.

CAPITALIZATION OF THE COTTAGE INDUSTRY

From the moment of wool purchase, the production process of Harris Tweed is entirely in the control of mill-owning capital, except for the slight loss of control during the outworking phase. Until a few years ago, the production process of Harris Tweed was owned and controlled by several small mills, often family firms, situated either in the town of Stornoway, or at Shawbost on the west coast of Harris, The scattering of many small mills throughout the Outer Hebrides had effectively ceased before the second world war; and consolidation of mill-owning capital led to a concentration upon Lewis, with its better infrastructure and port and harbour facilities. During the 1970's, the capitalization of the industry was further rationalized. Small family businesses were gradually taken over or merged, until the spinning interests were largely in mainland hands. In 1976, there were two mills remaining in Stornoway. One, trading as Kenneth Mackenzie Ltd, is the historical successor to the second Stornoway carding mill, built in 1906. This particular branch of the Mackenzie family (it is a common island name) retained managerial function and controlled a proportion of the shares. But in order to avoid losing the mill altogether because of death duties, the family firm was taken over in the early 1970's by Scottish, English and European Textiles. The group has a policy of investing in small family businesses, and its Chairman, Jock Mackenzie, paid lip-service to the cottage industry ethos by claiming distant relationship to the 'Kenneth Mackenzie' family. But the enterprise had nevertheless effectively passed out of family control. In addition, Jock Mackenzie has a controlling interest in London and Scottish Securities, which, despite its name, is a European investment group. Thus Kenneth Mackenzie Ltd has come under the control of national and international capital, and can no longer be described as a merchant-capital enterprise, or cottage industry.

The second Stornoway mill has had a curious recent history. Its present structure, as Clansman Holdings Ltd, is a mixture of local and mainland capital, with the main shareholding in the hands of a state agency, the H.I.D.B. Thus the state protection of the industry, which began with the Highland Home Industries Board, continues. In an interim phase, however, Clansman Holdings was formed from mergers of smaller mills, which caused many redundancies among mill workers. This was at the instigation of a local man, but one who had heavy involvements in international capital, multinational corporations and international trade in general. He attempted to bring the Clansman Holdings part of the Harris Tweed industry into direct competition with mainland textile producers, encouraging an entry into the bulk textile market as well as diversification into other textile fields, such as carpet manufacture. Local feeling ran heavily against these plans and union action by mill employees caused sufficient labour problems for this financier to withdraw his interest. The H.I.D.B. interest in this venture was therefore seen as something of a rescue operation to protect jobs. It was also part of an H.I.D.B. initiative taken with respect to Harris Tweed, because H.I.D.B. investment in industry in the Highland region was, at the time, being overshadowed by the heavier investment potential of the oil industry in the area.

Outside Stornoway, in the village of Shawbost, which lies at the centre of the heaviest concentration of weavers, though not of production, one mill remained in family control in 1976. Unlike larger Stornoway mills, this company had not been seeking large overseas markets and bulk orders. The directors had followed the policy of keeping the scale of production small, at the optimum size to survive economic recessions. Smaller mills, and mills which had attempted to expand with insufficient capital to tide them over periods of recession, had all been taken over or gone into liquidation. The decision not to enter the bulk market was not always due to wholly *capitalist* reasoning; on at least one occasion family feuds over control of the mill led to some members of the family selling property on the mainland in order to invest in the mill. But marketing policy was based on a conscious decision to remain within the traditional home markets for men's jacketings and coatings, so that any export of fancy produce provides only a bonus to basic income. The Stornoway mills, on the other hand, rely heavily upon foreign fashion and upholstery markets and are subject to consequent heavy fluctuations in seasonal demand. This had had a disastrous effect upon the supposedly symbiotic relationship between crofting and weaving because most weaving work is available during the months of heaviest agricultural activity. The conflict of interests has led both to a decrease in agricultural activity and the concentration of weaving in the urban area.

FACTORY WORKERS IN THE COTTAGE INDUSTRY

Because weavers are the pivot of the advertising of Harris Tweed, it is often forgotten that the mills employ a sizeable work force, which is engaged in the other operations of textile production. In 1971, the mills employed 1,000 members of the total Lewis and Harris employed work force of 7,500. Compared with this, the number of weavers at this time was about 900, but not all of these could be regarded as fully employed in weaving.

Mill workers, like weavers, are members of the T.G.W.U., but their union membership is more straightforward and they do not belong to the special weavers' branch, which really only operates as a negotiating structure. Nevertheless, union activity has a specific Hebridean flavour which is related to the typical Lewis deference/defiance attitude towards the mainland in general, as well as to the paternalism of the island industrial structure (Ennew 1978b). Shop stewards, secretary and branch chairman have, until recently, acted less as troubleshooters or agitators and more as collectors of dues and complaints. They are also channels of information (*from* management) rather than channels of communication between management and workers. Typically, they are incomers to the island or people with mainland work experience and typically they tend to send for mainland union officials to negotiate as soon as trouble brews. Their social relationships with workmates outside the factory, and the ideal of equalitarian relationships with the 'bosses', makes it difficult for them to cope with conflict and confrontation. When the 'bosses' themselves refer to 'the Union' they tend to mean, not shop stewards or labour force, but rather the outside officials who visit the islands in times of crisis and have a reputation for un-Lewislike troublemaking. The visiting officials have a corresponding tendency to view the islanders as troublemakers.

Island union officials and management, together with local spokesmen and councillors, will usually deny that there are trade-union problems on the island and may forget the occurrence of past strikes and labour problems when recounting the history of tweed production. One shop steward at a Stornoway mill stressed the continuity of union–management relations, while omitting entirely his own active participation in a recent strike, which had been well documented in the local press. 'My own boss' (the managing director), he recalled, 'told me when I took over as shop steward in 1962, that he was glad it was someone with common sense and to come straight to him if I couldn't get satisfaction with any gaffer [foreman]. I've done that ever since. I can go straight to the top any time. I've thought the world of him for that.'

Few local management personnel will go as far as the ex-millowner who claimed that 'The worst thing that ever happened to this island was the Transport and General Workers' Union.' But some staff, particularly those from the mainland, will admit to the existence of conflict. One man, who had been in management in a Stornoway mill, complained of the director's attitude to his labour force, under the egalitarian ethos, in these terms: 'It was a one-man band, he was going over my head to my staff.' He found it difficult to understand the Lewis labour force's attitude to trade-union activity and claimed that negotiated deals were often not accepted by the work force and that there was no worker solidarity. 'They are quiet because of unemployment.' He also claimed to have been present at a management meeting of all mill owners regarding a very small wage claim (in

1966–7, when the average weekly wage was £12). According to his account, one mill owner asserted that there was no need to offer mill workers an increase, because many of them were crofters, and he backed up this assertion with the words, 'They don't have to *live* on it, because they've got their sheep.'

THE LABOUR PROCESS IN THE MILLS

With respect to the actual labour process within the mills, the Harris Tweed industry definitely does not resemble the popular notion of a cottage industry. The machinery is large and noisy and the Stornoway mills occupy a large area of land, on which it is possible to drive from one section to another along internal roads. With the exception of designers and dyers (who in Mackenzie's, in 1976, happened not to be local men) and the small numbers of weavers employed in the mills to weave samples, the only skilled occupation is warping. But even this is only a semi-skilled occupation and requires no formal training. Simple warping can be learnt in about two days, although more complicated designs can only be warped by experienced men. Nevertheless, reliable warpers are in demand by the mills, who may keep them on the payroll during slack periods rather than risk them moving to employment at another mill. Carding and spinning machines, on the other hand, need only to be minded, and a watch kept for broken threads to be tied in. After the tweeds return from the weavers, they are examined and darned to repair any mistakes and then washed, shaped and pressed before being stamped with the Orb Mark by officials of the Harris Tweed Association.

These mill tasks are all semi-skilled, acquired through experience. For the various washing and milling operations, the work force is flexible, taking part in any or all of the processes as need arises during the course of a week. There are thus no demarcation problems and workers in nearly all parts of the factory seem to be more than willing to oblige management and accommodate themselves to the logistics of production at any one time. As demand is seasonal, there is little certainty of continuity of employment. Workers are subject to being laid off work, with no definite security about being re-employed. They also endure short-time working and week-about arrangements (working on alternate weeks) with consequent reductions in income. Rationalization of the industry led to massive redundancies in the 1970's, particularly when there was a decrease in demand for tweed between 1970 and 1977. Only warpers appear to have relatively secure employment, but even they can be laid off or made redundant.

6.4 Darning the woven tweeds, Stornoway factory

Despite uncertainties of employment, the mill workers appear to be relatively satisfied with their working conditions, for the mills provide some employment on an island with both unemployment and under-employment problems. Mill workers are also eligible for unemployment and sickness payments, unlike the weavers. They do not seem to join in the pessimism of weavers who frequently assert that 'there's no future in the tweed'. Instead of grumbling about slack periods and calculating their annual income to ta!·ε short-pay periods into account, mill workers describe their income in terms of the *weekly* rate during *good* periods. Slack times are accepted as integral to the nature of the industry; features for which 'the boss' is not responsible. The 'good' worker accepts the vagaries of the external world with resignation and trusts management to re-employ him when better times return.

THE ATTEMPTED TRANSFORMATION OF THE COTTAGE INDUSTRY

As we have seen, the capitalization and labour process of the Harris Tweed industry tend to belie the rural myth of the advertisements. It is now possible to look more closely at the events of 1976, which the *Nationwide* programme, alongside other media representations, implied was a case of a cottage industry refusing to enter the twentieth century.

A vital factor in the discussions of the double-width proposals was the special weavers' branch of the T.G.W.U. The chairman of this branch in 1976 was never heard to describe himself as an outworker, or to analyse his position, despite frequent references to the 'power of the mills'. Few other workers take the alternative stance of pride in being independent 'craftsmen' or even attempt to describe themselves as independent producers. Indeed, this latter description is usually applied to those few men who operate small workshops, employing one or two employees, and producing luxury cloth on mechanized looms outside the Harris Tweed structure. The Harris Tweed weavers, caught in a paradox, unable to fight for their rights as either independent craftsmen or proletariat, are 'grateful' for the tweeds sent by the mills; the work is monotonous but 'it brings in the coin'. They feel, as one weaver described it, 'a captive work force'. This is a description which can be applied to any wage labourer, but not one which is usually made by the worker himself, unless some militancy is involved; and in this case the worker is reduced to 'gratitude'. Indeed it could be argued that the freedom of labour under capitalism, by which the labourer is free to sell his labour on the market, without being tied by feudal or kinship obligations, is here denied. This is partly because high unemployment, and thus the lack of alternative work, ties the worker to the employers in the negotiations with trade unions (which can be modelled on kinship obligations) and the gratitude of employees for work is similar to feudal obligations. But it should be noted that this suggestion does not imply that these types of reaction are survivals of pre-industrial social relations; they are more likely to be produced by the situation of unemployment, which in itself is produced by the nature of capitalism in the United Kingdom (Ennew 1980a: chap. 3).

Events in 1976 showed that if weavers have the power to speak and act, they are capable of displaying solidarity and of manipulating that power. The proposed introduction of double-width, power weaving showed up many of the anomalies of the weavers' situation, while apparently trying to

195

solve them. The suggestions were made 'for the weavers' own good', by all the agencies interested in Harris Tweed production. From the mill owners' point of view, the introduction of power weaving would be one further step in the progressive rationalization of the industry; one which would enable them to gain control over the entire production process. The weaving population was expected to be contained, within set working hours, in small factories. In order to maintain the craft image, these were always referred to as 'workshops' during negotiations (at least by management and the Harris Tweed Association). They were to be situated at three points on the island and their purpose was to eliminate the ambiguities of the self-employed status, to control quality and maintain more efficient output.

For the H.I.D.B., and the Harris Tweed Association, double-width weaving would prolong their paternalistic state control of the industry, at the same time as fulfilling the long-term aim of solving part of the Hebridean unemployment problem. But they were hard put to explain how the workshops could be part of a symbiotic crofting/weaving relationship; to explain to part-time weavers that redundancy payments were better than occasional income from tweeds; and to justify how this industrial development fitted with the ideal of the 'crofting way of life'. The motivation of the T.G.W.U., whose mainland officials were involved in the development of double-width proposals, is even more obscure. Perhaps the intention was to serve the weavers' branch by removing the self-employed anomaly, and mainland officials made a great point of having secured redundancy payments for those previously self-employed weavers who would not be employed in the workshops. What was important to all agencies was the support of the weavers. Unless this could be obtained, the Board of Trade would not consent to changes in the legal definition of the Orb Mark, and the protected status of the Harris Tweed industry would be lost.

From the weavers' position, the double-width controversy arose suddenly and unbidden, threatening many with redundancy, while assuring permanent employment for a few. Nevertheless, it gave them the power of veto, the first power they had experienced in an industry which had been run 'for their benefit' for seventy years.

The suggestion that Harris Tweed should be made in a double width (rather than the meagre 29-in width produced on the Domestic Hattersley) arose from what were considered to be marketing problems in the 1960's. In bulk markets, for women's clothes and furnishing fabrics, the narrow cloth caused problems for machine cutting. Even hand cutting of garments from single-width fabric entails a great deal of wastage. In a textile market which is already threatened by competition from man-made fibres, the difficulty of selling narrow Harris Tweed to bulk buyers has been blamed for the decline in demand for the cloth in the 1970's.

The initial impetus for double-width manufacture arose within the Spinners' Federation, which represents the millowning interests. Clearly they had the most to gain from an increased demand for both yarn and finished cloth, if the industry could successfully compete in the bulk market. It is difficult to pinpoint an exact date or agent for the initiative. Discussions about the use of power for Harris Tweed production have been an integral part of the history of the fabric; and, in addition, the discussions and experiments took place in an atmosphere of secrecy. Nevertheless, rumours about double-width changes were current from the early 1970's, and discussions had probably been taking place, in private, ever since the Scottish Court of Session ruling over the Orb Mark in 1964. The first known strategy was initiated by the Harris Tweed Association, in close collaboration with millowners and management. A double-width '*hand*' loom was produced and subjected to trials. As expected by many of those involved in the trials, it proved too heavy to operate; the weaver could not provide sufficient motor power from the treadle to throw the shuttle the full width of the loom. But the use of power looms was prohibited by the terms of the Orb Mark. Thus these terms had to be adapted.

Although the millowners claimed that the old concept of the Harris Tweed production was outdated, and that what was needed for success in modern markets was increased rationalization of the industry and better machinery, most weavers seemed to prefer the economic theories which lay behind the idea of the protected industry which produces a luxury good. Paradoxically many weavers pointed to the small manufacturers on the island who produced other 'tweeds' for luxury markets, such as Jaeger and Aquascutum, in double width and without the benefits of the Orb Mark. Weavers argued that Harris Tweed should remain within the luxury market and not attempt to enter bulk markets. The success of some independent small producers demonstrates that entering luxury markets is one successful way of counteracting high transport charges. It could deny the need for the Orb Mark protection. But the Orb Mark does work for weavers around the island; it not only spreads the coin, it also spreads the work. Power weaving in three workshops would continue the geographical spread, but limit the number of men who were actually engaged in income-generating activity. Town weavers were as vigorous in protest as rural weavers, simply because they would suffer proportionately more redundancies than rural 'part-time' weavers. A further argument was that power weaving in sheds would necessarily entail an excess production of Harris

Tweed, even if fewer weavers were involved. Thus the textile could easily lose its unique rarity and thus its place in the luxury market. There is a fine line between luxury good and bulk market, which, once crossed, cannot be retraced; and this was one argument put forward by the weavers. They considered that 'modernization' was unnecessary and that the maintenance of the conditions of the Orb Mark only added a greater protection for the industry as a whole. For the weavers, the double-width power-driven loom did not seem to be a reasonable solution to their problems. They see the main difficulty as lying in the anomaly of the self-employed status. They argued that this could easily be moved by a revised definition as 'outworking employee', without threatening either the terms of the Orb Mark or the apparent 'craft' status of the industry. There is no logical reason why a craftsman has to be self-employed.

Amid all these considerations, the process of discussion and negotiation was long, often devious and frequently acrimonious. For five years, the weavers did not know what to think about their future employment and were provided with only partial information by the Spinners' Federation, T.G.W.U., H.I.D.B. and Harris Tweed Association. In 1976, a proposal for double-width reform was drawn up and presented to the weavers at two meetings. The first, a closed meeting, was addressed by the T.G.W.U. Scottish Secretary, who outlined the employment (and redundancy) prospects of the proposals. The second, a public meeting, was addressed by a Lewis-born public figure who was at that time a member of the Harris Tweed Association, the H.I.D.B., the Crofters' Commission and happened also to be the local newspaper proprietor. His oratory is well known on the island; thus a generally voiced opinion in Stornoway during the previous week was that weavers were expected to yield to his eloquence and accept the proposals. Yet weaver-power was absolute at this moment, for without their permission no proposals would be made to the Board of Trade. The choice which the speaker set before them at the meeting was simply one between total unemployment in the fact of declining demand for tweed on the one hand, and on the other redundancy pay for many but the incentive of becoming mill employees for the few who would be fully employed in the weaving workshop.

Much to the surprise of the agencies involved in drawing up the double-width proposals, weavers revealed no gratitude for these attempts to guarantee employment for a core of workers and 'save' the industry. Indeed, they revealed a strong distrust of those who had been trying to 'help' them. Despite the reluctance of most Lewismen to speak in public, they voiced their dissatisfaction with double-width proposals in words which were often incoherent, but which always had a very clear import.

Some weeks later they showed their dissent even more forcibly in a postal ballot with a 94-per-cent poll; 497 voted against the proposals and only 55 weavers were in favour. The *Stornoway Gazette* commented:

> Perhaps it was an indication of their confidence in the result that no weavers, other than the four involved in the count, bothered to turn up at the Harris Tweed Association Office ... to hear the result being declared. (*Stornoway Gazette* 24 May 1976)

CONCLUSIONS

This paper has had two intentions. The first is to link the development of marketing techniques for the Harris Tweed 'cottage industry' with the complex of ideological constructions which combine to form the Hebridean part of the Celtic Myth. This is more than a literary exercise, because it reveals that the positing of certain structures as 'traditional' has both economic and political consequences. The structure of the H.I.D.B. and the Harris Tweed Association alike show how the construction of the 'crofting way of life' produces certain policies of development, even defines which areas should be developed and the type of development which is regarded as correct. What is interesting about the development of the Hebrides is that it has a long and well-documented history of different kinds of development since the sixteenth century; Harris Tweed may be regarded as a particular case of this. The second aim is to illustrate that one of the more interesting aspects of the Harris Tweed cottage industry is the way in which state and private interests have combined, or at times been in conflict, in the production of the present structure of the industry. The case of the 1976 restructuring proposals is particularly interesting, because it shows how this structure produced an essential conflict of interest, in which workers were aligned against, not only state and management, but also the labour movement. The unique feature of the Harris Tweed industry in this context is not its 'authenticity' as a cottage industry, but rather that the protective legislation, which was derived from attempts to protect the employees against unemployment in one context at the end of the nineteenth century, actually worked to protect them against unemployment caused by possible redundancy in the very different situation of 1976. It is difficult to predict whether this protection will continue to operate to the workers' interest, or if the decision taken in 1976 was indeed the death knell of the Harris Tweed industry. But whatever the case, it should be obvious that the situation was far more complex than a simple conflict between the forces of tradition and those of modernity.[8]

NOTES

1 Introduction

1 See Quartey-Papafio 1913–14 for an account of the shift from kinship norms to money contract in apprentice–master relationship in nineteenth-century Ghana. See also Morgan 1966 for same process in Puritan New England.

2 In Kashmir the carpenters who made wooden window and door frames, and doors, were different from those who made furniture. There were stonemasons who cut stones for builders, others who fashioned grindstones and quirnes, and others who carved figures. There were iron workers who made cooking pots, others who made ploughs and hoes, others who made swords and daggers, others who made axes and knives and still others who made locks and keys. (Rybakov, quoted in Blum 1961; Baer 1964; District Officer's notebook, Kashmir 18th c.)

3 Geertz lists the following trades which involve commodity production (I am omitting those which involve only the selling of services or commodities): slipper maker, mason, saddle maker, weaver, potter, charcoal maker/seller, baker, floor layer/excavator, butcher, blacksmith, stone cutter/quarry worker, mule skinner, silk merchant/spinner, radio repairman, garage mechanic, shoemaker, tailor of ready-made Western clothes, tailor of cloaks (*jellabas* and *selhams*), sewing-machine tailor, kaftan tailor, watchmaker, ploughmaker, mattress factory, soap factory, modern carpenter/sawmill owner, weigher/measurer, carpenter, traditional plumber, tinsmith, button maker, cord maker, bicycle repairman, horseshoer, photographer, goldsmith/jeweller, Western-style tailor (different from tailor of ready-made Western-style clothes, above), glazier. (From Geertz 1979: Table A.2, pp. 269–71.)

4 The more one learns of this period the more it emerges as combining many important new trends (Cipolla 1976). Obviously I have had to be selective here.

5 This discussion is based on Carus-Wilson's long chapter in Postan and Rich (eds.) 1952 and on Thrupp's chapter in Cipolla (ed.) 1972. The Postan and Rich volume has been in the course of revision for several years, and I had hoped to be able to consult the new edition, but this has not proved possible.

6 The complete title is: 'The Clothier's Delight, or, the rich Men's Joy, and the poor Men's Sorrow, wherein is exprest the Craftiness and Subtility of many Clothiers in England, by beating down their Workmen's Wages.' Quoted in Mantoux 1961: 75–7.

7 Allusion to the truck system.

8 Special conditions of production in mining and metallurgy industries make these exceptions.

9 This has subsequently been given detailed documentation in Lis and Soly 1979.

10 Related inventions appeared: in 1598 an Englishman invented a machine for knitting stockings, the stocking frame. Ridiculed at first, both in England and France, by the beginning of the eighteenth century it had almost entirely displaced hand knitting of stockings for the market. Another key invention was a machine for twisting silk threads, invented in Italy sometime before 1621 when it was described in a treatise on mechanics printed in Padua. By what must have been one of the earliest instances of industrial espionage, drawings of the machine were procured by John Lombe early in the eighteenth century, and the first factory containing power-driven machines for spinning was built in England in the 1720's. Many more followed, and by the middle of the century there were several centres of production. But the silk industry never became important in England (due to the need to import the raw silk). But clearly during the sixteenth and seventeenth centuries there was already a lively interest in the design of machinery for various processes in the textile industry (Mantoux 1961).

11 When spinning wheels were first introduced in Europe (1298) there were regulations against the use of wheel-spun thread in warps (Baines 1977: 53).

12 This cloth went northeast to Bornu, north to the desert Tuareg and westward with caravans throughout the Sudan.

13 The government used cotton cloth for the army, and as salaries for government officials and employees. Cloth was also used to barter for horses and livestock with the northern nomads. Total government requirements were established at between 15 and 20 million bolts annually (Chao 1977:21).

14 The Blackburn Mission to China, which in 1896–7 travelled widely to study cotton textile production, discovered only one factory, in Szechwan. Cited in Chao 1977.

15 This is of course the same argument that Medick used in relation to the persistence of rural industry in Western Europe. The difference is that in the Chinese case the domestic group is not jointly involved in cottage industry, exploiting its own labour as a production unit in a single production process. Rather the women are 'exploiting themselves' for the cotton-textile industry, while the men are involved in other forms of production. Since poverty and debt drove the women to work for such low payment, presumably the men were not paid enough to support the family; they too were 'exploiting themselves'.

Perhaps Medick would argue that because the profit from the self-exploitation of the Chinese poor was not concentrated in the hands of a single merchant-manufacturer, but split between farmers and others who employed the men and the merchants who bought the women's thread and cloth, it did not form a sufficient differential profit to finance the establishment of cotton-textile factories. However, Chao specifically insists that there was capital available for such investment in China, and it was not a lack of capital that prevented the establishment of cotton factories.

16 These comments on Chinese textile production are based mainly on three secondary sources and cannot pretend to be more than exploratory. There may well be important material on China that would alter the picture given by these sources, though they are by scholars of Chinese economic history with wide command of primary sources.

2 On commoditization

1 A major attempt to tackle this problem was a collection of anthropological essays on African markets (Bohannan and Dalton 1962) whose editorial introduction was influential in the 1960's.

2 Sir John Hicks' universal history of the market (Hicks 1969) falls into this theoretical trap, but his insights are indispensable to the project outlined in the present paper.

3 There is an ancient debate over the logical/historical priority of steps 3 and 4. The early political economists derived the utility of commodities from the division of labour, whereas French sociologists such as Durkheim insisted on the independence of human sociability from any system of complementary material needs.

4 The relationship between commodity and form is explored at greater length, but still briefly, in a conference paper which is the basis for much of this one (Hart 1979).

5 Any parallel between my version of Marx and classical revisionism (of the kind laid out at the turn of the century by the German socialist Eduard Bernstein) is fully intentional. Social evolution seems to be more characteristic of industrial capitalist development than revolutionary class struggle.

6 The *locus classicus* is the opening chapter of the first volume of *Capital* (Marx 1965).

7 See Mauss (1967), Durkheim (1933) and Lévi-Strauss (1969).

8 There are two main English sources for this famous passage – the *Grundrisse* (Marx 1973: 471–514) and the edition introduced by Hobsbawm (1964).

3 Daboya weavers

1 I had been advised against working in Daboya by Gonja friends who said that there was no longer any weaving there. This misinformation

is a result of the pattern of marketing which is oriented to traditional buyers, and bypasses completely market stalls and modern stores.

2 It was to the Bakarambasipe elders that I was 'given' when I told the WasipeWura that I wanted to learn about weaving.

3 The Old Mosque is a small building standing between the Big House and the Small House and is used for religious services and the Koranic school by all the men of Bakarambasipe. It is, in a sense, neutral territory in terms of status contests between the three Bakarambasipe *kanang.*

4 Although, within a generation, age is the major principle of seniority, this is sometimes overridden by other factors. Mallam Asiiku is older than his full brother Mallam Abudu, yet it is the latter who is recognized as the senior within Bakarambasipe. At first I found this confusing. For instance, I was sent to Mallam Asiiku by the WasipeWura, but he told me to go home and come again in the morning. When I returned, it was Mallam Abudu who spoke to me. Gradually I realized, though this was never put into words, that publicly one referred to Mallam Asiiku, but it was really Mallam Abudu who managed the affairs of the Small House, and who was recognized within Bakarambasipe as the most senior elder. This is particularly clearly borne out by the fact that it is Mallam Asiiku who greets his younger brother in the early morning, and not the other way round. The *de facto* leadership of Mallam Abudu is due to his very evidently superior managerial ability which is reinforced by his four active adult married sons. Mallam Asiiku has no adult sons, and his adult daughter is married elsewhere.

5 The political significance of greeting in Gonja is discussed at length in 'Greeting, Begging and the Presentation of Respect' (E. Goody 1972).

6 The only time I found difficulty in combining the roles of pupil weaver and ethnographer was when I had learned the basic skills and, instead of sitting at the loom all day, would sometimes plead the need to greet a funeral or attend a case in the WasipeWura's court. 'You don't like to sit [at the loom] at all . . .', grumbled my teacher. By this time I was weaving on his thread, i.e. for his profit.

7 See E. Goody 1973 for a discussion of the concept of immediate authority.

8 This argument is interesting because the narrow cloth strips that come off the traditional West African loom must be sewn together to make the cloth which is then either worn as a cloth (by women) or tailored into men's smocks and gowns. However, most of the Daboya cloth is sold in the form of strips to itinerant traders. If cloth were woven in a width ready for wear or tailoring, this would alter the role of the visiting trader.

9 On my brief visit in 1976 I looked to see if a home-made Daboya version of the warping frame had been brought into use. There was no sign of one.

4 The tailors of Kano City

1 This paper is based upon fieldwork undertaken during 1974–6 when the author was resident in Kano City. It forms part of a Cambridge University Ph.D. thesis, entitled 'The Survival of Indigenous Tailoring among the Hausa of Kano City' (forthcoming).

I would like to thank the Canada Council for funding the fieldwork. I owe Dr Esther Goody a special debt of gratitude for her assistance in the writing of this paper. Thanks are also due to Dr Alan Frishman for providing me with data from his own research on small-scale industries in Kano.

2 Some areas of the city were called after the kinds of craftwork found in them. For example:
Dukawa – leather workers
Soron D'inki – tailors
Lokon Makera – blacksmiths
Kwalwa – cloth beaters and dyers.

3 These figures come from *British Government Colonial Blue Books* and *Nigerian Government Trade Reports.*

4 Other factors of importance in accounting for the survival of indigenous tailoring include (1) the growth in Hausaland's population over the past seventy years, (2) increases in *per capita* consumption of clothing by that population, and (3) the lack of investment by larger Nigerian and foreign capitalists in the local production of Hausa clothing styles. For reasons of space, I have omitted more detailed discussion of these factors.

5 Population size is a contentious issue in Nigerian politics. The figure of over 10 million is for 1977 and is based on estimates made by Davidson in the article cited in the text. *New African Magazine* (July 1977) gives a population figure of 8,126,000 for Kano State in 1976.

6 In 1976 a third firm, employing fifteen persons and specializing in the production of children's dresses and shirts, was established by a former Hausa employee of the Ministry of Trade and Commerce with financial backing from an American missionary. The aim of the firm's owner was to penetrate the northern market for children's clothes. This firm may mark a new departure in Hausa clothing production in that the owner used sophisticated sewing-machine equipment (albeit, second-hand), employed people, including non-Hausa women, on a time-rate basis, organized the production of exclusively non-Hausa-style clothing, and using his own car travelled throughout the north selling large quantities of clothing in the main towns and cities. However, in 1975 the plant was not fully operational.

7 These data on Kano City tailors should be considered as providing minimum estimates of the total number of people engaged in tailoring. My reasons for this are the following. First, not all wards were examined in the 1972 survey by students at Ahmadu Bello University and many were under-counted. In the three wards studied by the author,

the survey revealed a total of only 3 workshops and 9 tailors whereas my own count, in December 1975 and January 1976, showed a total of 133 workshops and 337 tailors. Second, the survey ignored the many hundreds, perhaps thousands, of secluded Hausa women who engage in tailoring on a part-time basis from the privacy of their homes. Third, the city also contains large numbers of Koranic students who do cap-making as a means of supplementing their meagre income. Fourth, many men who hold down full-time jobs outside tailoring also do tailoring as a part-time activity. Finally, in a number of villages close to the city there are many farmers who do tailoring either for direct sale in the city or who work on a putting-out basis for city-based merchants and other intermediaries.

If all these persons are included, the total number of tailors in the city or living close by and disposing of what they produce through the city, is considerably in excess of the 1,098 figure given in the 1972 survey. I would estimate the total to be over 3,000.

8 For reasons of space, I cannot deal in detail with women tailors. In summary, the position of women tailors is as follows:

(a) Women make a substantial contribution to the production of specific lines of clothing and women tailors can be found throughout the city.

(b) Much of this clothing is produced by secluded married women.

(c) Most women tailors are hand sewers although a few utilize sewing machines.

(d) The main item of clothing produced by women is embroidered caps known as *zanna bukar*, of which there are many styles. Women cap makers produce caps for private sale and for sale to the many male cap dealers in the market.

(e) There is some ward specialization among women tailors. Thus, in Soron D'inki one finds hand *jalala* embroiderers who sell to local horse-caparison dealers. In fact, hand *jalala* embroidery is increasingly regarded as women's work, although women have always done such work. In Yalwa women do hand embroidery of Eastern-style gowns on a putting-out basis for men. They also sew the inside seams of garments (*sab'iya*). In Hausawa women assist male tailors, usually but not always kinsmen, in cutting cloth shapes for caps, button-holing and the hand weaving of the *linzami* sewn into the necks of gowns.

(f) Cap making is usually own-account work, whereas other types of sewing, as in (e), is more commonly done on a putting-out basis.

(g) Money obtained from sewing, as from other work, is used by women to fulfil various female social obligations, particularly the purchase of household goods for female children which the latter take with them when they marry.

(h) Sewing is but one of a wide range of female economic activities which are largely hidden from the public eye, and which give women a measure of economic independence from their husbands.

9 Although all wards contain a few tailors, I estimate that the wards listed in Table 4.4 account for over 50% of all tailoring workshops in the city.

10 Alkali: Islamic judge

11 The increase in numbers of women hand *jalala* makers is part cause and consequence of the declining attractiveness of such work as a full-time male occupation. However, male embroiderers are still regarded as producing the best-quality *jalala*, and dealers can distinguish the work of male tailors from that of women.

12 Fika (Fika and Zubairu n.d.) reports that the man who originally settled here was from Kofa village in Kiru District, Kano Province, although he provides no explanation of why the man came to Kano. However, the explanation of how the ward got its name is substantially the same.

13 However, only the Emir could wear the *alkyabba* (burnous) with the hood up. In addition, some informants pointed out that nouveau-riche merchants who had become wealthy during their lifetime were admonished by members of the ruling class for wearing clothes of superior quality to those of their fathers.

Imam Imoru (Ferguson 1973: 314) also mentions a regulation against commoners (*talakawa*) using the more elaborately embroidered saddle covers.

14 Many workshops contain more machines than are being used at any one time. In addition, some of the larger workshops contain self-employed tailors working alone who are borrowing working space from bigger operators.

15 Exchange Rate (1975/6): 1 Naira = approximately 75 English pence. Average Daily Wage in Manufacturing (1975): N1.77 kobo.

During 1975 the national minimum wage for government employees increased from N312 p.a. to N720 p.a. This, and other increases within the public sector, sparked off a number of wage claims within the private sector leading to a general rise in wage rates throughout the formal sector of the economy. However, for the mass of the population incomes did not keep pace with the awards granted to the minority. In particular, none of the tailoring work force acquired increases in income through government action as the increases applied only within the industries possessing work forces with enough industrial muscle to force benefits from employers.

During 1975 there were major price increases as traders and merchants attempted to obtain some of the benefits that public and private sector employees had achieved. Among tailors, artisans raised their commission rates, while among market-oriented tailors attempts were made to raise the selling price of clothing. This move was, in part, a response to the increased prices such tailors were forced to pay to cloth merchants.

Industrial action was taken by a number of cap makers in Hausawa who were squeezed between rising cloth prices and stagnant market prices for their finished products. Some increase was obtained after a somewhat disorganized work stoppage among cap makers, both employers and employees. However, one or two producers were hard hit by this stoppage and many did not heed the call to stop producing, preferring instead to make their own private arrangements with market traders. This action, along with another employee withdrawal of labour in one workshop in Kwarim Mabuga ward, was the only case of industrial action I heard of during the period of fieldwork.

Food prices in Kano, November 1975	
Millet (measure)	N0.50k.
Rice (measure)	N1.60
Guinea corn (measure)	N0.50
Groundnut oil (beer bottle)	N0.85

Source: P. Lubeck: 'Labour in Kano Since the Petroleum Boom', *Review of African Political Economy*, 13, May–August, 1978, p. 41.

16 As good Muslims they neither eat nor drink during daylight throughout the month of Ramadan, so these very long hours must be especially tiring.
17 Training time is much less in some cases. For example, to become proficient at machine cap making can take as little as six weeks.
18 This is not perhaps surprising, as the workshop head considered it a waste of time to teach people who would leave at the first opportunity to do something more interesting.

5 Production and control in the Indian garment export industry

1 The field research on which this paper is based was carried out over three consecutive years, December 1976–January 1977, December 1977–April 1978, and December 1978–January 1979, and was financed by grants from the Social Science Research Council, the Smuts Memorial Fund and the University of Cambridge Travelling Expenses Fund. I am particularly indebted to the owners of Paville Fashions Pvt. Ltd for their hospitality and their unbounded generosity in giving me access to all their company's operations; to their employees; and to the handloom manufacturers and weavers of Cannanore.
2 Baker (forthcoming) cites a price of Rupees 15/- in the early 1900's, rising to Rupees 30/- by the late 1920's.
3 The main South Indian weaving castes are: the Kaikolans – mainly Tamil weavers who are also to be found in Telegu country speaking Telegu, and who are also known as Sengundars and sometimes take the

title Mudaliar; the Devangas – with both Canarese- and Telegu-speaking subsections, and also known by the titles or names Jadaru, Jada, Dendra, Devara, Dera, Seniyan, Sedan, Settukaran; the Sales – Telegu speakers scattered throughout the former Madras Presidency who have three subsections, Pattu Sale, Padma Sale and Karne Sale; and the Patnulkarans – a large 'immigrant' group of Saurashtrian weavers (Thurston 1909: *passim*).

4 Baker (*ibid.*) shows that by the 1940's some 40 Devengas controlled 1,600 looms in Coimbatore, and, in Madurai, 50 yarn dealers ran the industry led by 4 elite families.

5 There have been frequent government reports on the state of the handloom industry, from the first decade of this century to the present day. The idea of forming weavers' societies or cooperatives was first mooted in 1907, but not until the 1930's was the idea of cooperative organization adopted by the government, and some time later, in 1941, the first direct move towards a subsidy policy was made when the government decided to commission cloth rather than give relief at a time of great distress. During the 1940's the weaving cooperative movement began to develop. During the second world war and immediately afterwards the government introduced, removed and reintroduced regulations controlling the supply of yarn to the mill and the handloom industry, and developed a market-sharing policy (Somasundram 1967: vol. II, 3–4). In 1952 the independent Congress government, committed both economically and by policy to the support of the handloom industry, set up the All India Handloom Board.

6 Garment exports escalated from a value of Rupees 150 million in 1971 to Rupees 2,450 million in 1976 (Govt of Maharashtra 1977: 1) and the share of cotton apparel in the total exports of cotton-textile items increased from 11 per cent to 42 per cent in 1975 and 50 per cent in 1976. By 1976 74 per cent of all cotton garments exported were made from handloom fabric (*ibid.*: 54).

7 *Hobson–Jobson: A Glossary of Anglo-Indian Colloquial Words and Phrases* (Yule and Burnell 1903: 147) reinforces this impression, in its explanation of the word *calico*.

> The word appears in the 17th century sometimes in the form of Calicut [the Malabar trading port], but possibly this may have been a purism, for calicoe occurs in English earlier . . . The quotations sufficiently illustrate the use of the word and its origin from Calicut. The fine cotton stuffs of Malabar are already mentioned by Marco Polo (ii. 379). Possibly they may have been all brought from beyond the Ghauts, as the Malabar cotton, ripening during the rains, is not usable, and the cotton stuffs now used in Malabar all come from Madura.

8 The Izhavas (Ezhavas, Illavars, Ealavars), who are known in south Cochin and north Travancore as Chovans, in north Cochin and south Malabar as Thandus, and in north Malabar as Tiyyans (Tiyars, Tiars or Thiyyas), are the most numerous caste in Kerala, and have a repu-

tation for industriousness. Their hereditary occupation is usually given as toddy tapping, but the Travancore census of 1881 showed that approximately 50 per cent of the workers were general labourers; 20 per cent were 'put down under agriculture'; 19 per cent were toddy drawers; 2.5 per cent were cotton weavers; 2.85 per cent were traders and smaller numbers were stone quarriers, domestic servants, toddy contractors, boatmen, carriers, rope makers, astrologers, leaf plate makers, distillers and food manufacturers (Nagamaiya 1884: 219). In 1903 an Izhava uplift society – the Sri Narayana Dharma Paripalana Yogam – was formed, and this gave rise to a prosperous upper- and middle-class minority. The majority remain poor and are still employed as agricultural and industrial workers and toddy tappers (Rajendran 1974: 2–6). See also the classic studies by Aiyappan (1944; 1965).

9   The German Mission had industrial establishments in both Cannanore and Calicut. During the first world war these were taken over by the Commonwealth Trust. The Cannanore unit was later sold, but the one at Calicut is still an important concern.

10   A number of these families are closely interrelated.

11   I was told in 1978 that the cost of a jacquard fitted loom was Rupees 5,000, while the machine for punching cards was as much as Rupees 10,000.

12   The institution of 'master weaver' did not really exist previously in this region. The Cannanore manufacturers told me that they had consciously imitated the Tamil model.

13   The Factory Act (1948) ordinances apply to all units which employ ten or more persons on powered machinery, or twenty or more persons on non-powered machinery.

14   The garment company which features in this paper has its own fabric-development officer, who travels widely in South India, and a small unit for fabric development and sampling in Trivandrum.

15   I did though find a number of large units which depended on putting out winding work to households.

16   This figure was obtained from the primary data of a handloom census made by the Kerala State Government Department of Industries and Commerce in 1977.

17   *Beedi*-cigarette making, which is another small-scale industry, was on an upsurge in 1978. It is ideally suited to the deft fingers of young boys, and it was very clear that it was at that time providing a direct alternative to weaving, that some of the same kinds of manual skills were being used, and that some of the cigarette makers who were the children of weavers were, or could be, as deft on a loom.

18   In 1968–70, world trade in clothing was increasing fairly rapidly. The major producers and consumers were Western industrialized nations, but Japan and Hong Kong were emerging as increasingly large suppliers. India stood sixteenth in the league of world trade in clothing. Her strength lay in the production of cotton garments, but the proportion of cotton to synthetic fibres in world trade was declining.

Whereas the largest importing countries were the U.S.A. and Western Europe, over 50 per cent of India's exports were going to the U.S.S.R. and Eastern Europe. The first half of the 1970's showed a number of changes in this pattern. India's exports increased at a much faster rate than the world rate (though the growth of the clothing industry in Hong Kong, South Korea and Taiwan dwarfs hers), and this represents a vast increase in the number of manufacturing units (Govt of Maharashtra 1977: 26–30); the bulk of the exports are now sold to the U.S.A. and Western Europe; and fashion garments overshadow uniforms and utility clothing.

19 In April 1977 the son of the family moved to the U.S.A., which at the time was the company's major export market, to run sales from there, and in spring 1978 a managing director was appointed. He was a Saraswat Brahman and a relative of the family.

20 This was a 10-per-cent sample of each of the major work categories, as they stood in March 1978 – i.e. 52 tailors and 30 helpers. In the smaller groups higher percentages were interviewed, and selection was in some cases inevitably less random.

21 Some tailors did increase their income by working in sweat shops for an additional four hours a day in the morning or evening.

22 The justification made by the Director of the British Textile Confederation (Letter to the Times 16 May 1977) rested on the argument that India was passing off machine-made as 'genuine Handloom' products. His definition of handloom implied that the garment must also be hand sewn; that machine-sewn garments made of handloom cloth counted as machine-made; that the massive increase in shirt and blouse exports did not fall into the U.K.'s handloom quota, and thus exceeded the agreed quota for machine-made shirts.

23 A worker to be classified as permanent must have worked an established number of working days for a company in a twelve-month period, otherwise he/she has temporary-worker status, and less security. Many employers have deliberately exploited this loophole in the law.

24 These Delhi manufacturers were thought to be subcontractors and possibly nominees of much larger concerns.

25 In the winter of 1978 the company did begin to retail in India on a small scale, and established a shop in the newly completed trade centre in Bombay. During 1979 it extended its retail efforts further.

26 The number of cotton export garments made in Maharashtra rose from 13 million in 1973 to 42 million in 1976, while exports of non-cotton garments remained steady at 2 million. Cotton garments for the domestic market rose from 52 million units in 1973 to 95 million in 1974 but fell back to 90 million in 1975 and 88 million in 1976. Non-cotton domestic garments followed the same pattern, rising from 16 million units in 1973 to 44 million in 1974, then dropping to 40 million in 1975 and 1976 (Govt of Maharashtra 1977: 48). This pattern was typical of India as a whole. The following year (1977–8) the national export figures for cotton handloom garments show a drop of over 50

per cent in value from Rupees 1,736 million to Rupees 845 million (Source: Handloom Export Promotion Council).

6 Harris Tweed: construction, retention and representation of a cottage industry

1 The 1956 Crofters (Scotland) Act did not make any appreciable change in crofting tenure, although its intention was to consolidate small crofts into larger, more profitable holdings. This was resisted by the crofters themselves who formed the Crofters Union to lobby against the proposals. The 1976 Crofters (Scotland) Act has made it possible for a crofter to purchase the holding, or part of it, from the landlord, but this has not led to any large degree of private ownership by crofters of crofting land, particularly in the Western Isles.

2 Kelp is the generic name of a type of seaweed, as well as the name of the alkaline product of this seaweed when burned. This product is important in soap and glass manufacture. In the late eighteenth and early nineteenth centuries, when formerly cheap imports of barilla (a similar alkaline substance) from the Caribbean were prevented by the naval blockade of the Napoleonic wars, it was possible to make large profits from kelp production within the United Kingdom. Scottish lairds were not slow to encourage their tenants to leave their agricultural land in order to join the labour-intensive process of burning kelp on the seashore. The 'wages' for kelp burning were calculated in cash and offset against arrears of rent. Thus tenants were forced into a form of bonded labour for the landlord in this disguised type of wage labour (Gray 1957: 129–31; Ennew 1980a: 21–2).

3 Between 1599 and 1610, James I of England and VI of Scotland encouraged a group of mainland lords and mercenaries, known as the Fyfe Adventurers, to invade certain parts of the Hebrides and seize control of local fishing resources. After some setbacks, the expedition was successful and the lairdship of Lewis changed from 'local' Macleods to mainland Mackenzies. (Ennew 1980a: 19–20).

4 As can be seen on the map (Figure 6.2), Harris and Lewis are not separate islands, but different parts of the same island. Geographically, they are divided by a band of difficult, mountainous terrain; they also have quite distinct landscapes and agricultural characteristics. Lewis is largely peat bog, whereas Harris is bare granite with small patches of arable soil. Historically, they were the provinces of separate Macleod clans. Under state regulation, they were, until recently, administered by separate local authorities.

5 I have no information as to how Mrs MacDonald of Harris evades this legislation; but, as her product is well known, it would possibly be poor publicity for her to be prosecuted. Or it could be that she represents one instance of the rather generalized tendency towards permitted relaxation of administration in the Western Isles, some islands of which for instance, have no requirement for driving licences.

6 Mackenzie is a very common island name, resulting from the numbers

of mainland followers of the Seaforth family, who settled on the island after 1610. As clan kinship was often fictive, there is no need to assume that this or any other Mackenzie has any connection with the laird, or (as the name was originally mainland) have any local connections at all.

7 Under the British National Insurance scheme, which provides the government with the income for welfare payments (such as sickness, unemployment and retirement benefits), those in regular employment pay a proportion of their weekly income towards a 'National Insurance Stamp'; the remainder of the levy is made up from the employer's contribution. The self-employed naturally pay the whole of the levy from their income, at a different flat rate (1976).

8 This situation has undergone further changes since 1976, but the principle remains the same as when the data for this paper were collected.

REFERENCES

Abubakar, S. 1970. 'The Emirate of Fombina, 1809–1903', Ph.D. thesis, Ahmadu Bello University, Zaria

Adamu, M. U. 1968. 'Some Notes on the Influence of North African Traders in Kano', *Kano Studies*, 1:43–9

1978. *The Hausa Factor in West African History*, Ibadan

Adeleye, R. A. 1971. *Power and Diplomacy in Northern Nigeria, 1804–1906*

Aiyappan, A. 1944. 'Iravas and Culture Change', *Bulletin of the Madras Government Museum*, N.S., General Section, vol. V, no. 1; Madras 1965. *Social Revolution in a Kerala Village*, Bombay

Ajayi, J. F. A. and Crowder, M. (eds.) 1971. *History of West Africa* (2 vols.), London

Al-Hajj, M. 1968. 'A Seventeenth Century Chronicle of the Origins and Missionary Activities of the Wangarawa', *Kano Studies*, 1:7–16

Aliyu, Y. A. 1974. 'The Establishment and Development of Emirate Government in Bauchi, 1805–1903', Ph.D. thesis, Ahmadu Bello University, Zaria

Arnett, E. J. 1922. *The Rise of the Sokoto Fulani*, Kano

Baer, G. 1964. *Egyptian Guilds in Modern Times*, Jerusalem

Baines, P. 1977. *Spinning Wheels, Spinners and Spinning*, London

Baker, C. J. (forthcoming). *The Tamilnad Countryside*, Oxford

Balogun, S. A. 1970. 'Gwandu Emirates in the Nineteenth Century, with Special Reference to Political Relations: 1817–1903', Ph.D. thesis, Ibadan University, Ibadan

Barth, H. 1890. *Travels and Discoveries in North and Central Africa*, London

Bautier, R-H. 1971. *The Economic Development of Medieval Europe*, London

Bloch, M. 1967. *Land and Work in Medieval Europe*, Berkeley

Blum, J. 1961. *Lord and Peasant in Russia*, Princeton

Bohannan, P. and Dalton, G. (eds.) 1962. *Markets in Africa*, Evanston

Bowden, P. J. 1971. *The Wool Trade in Tudor and Stuart England*, London

Brackenbury, C. F. 1915. *Madras District Gazetteers: Cuddapan*, Madras

Braimah, J. A. and Goody, J. R. 1967. *Salaga: The Struggle for Power*, London

Brand Report, 1902. Report to the Secretary for Scotland by the Crofters

Commission on the Social Conditions of the People of Lewis in 1901 as compared with twenty years ago

Braun, R. 1966. 'The Impact of Cottage Industry on an Agricultural Population' in D. Landes (ed.), *The Rise of Capitalism*, New York

Broudy, E. 1979. *The Book of Looms*, New York

Buchanan, F. 1807. *A Journey from Madras through the Countries of Mysore, Canara & Malabar*, 3 vols., London

Bythell, D. 1969. *The Handloom Weavers*, Cambridge

Carter, A. T. 1974. *Elite Politics in Rural India*, Cambridge

Carus-Wilson, E. M. 1941. 'An Industrial Revolution of the Thirteenth Century', *Economic History Review*, XI, 1, reprinted in Carus-Wilson, *Medieval Merchant Venturers*, London, 1954

    1952. 'The Woollen Industry', in the *Cambridge Economic History of Europe*, vol. II, *Trade and Industry in the Middle Ages*, Cambridge

Census of India, 1961. vol. V, part VIIA, *Selected Crafts of Gujarat*, Delhi

Chamberlin, J. 1975. 'The Development of Islamic Education in Kano City, Nigeria, with Emphasis on Legal Education in the Nineteenth and Twentieth Centuries', Ph.D. thesis, Columbia University, New York.

Chandra Sekhar, A. 1971. *Census of India 1971*, Series 1 *India*; Paper 1 of 1971 – *Supplement: Provisional Population Totals*, New Delhi

Chao, K. 1977. *The Development of Cotton Textile Production in China*, Cambridge, Mass.

Chapman, M. 1978. *The Gaelic Vision in Scottish Culture*, London

Chaudhuri, K. N. 1974. 'The Structure of Indian Textile Industry in the 17th and 18th Centuries', *The Indian Economic and Social History Review*, 11: 127–82

Cipolla, C. M. (ed.) 1972. *Fontana Economic History of the Middle Ages, Europe*, vol. I, London

    1976. *Before the Industrial Revolution*, London

Coleman, D. C. 1969. 'An Innovation and its Diffusion: the New Draperies', *Economic History Review*, XXII: 417–29

Congested Districts (Scotland) Reports 1898–1904 (nos. 2–6)

Conlon, F. F. 1977. *Caste in a Changing World: the Chitrapur Saraswat Brahmans*, Berkeley

Cox, A. F. 1894. *Madras District Gazetteers: N. Arcot*, 2 vols., Madras

Dalal & Co. 1964. *Textile Industry in S. India*, 11th edn, Dalal & Co., Madras and Coimbatore

Das Gupta, A. 1967. *Malabar in Asian Trade 1740–1800*, Cambridge

Davidson, R. B. 1977. 'How Many Nigerians?', *West Africa*, 20 August

Deloney, T. 1929. *Jack of Newberie*, in *Shorter Novels*, vol. 1, *Elizabethan and Jacobean*, London

Dietrich, C. 1972. 'Cotton Culture and Manufacture in Early Ch'ing China', in W. E. Willmott (ed.), *Economic Organization in Chinese Society*, Stanford

Dobb, M. 1946. *Studies in the Development of Capitalism*, London

Dobbin, C. 1972. *Urban Leadership in Western India: Politics and Communities in Bombay City, 1840-1885*, London

Durkheim, E. 1933. *On the Division of Labour in Society*, New York

Elvin, M. 1973. *The Pattern of the Chinese Past*. London

Encyclopaedia Brittanica, 1857 edn

Ennew, J. 1978a. 'The Impact of Oil-related Industry on the Outer Hebrides', Ph.D. thesis, Department of Social Anthropology, Cambridge
  1978b. 'Gaelic as the Language of Industrial Relations', *Scottish J. of Sociology*, 3: 51–68
  1980a. *The Western Isles Today*, Cambridge
  1980b. 'Hebridean Self-image and Identity', *Cambridge Anthropology*, 6: 129–42

Fenton, A. 1978. *The Island Black House*, Edinburgh

Ferguson, D. E. 1973. 'Nineteenth Century Hausaland, being a Description by Imam Imoru of the Land, Economy, and Society of his People', Ph.D. thesis, U.C.L.A., Los Angeles

Fika, A. 1978. *The Kano Civil War and British Over-rule, 1882–1940*, Ibadan

Fika, A. and Zubairu, M. (n.d.). 'Kano City Notes', unpublished MS, Department of History, Bayero University, Kano

Fischer, E. and Shah, H. 1970. *Rural Craftsmen and their Work: Equipment and Techniques in the Mer Village of Ratadi, Saurashtra, India*, Ahmedabad: National Institute of Design

Frishman, A. 1977. 'The Population Growth of Kano, Nigeria' (unpublished paper)

Fuglestad, F. 1978. 'A Reconsideration of Hausa History before the Jihad', *J. of African History*, 19: 319–39

Fuller, C. J. 1976. *The Nayars Today*, Cambridge

Geertz, C. 1979. 'Suq: The Bazaar Economy in Sefrou' in C. Geertz, H. Geertz, and L. Rosen, *Meaning and Order in Moroccan Society*, Cambridge

Gilbert, B. 1970. *British Social Policy 1914–39*, London

Gilchrist, A. 1971. 'Chairman's Comment' in *North 7*, X, 10:3

Goody, E. 1972. 'Greeting, Begging and the Presentation of Respect', in J. S. LaFontaine (ed.), *The Interpretation of Ritual*, London
  1973. *Contexts of Kinship*, Cambridge

Goody, J. R. 1967. 'The Over-kingdom of Gonja', in D. Forde and P. Kaberry (eds.), *West African Kingdoms in the Nineteenth Century*, London

Govt of Kerala 1977. Report of the working group constituted by the Govt of Kerala as suggested by the Reserve Bank of India to study the problems related to the credit requirements of Handloom Primary Societies and Apex Society in Kerala State

Govt of Maharashtra 1977. *Readymade Garment Industry in Maharashtra*, Indian Institute of Foreign Trade, New Delhi

Gray, M. 1957. *The Highland Economy 1750-1850*, Edinburgh

References

The Harris Tweed Association, 1975. *Harris Tweed Handbook*
Hart, K. 1979. 'The Evolution of Commodity Economy', paper presented at American Anthropological Association meetings, Cincinnati (Dec.)
1982. *The Political Economy of West African Agriculture*, Cambridge
Headrick, J. 1800. Report on the Island of Lewis contained in a letter to the Rt. Hon. Lord Seaforth, the Proprietor
Heard, N. 1970. *Wool: East Anglia's Golden Fleece*, Lavenham, Suffolk
Heathcote, D. 1972. 'Insight into a Creative Process: A Rare Collection of Embroidery Drawings from Kano', *Savanna*, 1: 165–74
Helleiner, G. K. 1966. *Peasant Agriculture, Government and Economic Growth*, Homewood, Ill.
Hemingway, F. R. 1907. *Madras District Gazetteers: Trichinopoly*, Madras
Hicks, J. 1969. *A Theory of Economic History*, Oxford
Hill, P. 1972. *Rural Hausa*, Cambridge
1977. *Population, Prosperity and Poverty: Rural Kano, 1900 and 1970*, Cambridge
Hiskett, M. 1973. *The Sword of Truth*, London
Hobsbawm, E. (ed.) 1964. *Karl Marx's Precapitalist Economic Formations*, London
1968. *Industry and Empire: An Economic History of Britain since 1750*, London
Hogben, S. J. and Kirk-Greene, A. H. M. 1966. *The Emirates of Northern Nigeria*, London
Hogendorn, J. 1978. *Nigerian Groundnut Exports: Origins and Early Development*, Zaria and Ibadan
Hopkins, A. G. 1973. *An Economic History of West Africa*, London
Hunter, J. 1974. 'The Politics of Highland Land Law Reform, 1873–1895', *Scottish Historical Review*, LIII, 1: 45–68
1976. *The Making of the Crofting Community*, Edinburgh
Hunwick, J. O. 1971. 'Songhay, Bornu and Hausaland in the Sixteenth Century', in J. F. A. Ajayi and M. Crowder (eds.), vol. I: 202–39

Innes, C. A. 1908. *Madras District Gazetteers: Malabar and Anjengo*, 2 vols. F. B. Evans (ed.), Madras
1951. *Madras District Gazetteers: Malabar* [only 1 vol. in 1951 edn.], F. B. Evans (ed.), Madras
Irwin, J. 1955. 'Indian Textile Trade in the 17th Century', *J. of Indian Textile History*, 1: 5–33
1966. 'Indian Textile Trade in the 17th Century' in *Studies in Indo-European Textile History*, J. Irwin and P. R. Schwartz (eds.), Ahmedabad

Jaggar, P. 1973. 'Kano City Blacksmiths: Precolonial Distribution, Structure and Organisation', *Savanna*, 2: 11–25
Johnston, H. A. S. 1976. *The Fulani Empire of Sokoto*, London
Joshi, H. and Joshi, V. 1976. *Surplus Labour and the City: a Study of Bombay*, Delhi

Kellas, J. G. 1966. 'Highland Migration to Glasgow and the Origins of the Scottish Labour Movement', *Bulletin of the Society for the Study of Labour History*, 12: 9–12

Kemp, T. 1978. *Historical Patterns of Industrialization*, London

Kessinger, T. 1974. *Vilayatpur 1848–1968*, Berkeley

Knox, J. 1787. *A Tour through the Highlands of Scotland and the Hebrides Isles in 1786*, David and Charles facsimile, 1975, London

Landes, D. (ed.) 1966. *The Rise of Capitalism*, New York

Last, M. 1967. *The Sokoto Caliphate*, London

Launey, R. 1982. *Traders without Trade*, Cambridge

Leach, E. R. 1960. *Aspects of Caste in South India, Ceylon and North-West Pakistan*, Cambridge Papers in Social Anthropology, no. 2, Cambridge

Lenin. V. I. 1964. *The Development of Capitalism in Russia*, Moscow

Le Roy Ladurie, E. 1974. *The Peasants of Languedoc*, Urbana

Lévi-Strauss, C. 1969. *The Elementary Forms of Kinship*, London

Lis, C. and Soly, H. 1979. *Poverty and Capitalism in Pre-Industrial Europe*, Hassocks, Sussex

Logan, W. 1887. *Malabar*, 2 vols., Madras

Lovejoy, P. 1973a. 'The Hausa Kola Trade (1700–1900). A Commercial System in the Continental Exchange of West Africa', Ph.D. thesis, University of Wisconsin, Madison

1973b. 'The Kambarin Beriberi: the Formation of a Specialised Group of Hausa Kola Traders in the Nineteenth Century', *J. of African History*, 14: 633–51

1978a. 'The Role of the Wangara in the Economic Transformation of the Central Sudan in the Fifteenth and Sixteenth Centuries', *J. of African History*, 19: 173–93

1978b. 'Plantations in the Economy of the Sokoto Caliphate', *J. of African History*, 19: 341–68

1979. 'The Characteristics of Plantations in the Nineteenth Century Sokoto Caliphate', *American Historical Review*, 84: 1267–92

Lowe, N. 1972. *The Lancashire Textile Industry in the 16th Century*, Manchester

Lubeck, P. 1979. 'Islam and Resistance in Northern Nigeria', in W. L. Goldrank (ed.), *The World-System of Capitalism: Past and Present*, Beverley Hills

Mantoux, P. 1961. *The Industrial Revolution in the Eighteenth Century*, New York

Martin, B. G. 1977. *Muslim Brotherhoods in Nineteenth Century Africa*, Cambridge

Marx, K. 1954. *Capital*, vol. 1, Moscow

1965. *Capital*, New York

1973. *Grundrisse*, New York

Mateer, S. 1883. *Native Life in Travancore*, London

Mauss, M. 1967. *The Gift*, New York

References

Medick, H. 1976. 'The Proto-industrial Family Economy: The Structural Function of Household and Family during the Transition from Peasant Society to Industrial Capitalism', *Social History*, 1976, 291–315
Meek, R. 1967. *Economics and Ideology*, London
Mehta, F. A. 1976. *Second India Studies: Economy*, Delhi
Mendels, F. 1972. 'Proto-Industrialization: The First Phase of the Industrialization Process', *J. of Economic History*, 32: 241–61
Miller, E. 1965. 'The Fortunes of the English Textile Industry during the Thirteenth Century', *Economic History Review*, 18: 64–82
Miner, H. M. 1973. 'Traditional Mobility among the Weavers of Fez', *Proceedings of the American Philosophical Society*, 117: 17–36
Ministry of Trade and Industry, Kano State, 1974. *Kano State Commercial and Industrial Handbook*
Minutes 1895. *Minutes of Evidence taken before the Royal Commission Highlands and Islands in 1892*, vol. II, Edinburgh
Mitchell, J. 1883. *Reminiscences of My Life in the Highlands*, 2 vols., David and Charles facsimile, 1971, London
Morgan, E. S. 1966. *The Puritan Family*, New York

Nadel, S. F. 1942 (1969). *A Black Byzantium*, London
Nagamaiya, V. 1884. *Report on the Census of Travancore*, Travancore
Napier Report 1884. Report of Her Majesty's Commission of Enquiry into the Conditions of Crofters and Cottars in the Highlands of Scotland
Narayanan, K. 1973. *Census of India, 1971*, Series 9, *Kerala*; part XA, *Town and Village Directory*; part XB, *Primary Census Abstract; Cannanore District*, Trivandrum
Narayanaswami, M. and Sri Ram, V. 1972. *The Garment Industry in India*, Economic and Scientific Research Council, New Delhi
Neale, W. C. 1957. 'Reciprocity and Redistribution in the Indian Village: Sequel to Some Notable Discussions', in K. Polanyi, *et al.*, *Trade and Market in the Early Empires*, Glencoe
Nicholson, F. A. 1898. *Madras District Manuals: Coimbatore*, 2 vols. (revised by H. A. Stuart), Madras
Nicolas, G. 1975. *Dynamique sociale et appréhension du monde au sein d'une société hausa*, Paris
Nigeria, Annual Abstract of Statistics, 1973. Lagos
Nigeria Year Book, 1975. Lagos

Paden, J. N. 1973. *Religion and Political Culture in Kano*, London
Postan, M. 1972. *Medieval Economy and Society: An Economic History of Britain, 1100–1500*, London
Postan, M. and Rich, E. E. (eds.) 1952. *Cambridge Economic History of Europe*, vol. II, *Trade and Industry in the Middle Ages*, Cambridge
Power, E. 1941. *The Wool Trade in English Medieval History*, Oxford
Prebble, J. 1969. *The Highland Clearances*, London

Quartey-Papafio, A. B. 1913–14. 'Apprenticeship amongst the Gas', *J. of the African Society*, 12: 415–22

Rajendran, G. 1974. *The Ezhava Community and Kerala Politics*, The Kerala Academy of Political Science, Trivandrum
Rama Rau, 1978. *An Inheritance*, London
Richards, F. J. 1918. *Madras District Gazetteers: Salem*, 2 vols., Madras
Rybakov, B. A. 1948. *Remeslo drevnei Rusi*, Moscow

Samuel, R. 1977. 'Workshop of the World: Steam Power and Hand Technology in Mid-Victorian Britain', *History Workshop*, 3: 6–22
Scott Report 1914. Report on Home Industries in the Highlands and Islands
Select Committee on Emigration 1841. First Report together with minutes of evidence and appendix
Shanin, T. 1971. *The Awkward Class*, Oxford
Shea, P. 1975. 'The Development of an Export-oriented Dyed Cloth Industry in Kano Emirate in the Nineteenth Century', Ph.D. thesis, University of Wisconsin, Madison
Shenton, B. and Freund, B. 1978. 'The Incorporation of Northern Nigeria into the World Capitalist Economy', *Review of African Political Economy*, 13: 8–20
Skinner, G. W. 1964. 'Marketing and Social Structure in Rural China, Part I, *J. of Asian Studies*, XXIV, 1: 3–43
Slicher van Bath, B. H. 1960. 'The Rise of Intensive Husbandry in the Low Countries' in J. S. Bromley, and E. H. Kossmann, (eds.), *Britain and the Netherlands*, London
Smith, Abd. 1970. 'Some Considerations Relating to the Formation of States in Hausaland', *J. of the Historical Society of Nigeria*, 5: 329–46
1971. 'The Early States of the Central Sudan' in J. F. A. Ajayi and M. Crowder (eds.), vol. I
Smith, Adam 1776. *An Inquiry into the Nature and Causes of the Wealth of Nations*, 2 vols., London
Smith, M. 1954. *Baba of Karo: a Woman of the Muslim Hausa*, London
Smith, M. G. 1978. *The Affairs of Daura*, Berkeley
Smith, W. A. 1875. *Lewisiania or Life in the Outer Hebrides*, London
Somasundram, K. J. 1967. *Commodity Note, 'Handloom'*, vol. II, The Handloom Export Promotion Council, Madras
Steel, T. 1975. *The Life and Death of St Kilda*, London
Survey of Small-Scale Industry in Kano, 1972. Department of Economics, Ahmadu Bello University, Zaria (unpublished)
Sutton, J. E. G. 1979. 'Towards a Less Orthodox History of Hausaland', *J. of African History*, 20: 179–201

Tahir, I. 1975. 'Scholars, Sufis, Saints and Capitalists in Kano: 1904–74', Ph.D. thesis, University of Cambridge, Cambridge
Thirsk, J. 1961. 'Industries in the Countryside' in F. J. Fisher (ed.), *Essays*

References

in the *Economic and Social History of Tudor and Stuart England*, Cambridge

Thompson, E. P. 1965. *The Making of the English Working Class*, London

Thompson, F. 1969. *Harris Tweed*, Newton Abbott

Thrupp, S. L. 1963. 'The Gilds', in the *Cambridge Economic History of Europe*, vol. III, Cambridge

1972. 'Medieval industry, 1000 to 1500' in the *Fontana Economic History of Europe*, vol. 1, *The Middle Ages*, C. Cipolla, (ed.), London

Thurston, E. 1897. 'The Cotton Fabric Industry of the Madras Presidency', *J. of Indian Arts*, 7: 20–4

1906. *Ethnographic Notes on Southern India*, Madras

1909. *Castes and Tribes of Southern India*, 7 vols., Madras

Trevallion, B. A. W. *et al.* 1966. *Metropolitan Kano: Report on the Twenty Year Development Plan, 1963–1983*, Greater Kano Planning Authority

Usman, Y. B. 1974. 'The Transformation of Katsina, circa 1796–1903', Ph.D. thesis, Ahmadu Bello University, Zaria

Varkey, N. K. 1968. *A Handbook of Labour Legislation in India*, Institution of Works Managers, Bombay

Waldman, M. R. 1965. 'The Fulani Jihad: A Reassessment', *J. of African History*, 6: 333–55

Wallerstein, I. 1974. *The Modern World System*, New York

Wiser, W. H. 1936. *The Hindu Jajmani System*, Lucknow

Yule, H. and Burnell, A. C. 1903. *Hobson-Jobson: A Glossary of Anglo-Indian Colloquial Words and Phrases*, W. Crooke, (ed.) London